H
C
C
S

Harvard Contemporary China Series, 11

The Harvard Contemporary China Series, now under the editorial direction of Harvard University Press, is designed to present new research that deals with present-day issues against the background of Chinese history and society. The focus is on interdisciplinary research intended to convey the significance of the rapidly changing Chinese scene.

Zouping in Transition

The Process of Reform in Rural North China

Edited by

Andrew G. Walder

Harvard University Press
Cambridge, Massachusetts
London, England 1998

Library of Congress Cataloging-in-Publication Data

Zouping in transition : the process of reform in rural North China / edited by Andrew
G. Walder.

    p. cm.—(Harvard contemporary China series ; 11)

ISBN 0-674-96855-7 (cloth)

ISBN 0-674-96856-5 (paper)

1. Tsou-p'ing hsien (China)—Economic conditions.

2. Tsou-p'ing hsien (China)—Economic policy.

3. Tsou-p'ing hsien (China)—Social conditions.

4. Industries—China—Tsou-p'ing hsien.

I. Walder, Andrew George. II. Series.

HC428.T83Z68   1998

338.951'14—dc21   97-44907

To the people of Zouping County

Contents

Tables

Illustrations

Maps

Figures

Preface

The chapters of this book are products of the Shandong Field Research Project (1988–93), arranged jointly by the Committee on Scholarly Communication with China and the Shandong Academy of Social Sciences. The project was administered by the former organization and funded by grants from the Andrew W. Mellon Foundation and the Rockefeller Foundation. It placed researchers with diverse interests in Zouping County, Shandong province, for up to five consecutive years of research. We came from disciplines as varied as history, medicine, law, education, anthropology, sociology, economics, political science, veterinary medicine, and environmental science.[1] We did not work as a team, but we often collaborated with one another in the field and met irregularly in the United States. One such meeting, at the Wingspread Center in Racine, Wisconsin, in the fall of 1988, was sponsored by the Johnson Foundation. At that meeting we took stock of our first summer of research and presented preliminary papers. Another was held at the 1993 Annual Meetings of the Association for Asian Studies in Los Angeles, where two panels were devoted to research from Zouping, and where planning for this volume began. With such a diverse group of researchers, a representative collection of papers would lack thematic unity, while the independent nature of our investigations ruled out an integrated survey of change in the county.[2] So we have selected a subset of papers related to two issues that have featured prominently in scholarship on China's economic reforms: the evolving role of local governments in market-oriented economic growth, and the impact of reform on social inequality.

The Shandong Field Research Project began as an initiative of the Committee on Scholarly Communication with China in 1984, during a period when village sites for field research projects were almost impossible to arrange. The committee approached the Chinese Academy of Social Sciences in Beijing, which in turn asked for volunteers from among China's many provincial academies. Only the Shandong Academy of Social Sciences responded. The academy's president assigned the task of selecting a proper village to a deputy who was a native of Sunzhen, a township in the north of Zouping County. He selected the nearby village of Fengjia, which had relatively high incomes from its still-collective agriculture and a noteworthy village party secretary, Feng Yongxi, who had been a representative to the National People's Congress since the Mao era. What started as a village site, however, quickly expanded into a countywide project. By the time the first wave of researchers arrived in 1988, the county government's entire range of bureaus and enterprises were open to researchers, and by the 1990s the rest of the townships and villages were opened for research.[3]

Those of us who publish papers here are indebted to the members and staff of the Committee on Scholarly Communication with China, which worked so hard to place us in the field, to the Shandong Academy of Social Sciences, which provided continuing administrative and logistical support for many years; and to the foundations that gave such generous support to the project. Michel Oksenberg deserves special thanks for his strong advocacy of the project from its inception. We also express our gratitude to fellow Zouping researchers whose work is not represented here; we have learned a great deal from them.

Over the course of more than five years (many of us continue to visit the county for research), our group developed many obligations to people in Zouping. As repeated cooperation led to familiarity and friendship, we have all incurred heavy debts to many people, from the county's leaders down to members of ordinary rural households. There are too many people to thank by name in such a short space. One individual, however, was for many years directly responsible for arranging all aspects of our research and daily needs, and here we would like to record our gratitude to Shi Changxiang, head of the County Foreign Affairs Office (now retired). The leaders and people of Zouping treated us with a warmth and hospitality that is impossible to repay. As a small token of our gratitude, we dedicate this book to them.

Andrew G. Walder

Zouping in Transition

ANDREW G. WALDER

1 | Zouping in Perspective

This volume examines a single county in North China, but it offers general arguments about the economic transformation of rural China during the past two decades. During these years, a relatively uniform set of policies was implemented throughout the country. In the early 1980s, collective agriculture was abandoned in favor of household farms; the government monopoly on agricultural commerce ended; and peasants were permitted to set up their own businesses and to take jobs elsewhere. By the middle of the decade, county and township governments were given a share of tax revenues generated in their jurisdictions, providing new incentives and opportunities for local officials and paralleling those of peasant households. These policies applied to virtually all of rural China, but the consequent pace and nature of change has varied considerably across the nation's vast rural regions. This chapter seeks to characterize the distinctive features of Zouping County's transformation, before indicating the general lessons that we might draw from the findings of each chapter.

The authors in this volume address questions about China's rural transformation that are far from simple, and about which there is some controversy. Despite their complexity, the issues may be stated briefly. The first is about the role of local governments as economic actors. What is their role, how have they played it, and how can we explain their behavior? Have they dominated emerging market economies through public ownership of industry and local planning, or has the role of local governments diminished rapidly with the rise of market transactions and private ownership? The second is the relationship between market reform and inequality. Have rural cadres enjoyed large income advantages in the new market environment? Has the provision of such collective services as education and health care declined, leading to new forms of inequality? The chapters in Part One, about local governments as economic actors, address the first of these issues. Those in Part Two, about the potentially inegalitarian implications of markets and growth, address the second.

Zouping's Unexceptional Distinctiveness

Zouping has the distinctive characteristics of its region, but it is unexceptional in either the pace and nature of change over the past fifteen years or in its historical and geographic endowments. Like many counties in the Yellow River Valley, Zouping has a long, documented history. With the exception of an interregnum of a mere century and a half during the Northern and Southern dynasties (420–589), records identify of a county named Zouping in this location since the Western Han (206 B.C.–A.D. 25).[1] With the addition of part of Changshan County in 1954 and Qidong County in 1958, present-day Zouping includes within its borders a variety of north China economic regions of the late nineteenth and early twentieth centuries. The Northwest, most of which was originally Qidong County, is a flat, alluvial plain on the southern bank of the Yellow River, and is subject to flooding, drought, and poor drainage.

The predominant crops have been wheat and corn, and the primary cash crop, after the turn of the century, cotton.[2] This has traditionally been a region of smallholding subsistence farmers, the kind of ecologically unstable and impoverished region that Joseph Esherick has designated as the cradle of the Boxer Rebellion in 1900.[3]

The Zouping County of this period, covering a smaller area that is now the core of present-day Zouping, was a transitional region with a greater degree of commercial development, more diversified agricultural economy, and higher incomes.[4] The northernmost of two roads around the Baiyun Mountains from the provincial capital, Ji'nan (fifty miles to the west), to the thriving eighteenth- and nineteenth-century market town and silk-weaving center of Zhoucun and continuing on to Yantai on the Bohai Gulf, passed directly through Zouping town.[5] Even though the main route from Ji'nan to Zhoucun by the eighteenth century was the southern one, Zouping benefited from the traffic on the less hilly northern route.[6] As a result, thriving markets grew up outside Zouping town's western and especially eastern gates.

The current southwestern third of the county, by contrast, is the northern half of the properous Qing- and Republican-era county of Changshan. The former county seat, Changshan town, is now one

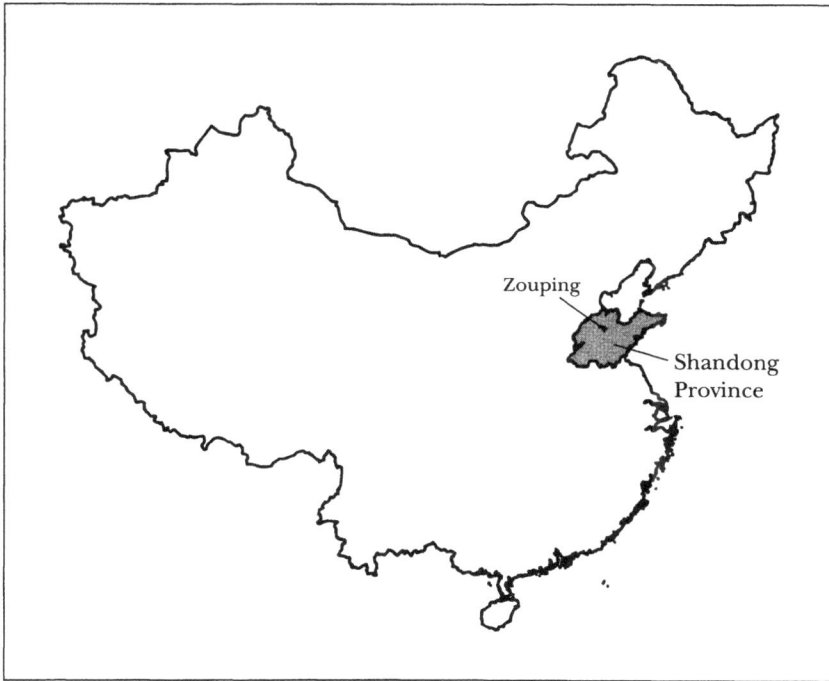

Map 1.1 China, with Shandong Province and Zouping County

of Zouping County's seventeen townships. On the eve of the Japanese invasion, Changshan had a thriving economy and was a local center of education and culture. Even so, it was overshadowed after the eighteenth century and up to the 1930s by Zhoucun, now just across Zouping's southwestern border.[7] Zhoucun, with a population of 296,000, is now an urban district on the western edge of the municipality of Zibo, a sprawling new industrial center of 2.5 million, whose city center lies another twenty miles to the east.[8]

The legacy of Zouping's modern economic history is therefore mixed: it contains some of the poorer types of northern China regional economies, as well as areas that were once among the region's more commercialized and prosperous. None of these areas, however, could match the wealth and commercial activity of the lower Yangzi Valley, or many southern coastal regions from the late Qing Dynasty to the 1930s. Moreover, Zouping was never tied closely to international trade and investment, as was true historically of the coastal regions that have grown so spectacularly after 1978. While the northern overland route from Ji'nan to Zhoucun passed

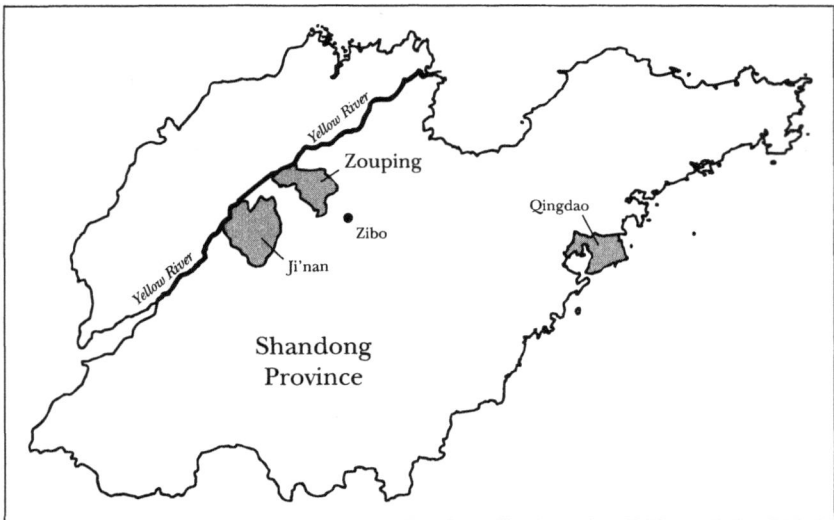

Map 1.2 Shandong Province

through Zouping, the railway, built early in the twentieth century, linked Zhoucun directly with Ji'nan and Qingdao, bypassing the county seats of both Zouping and Changshan. Beginning in the late 1930s, bombings by the Japanese air force and war among Communist, Nationalist, and Japanese ground forces devastated and depopulated the region and virtually destroyed Zouping town, including its massive town walls, of which there are now few traces.[9]

The Mao-Era Legacy: Zouping in 1978

After 1949, Zouping began a long, slow recovery from the devastation of invasion and civil war. Agriculture recovered, and real output value climbed steadily from 1949 to 1955, increasing by a total of 60 percent, and stayed at this plateau until 1959. Industry, too, began a steady but gradual development. The first factory, state-owned, was

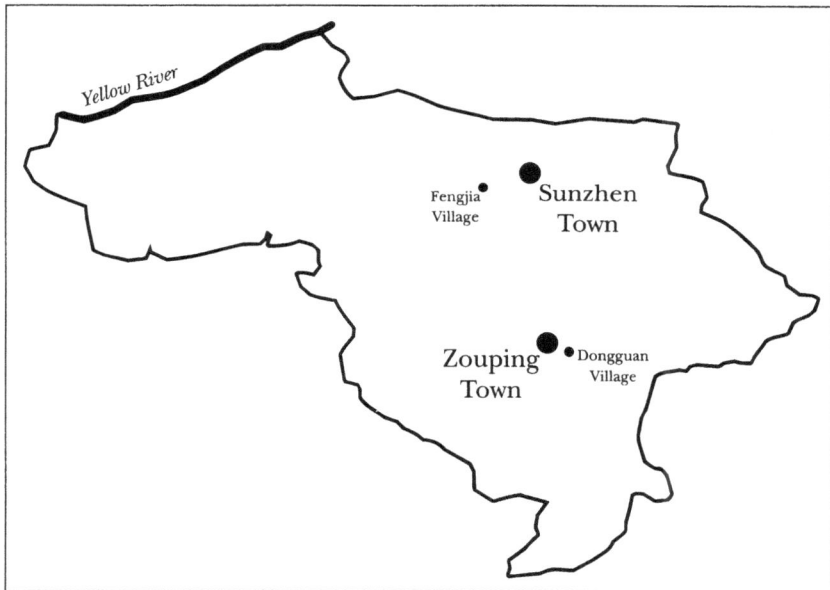

Map 1.3 Zouping County

established in 1950, and by 1957 the country had thirty-three small factories.

Like so many rural regions, Zouping was devastated by the Great Leap Forward of 1958 to 1960, and the consequent famine was one of the greatest human catastrophes in its long history. The grain harvest, 157,000 tons in 1956, declined to 69,000 by 1962. The grim demographic consequences of the famine are plainly evident in population records. Twenty-five percent of Zouping's population disappeared within two years.[10] Not until 1967 would the grain harvest return to the level of 1957. Not until 1974 would Zouping's population return to its 1959 level.

The 1970s were years of steady progress for Zouping agriculture. Increases in output during that decade left Zouping's 1978 real value of output at 25 percent above that of 1957. The grain harvest, now 221,000 tons, was 41 percent higher than in 1956, a per capita increase of 60 percent.[11] As Huang and Odend'hal show in their study of Fengjia village, these advances were due to investment in irrigation works and the introduction of new seed strains.[12]

Local industry suffered the same kind of prolonged depression that the Great Leap Forward caused elsewhere in China. The number of factories in the county quadrupled in 1959, as large numbers of small firms were established hastily in order to produce steel and other products that were of poor quality and unusable. Supplies, parts, and fuel were exhausted in the initial push, as massive production increases (much of it probably false) were reported for 1958, 1959, and 1960, each year producing 2.5 times the output of 1957. By 1961, this wasteful charade could no longer be sustained, and reported output dropped back to 1956 levels, not surpassing them again until 1965. After a brief pause during the political struggles of the late 1960s, the county steadily developed rural small-scale industry. As the reform era began in 1978, the county had an industrial base of 31 factories under the county government, 97 run by its 18 communes, and another 427 spread over more than 800 brigades (villages).[13]

At the outset of reform, Zouping was therefore a typical product of the grain-oriented subsistence regime enforced by the commune system and by the program of rural industrialization that accompanied it. Moreover, Zouping had suffered some of the worst effects of the ill-conceived national policies of the Great Leap Forward and political turmoil of the late 1960s.[14] The population was poor but comfortably above subsistence levels established by both the Chinese government and international agencies. The economy was overwhelmingly agricultural: only 6 percent of the county's labor force was employed outside agriculture, and less than 25 percent of total output came from industry.[15] The rural communes showed the heavy emphasis on grain production of the Mao era: in 1978 more than 80 percent of total agricultural output, including industrial sidelines, came from crops, the vast majority of that from wheat and corn (Table 1.1). Household sideline activities, which had grown during the mid-1970s to reach a meager 4.5 percent of rural output by 1976, were subsequently strangled almost entirely by 1978 in a fit of early post-Mao ideological rectitude (see Table 1.1).

The restricted material development of the county was reflected in its striking lack of modern amenities. In 1978 only eighty-one trucks and nine passenger sedans existed in the county. The vast majority of transportation was by means of tractors with attached carts. The first goods trucks and passenger cars arrived in the county only in 1970. They traveled on a road network that was almost entirely unpaved, as by 1977 the county had only ninety-two kilometers of asphalt roads (up from only ten kilometers in the late 1960s). Communication was still primitive: only 900 telephones were available for a population of more than 627,000.[16]

Zouping's economic profile at the end of the Mao era was unexceptional. It was somewhat below national averages for nearly all measures of development and living standards.[17] Zouping's per capita rural output in 1978, 376 yuan, was virtually identical with the national average of 379 yuan.[18] The per capita annual income of rural residents in 1980, 105 yuan, was below the national average of 113 yuan.[19] Zouping's industrial base—almost entirely in cotton textiles and foods—was also below average for China's rural regions. Per capita output of rural industry was 81 yuan nationwide, 73 yuan in Zouping.[20]

Rapid Growth and Transformation after 1980

Grain production responded immediately to liberalized agricultural policies. State procurement prices rose an average of 44 percent from 1979 to 1984,[21] and while Zouping began experiments with household production contracts as early as 1980, the final conversion from collective to household agriculture was relatively late, at the end of 1984.[22] As in other areas of China, grain production responded dramatically, and in Zouping it began to do so even before the dismantling of collective agriculture. Grain harvests (almost entirely wheat in June and corn in October) increased 52

Table 1.1 Growth and diversification of Zouping's rural economy, 1976–1993

	1976	1978	1980	1986	1988	1990	1993
Gross output value (millions constant 1980 yuan)							
Crops	78.8	97.8	143.3	230.1	197.9	235.6	246.2
Livestock	9.9	8.1	13.8	24.2	36.8	61.5	148.1
Fisheries	0.02	0.01	0.01	0.4	0.7	0.8	4.4
Forestry	5.1	1.6	7.8	5.7	5.3	5.3	11.9
Household sidelines[a]	4.4	0.4	25.5	25.6	36.0	28.7	—
Household (*geti*) and cooperative (*hezuo*) industry	—	—	—	30.4	80.4	149.4	396.7
Township and village industry	—	—	20.0	88.5	188.9	269.0	513.8
Total	98.2	107.9	200.1	404.9	546.0	50.3	1,321.1
Physical output							
Grain, primarily wheat and corn (thousands of metric tons)	—	219.4	—	334.5	—		422.0
Summer harvest (i.e., wheat)	—	92.2	—	163.4	—		205.3
Fall harvest (i.e., corn)	—	127.2	—	171.1	—		197.0
Cotton	—	12.4	—	14.1	—		9.8

Sources: Zouping County Statistical Bureau, *Zouping tongji nianjian 1980* (Zouping statistical yearbook [Ji'nan: Zouping xian tongjiju, 1981]), 31–33, 36–43, 114–116, 120, 232–233; *Zouping tongji nianjian 1988,* 41, 44–45, 52–61; *Zouping tongji nianjian 1990,* 19, 172; *Zouping tongji nianjian 1993,* 11, 24–25, 38–47; local statistical materials supplied to researchers.

a. Figures for 1976 and 1978 include value of household sideline production and output for production brigade industry. Figures from 1980 to 1990 include all household sideline activities only. The category of household sideline activity does not appear in 1993 records. Figure for 1993 includes only individually registered village household industry.

percent between 1980 and 1988 and, despite relatively stagnant prices after the mid-1980s, increased another 26 percent by 1993 (Table 1.1).[23]

The Rapid Diversification of the Rural Economy

After the shift to household farming, agriculture diversified rapidly as household activities suppressed under the communes grew much faster than the output of staple grains. Sideline production grew quickly after commune households were permitted greater freedom in sideline production after 1978, and faster still after the shift to household agriculture was "consolidated" in most of the county in 1984. Real output value of livestock tripled between 1978 and 1986, but grew sixfold again from 1986 to 1993 (Table 1.1). Household sideline production, most of which comprised handicrafts, also grew quickly after the liberalization of commune rules after 1978, and by 1986 it had reached a figure almost six times larger in real terms than a decade earlier (Table 1.1). Eventually emerging as a legal private sector of 1,099 household enterprises that produced eleven million yuan of output in 1985 (alongside the twenty-five million still classified as sidelines), it thereafter grew explosively into a thriving sector of more than 5,000 enterprises producing 470 million yuan of output by 1993—a thirteen-fold increase in constant yuan over eight years (Tables 1.1 and 1.2). This rapid diversification led to a 3.4-fold real increase in per capita cash income of rural households between 1980 and 1993.[24]

The Rapid Growth and Ruralization of Industry

At the end of the 1970s, the county's industrial production, composed primarily of cotton yarn and cloth, ginned cotton, cottonseed oil, and some beverages and foods, was heavily concentrated in state enterprises in or near the county seat. Almost 70 percent of the county's annual output was produced by the twenty-one state enterprises owned and operated by the county government. One of these enterprises overshadowed all the others: the cotton textile mill that was established with a large investment by provincial authorities in

1977.[25] In 1980 the mill was by far the largest enterprise, employing 1,440 (the next largest employer had 560), and alone it produced 19 percent of the county's entire industrial output value.[26]

By 1993, more than a decade of frenetic growth had transformed the scale and distribution of Zouping industry beyond recognition.

Table 1.2 Growth of industry in Zouping, by level of ownership, 1980–1993

Category	1980	1985	1986	1987	1988	1989	1990	1992	1993
County level									
State									
No. enterprises	21	16	17	17	20	20	20	23	31
Gross output (millions)	45.8	53.4	58.1	70.5	96.0	109.5	124.8	184.1	229.7
Collective									
No. enterprises	10	18	21	21	22	25	30	29	37
Gross output (millions)	7.4	123.2	104.8	115.3	116.6	129.8	135.1	148.2	151.2
Total county									
No. enterprises	31	34	38	38	42	45	50	52	68
Gross output (millions)	53.3	176.6	162.9	185.8	212.6	239.2	259.9	332.3	380.9
Township (commune)-run									
No. enterprises	86[a]	89	82	91	99	99	115	124	259
Gross output (millions)	20.0	17.1	22.2	31.3	52.0	77.6	101.0	126.1	500.2
Village (brigade)-run									
No. enterprises	—	259	280	353	405	344	311	390	320
Gross output (millions)	—	36.5	66.3	85.8	136.9	149.3	168.0	238.4	110.3
Village cooperative									
No. enterprises	—	193	542	618	637	356	609	349	637
Gross output (millions)	—	6.7	15.2	16.1	18.0	16.7	17.9	39.9	97.7
Individual—private									
No. enterprises	—	1,099	2,283	6,242	3,339	2,749	2,900	4,214	5,030
Gross output (millions)	—	10.9	15.2	26.7	62.5	96.7	131.5	240.6	471.5
Total output value (millions)	67.5	247.7	281.2	345.8	482.0	579.4	678.2	977.3	1,561

Sources: Zouping tongji nianjian 1980, 168–169, 180–181, 232–233; *Zouping tongji nianjian 1988,* 227; *Zouping tongji nianjian 1989,* 225–229; *Zouping tongji nianjian 1990,* 171–173; *Zouping tongji nianjian 1992,* 121; *Zouping tongji nianjian 1993,* 2, 117. All output figures are in constant 1980 yuan.

a. Includes brigade (village) industry.

Industrial output grew almost seventeen-fold in real terms (see Table 1.2). The output of the county government's own enterprises increased seven-fold in constant prices. The formerly dominant cotton textile mill, which still employed far more than any other enterprise, was itself now overshadowed in total output by a new brewery, which began production in 1984 after county officials decided in 1982 to close and convert an unprofitable chemical fertilizer plant.[27] Despite the respectable growth of the county government's industry, however, these county firms by 1993 contributed only 24 percent of the county's total (in 1980, it was 79 percent), and the state sector provided only 15 percent of the total (in 1980, 68 percent).

This remarkable shift in the relative weight of county industry indicates the explosive growth in townships and villages. Zouping's rural industrial sector of several hundred enterprises grew to more than 6,000, and where total output of rural industry (including household sidelines) was only 39 million yuan in 1980, it was almost 1.2 *billion* in constant yuan by 1993. Rapid industrial growth therefore involved the establishment of thousands of small enterprises. Where there was an average of twenty nine per commune (township) in 1980, there were 367 per township in 1993.

During the 1980s the rapid thrust of industry into rural areas was led by township and village governments. As late as 1988, enterprises owned and operated by township and village governments still produced 70 percent of all rural industrial output. Thereafter, however, the rapid formation of thousands of small private enterprises increased the private sector's total to the point where it was almost as high as that of the public sector. Not until the mid-1990s, then, would the rural private industrial sector come to surpass the rural public sector in output (Table 1.2).

The rapid shift from agriculture to industry did not lead to the urbanization of the county: industry, instead, moved to the villages. Agriculture's contribution to the county's tax revenues dropped from 74 percent of industry and commerce's contribution to only 8 percent (Table 1.3). While the agricultural labor force declined only slightly, the number of people who worked outside agriculture increased more than ten-fold. The urban population doubled, but was still only 7.6 percent of the county's total (all figures calculated

Table 1.3 The shift from agriculture to industry in Zouping, 1980–1993

	1980	1986	1988	1990	1993
Gross value of output (millions 1980 yuan)					
Agriculture	190.4	286.0	276.7	331.9	410.6
Industry	67.5	281.2	481.9	678.2	1,560.0
Ratio agricultural to industrial output	2.8	1.0	0.57	0.49	0.26
Contribution to county tax revenues (millions 1980 yuan)					
Agricultural taxes	2.0	—	2.4	2.3	2.7
Taxes on industry and commerce	2.7	—	17.8	21.7	34.4
Ratio agricultural to industrial taxes	0.74	—	0.13	0.11	0.08
Employment (thousands)					
Agriculture	260	—	262	—	243
Nonagricultural employment	18	—	87	—	149
Total employment	278	—	349	—	392
Nonagricultural as percent of total	0.06	—	0.25	—	0.38
Percent of population urban	0.034	—	0.064	—	0.076

Sources: Tables 1.1, 1.2, and 1.4; *Zouping tongji nianjian 1980,* 1, 4; *Zouping tongji nianjian 1988,* 1, 488; *Zouping tongji nianjian 1993,* 11, 305, 301–331; statistical materials provided to researchers.

from Table 1.3). The rural character of the county's population was evident during our research visits in the summer months, as many county-run enterprises closed down during the summer wheat harvest.

Rising County Revenues and Investment in Infrastructure

The impact of this rapid industrialization on the revenues available to county officials has been enormous. In 1980, Zouping needed large subsidies from higher levels of government to meet its annual budgetary expenditures. Total subsidies amounted to 59 percent of all locally generated budgetary revenues in 1980. Because China's fiscal system, reflecting its Soviet inheritance, is founded on taxes on industrial enterprises (agriculture being "taxed" by unfavorable prices), Zouping's rapid shift to industry has yielded massive increases in county revenues. The county's total budgetary and extrabudgetary revenues have increased in real terms from sixteen million to sixty-seven million yuan between 1980 and 1992 (Table 1.4). By 1992, subsidies from higher levels, which no longer serve to cover Zouping's general expenditures but are designated for specific infrastructure projects, had declined in absolute terms and were only 15 percent of locally generated budgetary income. By 1992, Zouping was contributing an amount to the prefecture equal to 5 percent of locally collected budgetary revenues.[28]

Real expenditures on government and party administration, education, and health more than doubled. Investment in infrastructure soared. The main streets of the county seat were relaid to in-

Table 1.4 Zouping County fiscal and budgetary trends, 1980–1992

Item	1980	1988	1990	1992
Sources of Public Revenue (millions constant 1980 yuan)				
Taxes on industry and commerce	2.7	17.6	21.7	27.5
Products tax	—	2.3	2.8	4.0
Value-added tax	—	3.0	4.9	5.7
Business tax	—	5.0	6.2	7.8
Collective enterprise income tax	—	3.6	3.7	4.5
State enterprise income tax	—	2.5	2.2	2.5
Other taxes	—	1.2	2.0	3.0
Agricultural taxes	2.0	2.4	2.3	2.6
All subsidies from upper levels	7.9	4.4	5.2	6.0
Total budgetary revenues	13.2	24.4	29.2	36.1
Extrabudgetary revenues	2.8	23.7	21.0	30.6
Total revenues	16.0	48.1	50.2	66.7
Selected Expenditures (millions constant 1980 yuan)				
Government and party administration	2.5	3.3	3.9	6.1
Education	4.6	7.1	7.3	9.8
Health and medicine	1.3	1.8	2.7	3.3

Sources: *Zouping tongji nianjian 1980*, 285–289; *Zouping tongji nianjian 1988*, 381–385; *Zouping tongji nianjian 1990*, 394–401; *Zouping tongji nianjian 1992*, 261–267.

clude sidewalks and poplar and willow trees, and new sewer and drainage systems were installed. A new express highway crossed the county and connected it with Ji'nan and Zibo; the old provincial highway (which largely followed the historical northern road around the White Cloud Mountains) was improved, and the county road network was further paved. By 1993 the network of paved roads had increased seven-fold over 1977.[29] There were now almost 2,000 trucks (eighty-one in 1978) and eighty-four passenger cars (up from nine).[30] County residents now had access to almost 3,600 telephones (900 in 1978).[31]

Zouping's Transformation in National Perspective

Despite its rapid growth, Zouping in 1993 remained near national averages for rural areas in most indicators of development. Somewhat slow in getting started in the early 1980s, Zouping began to catch up after 1985 as its industry grew at considerably higher rates than the nation as a whole.[32] Nonetheless, Zouping is still just below national averages for many measures of development and income (Table 1.5).

To give a clearer sense of how far Zouping is removed from China's more spectacular coastal success stories, we might compare it briefly with one of Guangdong Province's more prosperous—Nanhai County in the Pearl River Delta, south of Guangzhou. In 1993, Nanhai's per capita rural gross domestic product was almost four times that of Zouping, and its per capita industrial output almost seven times that of Zouping. Nanhai had five times Zouping's number of township and village enterprises and produced ten times its output (See Table 1.6). Zouping today is just reaching the level of development that Nanhai attained almost a decade ago.

The Contributions of This Volume

In a rural economy as vast and as varied as China's, where the gap between a rapidly developing Zouping and a poor county in the interior can be as great as that between Zouping and Nanhai, one must be circumspect when drawing general conclusions. The chapters that follow this introduction do offer important general lessons for the study of China's rural transformation, but not because Zouping's trajectory of change is characteristic of an "average" Chinese county. Instead, they contribute in two distinct ways. First, they provide grounded generalizations about the process of reform and economic growth—generalizations that may serve as hypotheses to be evaluated and either modified or rejected in studies of other regions where conditions may vary greatly. Second, they help us to recast the questions that we have asked and the conceptual tools with which we have framed them. The authors make both kinds of contributions to the two issues that preoccupy us in this book: the role of rural governments as economic actors (Part One) and the impact of reform on rural inequality (Part Two). In the remaining pages of this introduction, I briefly characterize these issues and identify the contributions.

Table 1.5 Zouping's rural development compared with national averages, 1993

Measure	Zouping	China
Nonagricultural labor force proportion of rural labor force	38%	33%
Crop cultivation as proportion of total agricultural output	63%	60%
Animal husbandry as proportion of total agricultural output	33%	27%
Per capita cash income of rural residents	836 yuan	910 yuan
Per capita rural gross domestic product	2,306 yuan	2,926 yuan
Rural industrial output per member of rural labor force	3,007 yuan	7,136 yuan
Township and village-run enterprises as % of rural industrial output	52%	73%

Sources: *Zouping tongji nianjian 1993*, 6, 11, 93, 117, 352, and Tables 1.2 and 1.3; State Statistical Bureau, *Zhongguo tongji nianjian 1995* (China Statistical Yearbook [Beijing: Zhongguo tongji chubanshe, 1995]), 27, 32, 84–85, 280, 332, 365, 375.

Local Governments as Economic Actors

All of the chapters in Part One point to a single conclusion: one cannot explain the rapid development of Zouping without reference to the role of local governments and officials as economic actors.[33] In Chapter 2, Jean Oi specifies the role played by county, township, and village officials in mobilizing investment funds, targeting enterprises and industries for growth, gathering information about market opportunities, and acting as brokers for contracts with distant enterprises and provincial marketing agencies. Moreover, she portrays a coordinated effort between different levels of government to promote specific promising sectors for further development—sectors that in recent years have included private village industry, which township officials have promoted by establishing quotas for villages to meet. In all of these activities, local government acts as an inter-

Table 1.6 A comparison of Zouping with Nanhai County,
Guangdong, 1993

Indicator	Zouping	Nanhai
Proportion of population in urban areas	7.6%	26%
Per capita rural gross domestic product	2,306 yuan	8,063 yuan
Per capita industrial output, entire county	2,329 yuan	14,989 yuan
Agriculture as proportion of county's total social output	30%	9%
Industry as proportion of county's total social output	47%	75%
Number of industrial enterprises	6,246	30,727
Gross output value of industry	1,179 million	11,794 million

Sources: Zouping tongji nianjian 1993, 2, 352, and Tables 1.1 and 1.2; Guangdong Province Statistical Bureau, ed., *Guangdong tongji nianjian 1993* (Guangdong statistical yearbook [Beijing: Zhongguo tongji chubanshe, 1993], 467, 472, 490, 494, 510.

esting variant of the East Asian developmental states, actively promoting and guiding local industry in a variety of ways.[34]

As Oi has emphasized in other published work based in part on Zouping,[35] and as I describe in Chapter 3, rural officials also directly manage a subset of the most important enterprises in their jurisdiction. In doing so, a rural government comes to resemble an industrial corporation. While this has often been noted for village and township governments, I show in Chapter 3 that county officials in Zouping manage their key industrial enterprises in a similar way. The relationship between the county and this subset of key public enterprises is decidedly not that of a government that retreats to the role of an increasingly distant regulator of autonomous firms. Instead, county officials monitor their key enterprises closely and participate in all important decisions that affect their future. In the case of the most successful and largest enterprise, the brewery, the enterprise itself was created by county officials in response to perceived market demand, and top county officials act as the leading management group of the firm, with the plant director in charge primarily of day-to-day operations. Despite the fact that the brewery and other large enterprises compete fiercely in domestic product markets, there is no evident trend toward greater autonomy of firms from the "interference" of meddling government officials. Far from it: Zouping officials behave as if they are hard-driving business executives vitally concerned with profitability and market share.

A similarly dominant economic role has been played by the party secretary of Fengjia village, Feng Yongxi, whose management of village assets in the 1980s is described by Huang and Odend'hal in Chapter 4. Secretary Feng in fact was able to delay the full implementation of household agriculture until the late 1980s, and even at that late date the villagers still harvested and sold most of the crops grown on family land as a group. One reason that this was so is that Secretary Feng, a national model and former National People's Congress member from the Mao years, was able to use his connections to obtain a lucrative contract to supply provincial research stations with high-quality seed grain at premium prices, and was able to gain permission to establish a cotton mill within the village—a rare exception to a jealously guarded state monopoly on cotton purchasing and first-stage processing (as described in Sicular's Chapter 5).

The continuing collective management of assets could probably not be maintained were it not for these special market advantages gained through political pull. Fengjia industry, more in line with county and with national practice, continued to be managed directly by the village government, in a pattern not unlike that at the county level. Only the smallest and least lucrative of the village's nine enterprises were leased out to families to operate independently, to become part of the new "jointly operated" sector. Not until the early 1990s, after the end of Huang and Odend'hal's period of observation, would private enterprises be established on a significant scale in Fengjia (again, some four to five years after the norm for the county). Despite Fengjia's "backwardness" in terms of its shift toward household independence in economic affairs—or perhaps because of it—Fengjia village nonetheless remains to this day one of the wealthiest villages in the county, ranking eighth (out of more than 850) in per capita income in 1993.[36]

Terry Sicular turns our attention from the role of officials in local governments to the continuing dominant role of state commercial agencies in the purchase and sale of agricultural commodities. While it is commonplace to characterize China's reforms as a shift from plan to market, Sicular shows in concrete detail how greatly these blanket terms mask the actual process of commercialization. While her survey and aggregate data show the deep involvement of rural households in commercial sales, her study of local commercial institutions shows that state commercial agencies still dominate markets for corn, wheat, and cotton, and that local governments are still deeply involved in the setting and enforcement of quotas for key agricultural commodities. More important for our understanding of the actual process of reform in rural China, Sicular shows that while it is true that there has been a proportional increase in transactions on markets, it is not justified to assume that this marks a corresponding proportional decrease in the power and activities of state agencies. Sicular shows that there has been a *qualitative* change in the behavior of state agencies in the rural economy—especially now that they operate within, and respond to, market incentives—but that as of this writing they continue to dominate rural markets.

The overriding point of these chapters is not the already familiar observation that rural governments have played a central role in economic development in the reform era. This argument has appeared in print for the better part of a decade, and the closely related argument that economic development in rural China has commonly proceeded under the umbrella of a local "corporatist" form of government is also by now a familiar one.[37] These chapters suggest, more fundamentally, that local government officials and agencies are economic actors just as surely as are peasant households and rural industrial enterprises, and that the incentives and constraints under which they operate are just as central to an understanding of China's rapid development, for the behavior of officials can have enormous economic consequences. In other words, the question is not really whether the role of local government has been large; the question is why and how local governments have played the role that they have, and why this high degree of state involvement has ended up promoting rapid market-oriented growth instead of serving primarily as a barrier to it.

While students of China have become accustomed to these observations about the roles of rural government, it is important to note that China's reform experience—and the pivotal role played by government as an economic actor—has either been ignored or distorted in many prominent scholarly writings about the "transitional economies." It is an item of faith among many social scientists—especially those who comment on the transformation of Eastern Europe's post-Communist economies—that market reform can succeed only if, or will succeed best when, governments actively privatize their public firms and stand back from efforts to carefully regulate economic activity.[38] Communist (or post-Communist) governments, according to this line of thinking, are motivated by cadre privilege, and will seek to block any genuine economic reforms, no matter how potentially beneficial, in order to maintain their power and privilege.[39]

This same line of analysis interprets China's rapid rural growth as the result of an early "big bang" reform in agriculture, in which rapid privatization of farming and the emergence of free markets for agricultural produce were responsible for rapid rises in output;[40] furthermore, rural industry is claimed to be a "nonstate" sector that is "semi-private," "de facto private," an evolutionary form of property midway between state and private ownership that enjoys far greater autonomy and is subject to far more intense market competition than is true in planned economies.[41] These interpretations of China's rural economy buttress the claim that government is a barrier to economic reform, that "partial reform" (as opposed to a hypothetical "full" reform) is a flawed strategy, and that government ownership and control is incompatible with the market mechanism.

These generalizations about China's reforms appear plausible only from a distance. The process of reform in Zouping fits with these statements only in the most superficial of ways. First, while it is true that free markets for agricultural products have revived in rural China (though not for cotton), and that peasant households now participate in rural commerce to a very great extent, it is also true that the same state purchasing agencies that monopolized rural commerce in the 1970s still dominate that trade today (Sicular documents both trends in Chapter 5). This continuing deep involvement of state agencies and local government in agricultural planning through price and quota setting is precisely the gradual approach to reform that some tell us has no hope to succeed. And Sicular notes that these same state agencies have transformed their behavior in the face of new market incentives and constraints—something not anticipated by some analysts of transitional economies.

Second, while it is true that peasant households have gained control over family farms, the rapid rise in grain output in much of China antedated the final push toward household agriculture: by the time this was consolidated in Zouping in 1984, the county's grain production had already seen its largest increase (perhaps due, as some have argued, to the rise in state procurement prices). (Fengjia village agriculture, which retained collective control over cultivation and marketing into the late 1980s, is highly unusual, even in Zouping County.)

Third, the characterization of rural industry as partially private in character, or the claim that it enjoys greater autonomy from government "interference," is at odds with the widespread pattern of direct official industrial entrepreneurship at the county, township, and village levels observed in Zouping throughout this period. As I argue in Chapter 3, it is only in these smaller government jurisdictions, where there are few firms to oversee and where the economic interests of government in having competitive and profitable firms is clear and pressing, that government officials are able to behave in many ways as if they are private entrepreneurs or professional, profit-oriented managers.[42] This is not typical of all enterprises, especially the many new small private and jointly owned ones that grew so rapidly in number in the 1990s. Still, this mode of behavior characterized the key local firms that took the lead in responding to new market opportunities throughout the 1980s.

The evolution of Zouping's industry in the course of reform and rapid growth shows that any descriptive generalization about the relative role of government entrepreneurship is likely to be accurate only for a certain period of time. For in aggregate terms, the weight of government-owned and -operated industry has declined rapidly since 1988. During our group's first research in Zouping that year, enterprises owned and operated by county, township, and village governments dominated local production, and the vast majority of economic growth that had occurred since 1980 was in this government sector. While the government sector has continued to grow rapidly since then, those rural firms under private or mixed forms of ownership have grown at much higher rates: where they comprised only 16.7 percent of total output in 1988, they comprised 36.5 percent of total output by 1993 (See Table 1.7). The rapid formation of thousands of small enterprises run by families or several entrepreneurs, and the apparent reclassification of village-operated factories as they are leased out to private individuals (see Table 1.2), has led to a rapid aggregate shift of output toward the truly nonpublic sector. But this has occurred only after a decade of energetic, public-led growth, and even today the public sector still produces almost two-thirds of Zouping's total output and remains the bedrock of the county's fiscal system.

Clearly, local "corporatism" is evolving, as Zouping County moves for the first time toward a truly mixed economy. At present, county, township, and village officials run a still vital and rapidly growing sector of larger market-oriented enterprises. Control of capital remains concentrated in the hands of public officials at all levels. While county, township, and village governments have sought to divest themselves of direct responsibility for the smaller and less promising firms, they continue to hold tightly the larger and more prosperous ones. Rapid industrial growth was not achieved in Zouping through either covert or hidden privatization: the rise of private firms and leasing arrangements have occurred only near the end of the first decade of frenetic economic growth.

What the eventual "equilibrium" level of public versus private ownership will be, and whether most public firms will eventually be forced into bankruptcy and privatized owing to market competition, cannot be easily foreseen. Proponents of rapid privatization and limited government might find solace in the assertion that public industry is doomed to eventual extinction under market competition, and that is indeed one possible path of evolution for the Chinese economy. But this is small solace indeed, for it is an admission that a transitional strategy of gradual reform and limited privatization is in fact a feasible strategy of reform. Zouping's record, not untypical of rural China, speaks for itself. For the crucial early period of reform, government officials have played an array of centrally

Table 1.7 The shift from public to private industry in Zouping, 1980–1993

Category	Value of output (constant 1980 yuan)								
	1980	1985	1986	1987	1988	1989	1990	1992	1993
Public ownership (state, collective village-run)	67.5	230.2	251.4	302.9	401.5	466.1	528.9	687.8	991.4
Private (*geti*) or mixed (*hezuo*) ownership	0	17.6	30.4	42.8	80.5	113.4	149.4	280.5	569.2
Private or mixed as % of total	0	7.1	10.8	12.4	16.7	19.6	22.0	29.0	36.5

Source: Table 1.2.

important, and highly effective, entrepreneurial and regulatory roles.

Together, the essays in Part One point toward a new phase in the analysis of China's rural development, one in which we will be motivated not by a desire to arrive at descriptive generalizations about the role of the state, or to rebut more doctrinaire versions of economic orthodoxy about transitional economies, but to explain the behavior of government officials as economic actors. Why have local officials in places such as Zouping proved to be active promoters of market-oriented reform instead of barriers to it? One answer implicit in these chapters is that officials and their firms are subjected to rather intense competitive pressures. There is no input-output planning in Zouping; it is too small a locality. Virtually all of its produce must be marketed independently outside of the county's boundaries, and this is especially true for the county government's foray into the highly competitive brewing industry. The position of local government is therefore not unlike that of a firm in a competitive environment.

But what connects the interests of officials to the competitiveness of their firms? An answer implicit in several chapters, and in this introduction, is the revenue imperative.[43] Profits accrue to governments as owners in the form of taxes and profit remittance. The translation of rapid growth into the expansion of government revenues is immediate and direct: while individual cash incomes have almost tripled in real terms, county government revenues from industry have multiplied by a factor of more than ten (Table 1.4). These increased revenue flows have vastly expanded the funds that local officials can use for local construction and other government expenditures—and these, not unimportantly, include office buildings, automobiles, fax machines, long-distance and international telephone lines, and expanded housing for government officials.

Why, then, if local public industry is such an important source of revenues and public spending, would local officials not be hostile to the potential threat presented by a private sector? In fact, they were at best suspicious of the private sector through much of the 1980s, and to this day are opposed to the systematic privatization of public industry—except of those firms judged unpromising. What, then, can explain the relatively late conversion of local officialdom to the private sector? The answer may well be that they already have a thriving public sector under their control and that the expansion of a small-scale private sector is unlikely to challenge them in the same product markets (brewing, cotton textiles, mining). A thriving public industrial base may be an important way in which official suspicion of a private sector is broken down. In addition, as Oi suggests in her chapter, private enterprise is an important new source of tax revenues to the locality. In this case, the early equation of industrial growth with rising revenues may whet the appetite of officials for even higher revenues—whatever their source. And when market performance becomes so intimately linked to revenues for government agencies, government officials increasingly become market-oriented actors. Sicular's account of the way that the traditional state commercial agencies become enmeshed in markets and subject to market pressures and incentives is an excellent illustration of this line of argument.

In sum, the papers collected here point beyond recent debates about descriptive generalizations and toward a new emphasis on explaining why the process of reform in China has proceeded in the way that it has. And they do so by conceiving of government officials as economic actors whose incentives and constraints must be understood just as surely as those of households and firms.

Market Reform and Inequality

At the end of the Mao era, rural China had some of the lowest levels of income inequality ever measured. The commune system leveled incomes within villages and townships to a remarkable degree, such that most measured inequalities were those between richer and poorer rural regions, not among individuals within communities. Moreover, the commune system had succeeded in delivering basic preventive health care to rural areas more successfully than in other countries with similar levels of income, and it had presided over a remarkable expansion of rural education up to the secondary level. For some, the dismantling of collective agriculture and the shift toward market mechanisms portended a rapid rise of income inequality, and potentially the collapse of collective rural programs that had supported the delivery of preventive health care and mass rural education.

These questions have stimulated considerable research and controversy in recent years, especially in the area of income distribution. Somewhat unexpectedly, aggregate measures of inequality in fact declined in the early years of reform, primarily because the large gap between city and countryside, and between different rural regions, began to narrow. The steady declines of the early to mid-1980s, however, have been followed by a reverse trend of rising inequality, as some rural regions have grown much more quickly than others, as wage labor and industry have spread unevenly across the land, and as differences between rich and poor within villages have grown.[44] The essays collected in Part Two contribute to two distinct issues about changes in inequality owing to market reform.

The first of these issues is whether rural cadres and their families have advantages over ordinary rural residents as a collective economy moves toward household enterprise in a market environment. This question has preoccupied sociologists interested in a number of transitional economies, not solely China's. One group argues that those with political power and connections are able to use these attributes to their advantage during market reform and are therefore more likely than ordinary households to end up among the higher paid and more prosperous in future years.[45] A contrary argument emphasizes the fact that markets open opportunities to those formerly monopolized by political officials, and that as markets spread, the relative advantages of officials or former officials will decline.[46]

The findings so far have been mixed. Victor Nee finds that the income of rural officials in two suburban counties outside Xiamen grew more slowly than that of ordinary peasant households in the early 1980s, that rural officials were not more likely to end up in the top income quintiles than others, and that cadres were not more likely to become private entrepreneurs than others.[47] Yet Nee also finds that cadres who entered into private entrepreneurship earned higher incomes than those from nonpolitical backgrounds, and in a later national survey he finds that cadre incomes increased at faster rates than ordinary peasants in most of the country up through 1989, while nowhere did it show the kind of decline reported earlier for suburban Xiamen.[48] Yu Xie and Emily Hannum find that the income advantages of urban party members do not decline with the advance of market reform because these advantages remain undiminished in areas where economic growth has proceeded the fastest.[49]

Sarah Cook's Chapter 6 contributes to this research in two novel ways. First, she has data on household income and economic activities that are much more detailed and arguably much more reliable than those used in the studies cited earlier. Previous findings usually have been based on self-reporting of household income in the present and in the past. It is notoriously difficult to get accurate income data from rural populations, especially when those data are based on recollections of incomes five or ten years earlier. Therefore research findings have been troubled by a nagging suspicion that higher-income households, especially cadre households, might underreport their incomes to a greater extent than others. The analysis presented in Cook's chapter is based on a careful survey of households in Zouping County in which very rich and detailed data on a wide range of household economic activities were recorded and checked for consistency. Second, instead of analyzing the determinants of change in net household income over two points in time, Cook uses a much different and more unobtrusive economic measure of political advantage: whether income returns per unit of labor are higher in politically connected households than in others.

Cook selects a difficult test case for the hypothesis that cadres have advantages in a market economy, for she examines the earnings of rural households. If one would predict advantages for political connections, one would expect them in the more lucrative rural economic activities—in gaining access to highly paid managerial jobs, or in more lucrative and large-scale forms of private entrepreneurship. If one can find that the politically connected enjoy significantly larger returns even to their labor in rural household activities, this represents a clear-cut finding of political advantage even in the kinds of activity in which one would least expect it.

Cook does find significantly larger returns to labor for politically connected households, with dramatic average increases in marginal returns to labor of just under one yuan per day in agriculture to seven to eight yuan per day for nonagricultural work. For self-employment, households with party members have on average double the returns to labor as households without party members. This suggests that different measures and more detailed and accurate data on incomes will go far toward reconciling currently contradictory findings and, more important, will specify the mechanisms through which political advantages do and do not have their effects. Cook's analysis indicates that political connections provide a key route out of low-paying agricultural work.

The final two essays in Part Two shift the focus from income to changes in access to preventive health care (and changes in health status) and educational opportunity. These subjects have remained relatively unexplored in the existing literature on inequality under Deng Xiaoping, despite the fact that there is no more direct and sensitive measure of social inequality than physical well-being, and despite the fact that educational systems play a universally recognized role in shaping patterns of opportunity in societies of all kinds. In their detailed examinations of preventive health care and access to education in Zouping, Gail Henderson and T. Scott Stroup (Chapter 7) and Lynn Paine (Chapter 8) shed considerable light on relatively neglected and still poorly understood dimensions of inequality.

Henderson and Stroup find some evidence of the expected decline in basic preventive services, but hardly the major ones that some observers feared would result from the dismantling of the commune system. There has been a switch to more market-oriented health services, however, and a shift toward the treatment of chronic diseases rather than preventive care, and some decline in the number of village-level health personnel. But the rural health network has not deteriorated. The reason is clear: Zouping's rapid development has raised government revenues and spending on health care, while at the same time improvements in diet have independently improved the health of the entire population. In fact, Zouping is already making the shift from acute to chronic disease as a leading cause of mortality. In effect, Henderson and Stroup portray a race between a tendency for rural health services to decline and economic development that raises funding for these same services. Zouping's decline in services is checked by rising government revenues and health expenditures and by rises in living standards. Stated this way, the implications for the rest of rural China are fairly clear: those areas that have grown as rapidly as Zouping are not likely to have experienced deteriorating rural health. In those areas that have not grown as rapidly as Zouping, however, and especially in those regions whose economies remain stagnant, serious inequalities and declines in health status might be expected.

Finally, Lynn Paine portrays an educational system that has shifted dramatically from one designed to universalize middle-school education and serve rural development to one designed to train top students for entry into China's universities. Middle-school enrollments have declined precipitously as schools have closed, while expenditures on education have increased considerably in real terms. The number of students who graduate from Zouping's elite schools and who are admitted to universities every year has risen steadily. Paine finds that modernizing reforms in Zouping education have improved schooling and made the system more accessible and responsive to parents, and more rationally organized. On the down side, however, the former ideal of mass education in rural areas has now fallen by the wayside, producing more inequality and new forms of it. The advantages of those from higher-income and well-educated families are likely to increase given this striking shift in the organization of public education.

Conclusions

One county in central Shandong is not a microcosm of rural China, and therefore our descriptive findings in themselves do not have national significance, except perhaps as benchmarks against which to compare the findings of other regions. The issues that we address in the context of Zouping, however, and the analyses we have pursued, are generic ones that apply to any Chinese region. We have sought not only to describe what has happened in Zouping but to understand why. Therefore our findings immediately raise comparative questions about variation and change—questions that must be asked about a nation as vast and varied as China, questions that must be sharpened continually before we can make the kind of informed and nuanced national generalizations that would match the importance of the issues involved.

It is therefore not very helpful simply to describe Zouping as an area in which local government has played a pivotal role in market-oriented economic growth since the late 1970s. Why did Zouping develop in this fashion? The fact that it had a significant base of commune and brigade industry at the outset of reform meant that there were assets in the hands of rural officials with which to begin a program of industrialization under public ownership and cadre control. The fact that the political leadership was at the outset politically conservative—indeed, hostile to private enterprise—and that it carried out the dismantling of collective agriculture slowly and reluctantly served to retard private enterprise throughout the first decade of reform. And finally, as an area closed to foreign investment throughout the first decade, far from thriving special economic zones or Hong Kong and without a large overseas population that would transfer capital and skills back into the county through kinship networks, Zouping did not have the same opportunities to develop small-scale capitalist enterprise that many southern coastal regions enjoyed.[50] Nonetheless, Zouping grew very rapidly, and throughout the 1980s it built an impressive record of industrialization under public ownership and cadre leadership.

While we describe Zouping's model of rural industrialization as one in which government has played a centrally important role, we also emphasize important qualifications. First, government officials do not exercise the same degree of control over all local enterprises. They tend to concentrate on those that are large and important sources of revenue; they tend to hold at an arm's length the smaller or less promising ones. Indeed, as rapid growth makes the government's tasks of monitoring enterprises more difficult, officials exhibit an increasing willingness to divest themselves of troublesome assets by contracting, leasing, or selling them to individual entrepreneurs who will assume control and risk. Second, while the relatively large-scale public sector has grown rapidly in the 1980s, the small-scale private sector, after a slow start, has grown much faster after the late 1980s, leading to a rapidly shrinking total share of industrial enterprise owned and operated by rural governments. Successful public industry in Zouping appears to have overcome initial cadre reluctance to permit the rapid expansion of the private sector. Through time, with more public enterprises to supervise than they can handle, and increasingly faced with competitive pressures on product markets, local officials have encouraged private enterprise growth as a new and rapidly growing source of tax revenue—but only in areas that do not compete with the government's industrial core of cotton textiles and alcoholic beverages.

Has the emergence of a market economy led to increasing inequality? Again, the studies in this volume sharpen the questions we ask and suggest resolutions to complicated debates. Regarding income advantages for the politically connected—a question that has been approached primarily by looking at aggregate income trends—research results have been ambiguous and contested.[51] When the question is asked somewhat differently, however—not whether incomes of the politically connected are growing faster than other groups but whether the politically connected receive higher returns to their labor—the advantages of political connections appear to be large and clear. With regard to possibly rising inequality in health status and the decline in health services, the answer appears to depend on local economic growth. Places that experience sustained rises in income and improvements in diets will not suffer in this regard; places that are economically stagnant, however, may not be so fortunate. And with regard to access to education for rural citizens—and related questions about the intergenerational transmission of status—successful efforts to upgrade rural schools in order to prepare students for university do appear to have reduced school enrollments and introduced less equality of opportunity. It is not clear, however, whether this outcome is inherent in a market economy or whether it hinges on local educational policy—a perennial question about educational systems around the world.

Our research on Zouping has made us wonder about variation and change in other rural counties—counties that did not have a legacy of political conservatism, that lacked a significant base of commune industry, that received large amounts of foreign investment, that grew much faster than Zouping or much more slowly, or that had thriving ties with large communities of overseas relatives. It makes us curious about the reasons for local variation, and the causes at work behind a local trajectory of change, and suggests to us a strategy of relating local studies to one another in an effort to build toward more nuanced generalizations about rural China as a whole. We hope that our research has the same effect on our readers.

1 | Local Governments as Economic Actors

JEAN C. OI

2 | The Evolution of Local State Corporatism

During the 1980s, the rural governments of Zouping County, like those of many other Chinese regions, guided the rapid development of industry through the corporate management of public enterprises and the pooling of community resources.[1] In past work I have labeled this type of government-led growth, in which privatization and the formation of new private firms play a distinctly secondary role, *local state corporatism*. In this chapter I show that this local corporatism has not been static: in Zouping it has evolved continuously from the late 1970s to the mid-1990s, as the increasing scale of the local industrial economy and increasing market competition alter and erode the simpler forms of direct cadre governance.

Township and village governments have moved toward more indirect forms of governance over public enterprises, reserving more direct control to the more important and more successful enterprises. During the early 1990s, cadres ended their earlier suspicion of private enterprise and now actively promote it in ways that were previously reserved exclusively for the public sector. In the mid–1990s they have begun to privatize township and village enterprises by either leasing them or selling them outright. Through time, Zouping has moved from the simpler and more cadre-centered forms of governance to a mixed model appropriate to the vastly larger industrial economy of the mid-1990s. In this chapter I describe Zouping's evolution and suggest the reasons for it.

For most of the 1980s, Zouping, like many counties in Jiangsu province documented by other researchers, was heavily biased toward collectively owned township and village enterprises and direct cadre involvement in their management.[2] Private business, discriminated against and periodically criticized, received little or no help in securing loans or production inputs. During the economic recession of 1988–1989, the private sector was hit much harder by bankruptcies and closures than the public sector.[3] As a result, growth from 1980 to 1988 was concentrated in the public sector.[4]

Despite the success of public enterprise in the 1980s, by the end of the decade it was no longer economically advantageous to rely exclusively on collectively owned township and village enterprise. By the early 1990s, private firms became a new target of local plans, and the sector began to receive the kind of preferential treatment earlier reserved for public firms. The result has been a rapid expansion of private industry that is taking the lead in creating new growth.[5] To grow beyond the smallest of undertakings, industrial enterprises require capital, technical expertise, market opportunities, and a favorable business environment for licensing, credit, and the procurement of supplies. Private entrepreneurs may have ideas and initiative, but only in favorable circumstances will they have the resources and the willingness to assume the risks required to develop rural industry of any scale. In Zouping, local cadres did not simply proclaim their approval of private industry and step back to watch the sector grow. Just as they earlier assisted collective enterprises, local cadres have worked hard to mobilize capital and credit, to provide technical assistance, to search out market opportunities, and to facilitate licensing to promote the development of the private firms within their jurisdictions.[6]

The Early Dominance of Collectively Owned Enterprise

In the 1980s, Zouping made the most of available resources to develop rural industry in the fastest manner possible. This meant using methods and institutions inherited from the Maoist past; in particular, the existing bureaucratic network and the still-strong political institutions of the county's townships and villages.[7]

The early decision to promote township and village enterprises reflects the dominance of local governments, the strength of the collective, and the county's gradual approach to change. While some counties in China moved to household agriculture in the late 1970s, Zouping waited until 1983—the year that decollectivization was declared basically complete throughout China—to begin the task. Some villages, such as the prosperous Fengjia, delayed until 1984. Such villages that had done well in the later part of the Maoist period saw little reason for radical change. The collective system in Zouping was successful enough that all communes had managed to establish at least one enterprise in the 1970s.[8] As Table 2.1 shows, 331 commune and brigade enterprises were already in operation by 1979, an average of 18 per commune (later township), although variation within the county was significant.[9] As collective agriculture was coming to an end, officials decentralized the management of these commune and brigade enterprises. But every effort seemed to be made to keep some form of the collective as the unit of produc-

Table 2.1 Commune and brigade industry in Zouping, 1976–1983

Year	Total no. of enterprises	No. of commune enterprises	No. of employees	Gross output (million yuan)	Realized profit (million yuan)
1976	77	77	3,566	6.4	n.a.
1977	405	80	10,838	20.0	n.a.
1978	524	97	13,167	23.6	5.6
1979	331	107	9,977	19.5	3.9
1980	264	115	9,463	23.9	4.3
1981	437	103	11,139	23.7	4.0
1982	364	104	11,046	26.9	3.9
1983	297	110	9,540	27.6	3.6

Source: Interviews with county agencies.

tion and accounting. In 1981 and 1982, enterprises were contracted out *(chengbao)* to collective groups *(jiti),* usually meaning all of the workers and managers of a factory.[10] Only in 1983 did the county allow contracting to individuals.

Even when individuals were allowed to contract enterprises, the first contracts were only a modification of the collective group contracting system. The new system was known as the "individual leading the collective contracting" *(geren daitou jiti chengbao).* To protect peasants within the collective factories, managers could not fire any of the existing workers. The shift to individual contracting was simply to institute greater incentives and therefore to give greater responsiblity to one person for meeting quotas and running the factories efficiently. Nevertheless, all the workers of a factory were considered partners in this endeavor. As late as 1988, more than 60 percent of all the township and village enterprises in the county were contracted under this system. Only about 30 percent used individual responsibility contracts. Of the remaining collectively owned township and village factories, not more than 5 percent were leased out, and not more than 5 percent were sold. The latter were usually the very small repair shops, such as those servicing agricultural tools, that were difficult to control. According to county officials, there were still a few enterprises not yet contracted out.[11]

The decision to go with contracting rather than leasing further indicates the continued hold of the collective even as land was distributed to the households. Leasing *(zulin)* is a contractual arrangement where management's rights over collectively owned firms are delegated to individuals who decide how to dispose of all income after rent is paid to the township or village owners.[12] Contracting restricted the contractor's autonomy in making major decisions about existing capital equipment and significant new investments and kept the rights over the distribution of profits in the hands of the township or village. Local governments made use of individual management incentive schemes, but as owners, they keep property rights over the use and redistribution of profits, over and above the contracted fees.[13]

Contracting allowed townships to directly benefit from the revenue of these enterprises, in addition to any taxes that these enterprises paid. Once revenue sharing was extended to townships in 1986, the townships could keep surplus tax revenues once quotas were met, just like the county. The more rural enterprises a township had, the higher its revenues.[14] Villages are not allowed to keep any taxes. They are not considered a fiscal unit and do not practice revenue sharing. For villages, these enterprises represented the one source of income to which the village government had legitimate access after the shift to household farming. While townships used the nontax revenues taken from their enterprises in the form of fees, rents, and profits to supplement their tax income, this was the primary source of income for villages.

Contracting as a Form of Management and Fiscal Regulation

To ensure their control over township and village enterprises, local officials altered the contracting system during the 1980s. Under the early contracts, often called *dabaogan,* the contractor paid a predetermined lump-sum "rent"—the contract fee *(chengbao fei)*—to the collective for the right to run the enterprise and to keep remaining profits.[15] Rather quickly, however, township and village governments changed the terms of the contracts.[16] Officials complained that under the lump-sum system, contractors took a short-term view of profits, striving to make as much as possible before the contract expired. Village property suffered—machines were poorly maintained, accounts were poorly kept, and sometimes the factory stock was illegally sold.[17]

In response, many townships and villages changed to a percentage system to guarantee themselves a share of unexpected increases in profitability and spread the risk between the contractor and the collective. This eliminated the need to correctly estimate the potential profits of an enterprise and allowed local authorities better control over the property and accounts of their enterprises. Instead of paying a simple lump sum at the end of the year, the rent is stated as a set percentage of a fixed quota of the profit that the contractor agrees to generate. That quota is individually set for each enterprise based on a calculation of estimated profits, taxes, and costs. In addition, most township and village governments give each contractor a list of mandatory quotas for output value and sales. Factory managers who fail to meet the quotas have their contracts terminated and are relieved of their position. To ensure that contractors take care of the collective assets, some villages have audit teams go to each factory twice a year to check on the factory's funds, accounts, and machinery.[18] Moreover, the contracts specified the share of the after-tax profits to be allocated to the government, enterprise, and workers.[19]

The strength of the government is exhibited again when the contracting system undergoes further modifications in those villages where contractors have successfully managed collectively owned factories and earned large bonuses. Villages with many enterprises—for instance, Dongguan—set up a special body, often headed by the village party secretary, to oversee these enterprises. Called the village industrial committee in Dongguan, this body set contract terms for each of its enterprises. When factory managers were felt to be making too much money, the committee limited factory manager salaries by pegging them to the average earnings of workers in the factory.[20] Factory managers under such arrangements were essentially hired managers with a good incentive plan.

Government Guidance of Township and Village Enterprises

The rapid development of township and village enterprises in Zouping was due to entrepreneurship by the county, township, and village governments that owned these enterprises. Township and village leaders raised the initial capital for new enterprises and closely supervised and assisted in their subsequent growth. Using their political authority, they mobilized capital for investment, arranged and allocated credit, and provided market information and technical expertise well in excess of what was initially present in the locality. The overlapping political and economic authority in the collective sector allowed for corporate solutions to business problems and provided public firms with a competitive advantage over private firms. Local governments used their political authority single-mindedly to promote local industrial development. During the

1980s, local officials became entrepreneurs who assumed the burden of political and economic risks.

The Formation of Capital by Townships and Villages

Unlike private enterprises, collectively owned enterprises were able to use the corporate funds of their parent organization—either the township or the village. Because these enterprises remained collectively owned, township and village officials could pool the assets of their collective enterprises and could raise additional funds from within the collective. This strategy allowed collectively owned enterprises to develop in villages and townships regardless of whether willing and able individuals were on hand to raise enough capital to fund a private enterprise.

Redistribution of Enterprise Funds. Townships and villages raised capital by "borrowing" and redistributing profits from one enterprise to another. Richer enterprises could support weaker enterprises during downturns in the market or provide the capital to start new enterprises or to expand the operations of enterprises that were doing well. This is how Sunzhen township repaid the 120,000 yuan debt left by one of its enterprises when it only had 60,000 yuan on hand. To make up for the difference, the commission divided the remainder of the debt and collected the amount from its other township enterprises.[21] Yuancheng township, which is more industrialized and richer than Sunzhen, asked some of its factories to pay contract fees in advance to start new factories.[22]

Even Dongguan, one of Zouping's wealthiest villages, raised 1 million yuan for its new cotton mill in 1989, during the nation's economic retrenchment, by borrowing from its other enterprises.[23] It secured a 250,000-yuan loan from the forging plant, one of the village's richest enterprises. In this case, one can sense that there are divergent interests within the village corporation—every enterprise has its own interests as well as that of the larger collective to consider. The manager of the forging plant initially resisted, but in the end he was "persuaded" to make the loan. In this particular case, the request was much more urgent because the mill, which was just getting under way, had not yet been contracted out, and the village party secretary, who was negotiating the loan, was personally running the operation. Dongguan's party secretary, who was acutely aware that each factory wanted to protect its own resources, tried to make this as palatable as possible. He arranged to repay the forging plant in three years, at 15 percent interest on the loan.[24]

Borrowing from Collective Members. When a village cannot raise sufficient capital from its enterprises, it can also borrow from villagers. This is often simply called "collecting funds" (*jizi*). Sometimes it means selling shares or bonds to the workers; other times it is simply a savings scheme. This practice has been criticized as placing extra burdens on peasants, especially in poor areas, but has been an important way to raise funds for enterprise development in Zouping.

In the late 1980s, to amass funds for its village enterprises, Dongguan sold bonds to its workers and crafted a savings scheme offering high interest rates.[25] The village was able to raise approximately 700,000 yuan in the first half of 1989 alone using a combination of bonds and savings plans.[26] In 1991, approximately 80 percent of the village's enterprises were still engaging in various forms of *jizi*. At that time, Dongguan was able to mobilize approximately 3 million yuan.[27] By 1995, Dongguan had eighteen village enterprises, with total annual profits of more than five million, and it still continued to raise approximately 2 million yuan per year from its savings schemes.[28]

The Pooling of Risk and the Guaranteeing of Bank Loans. The same principle of corporate management and funding applies when outside funds are needed. The township or village uses its collective resources and the name of the collective to guarantee loans. Factory managers may formally apply for a loan and commonly sign the loan papers, but in all cases, local officials play a crucial role. In some instances, townships or villages prearrange and negotiate loans on behalf of their enterprises. The powerful Zouping township, for example, secured agreement from the county Agricultural Bank and the prefectural Finance Bureau to provide 1 million yuan in low-interest loans for one of its enterprises.[29] Sometimes the village industrial committee secures the needed funds for all its village industry and then divides the funds.

Regardless of whether the factory manager or the collective signs for the loan, the owner of the firm—the township or the village government—bears the financial responsibility for the debts of its enterprises.[30] During most of the 1980s, the township economic commission could sign as the guarantor of loans to its enterprises.[31] The township was obligated to bear the risks and ultimately had to repay the loan. This is why in 1987, when four Sunzhen township enterprises closed, the township economic commission was responsible for repayment.[32] Village governments are in the same position with regard to the enterprises that the village has contracted out for individual management.

Corporate funding and management allowed township and village enterprises to develop, but it also meant that local governments rather than enterprises assumed the risk of loans. In an economic downturn, if the factory defaults and the township is unable to mobilize sufficient funds for repayment, the loaning agency is left without recourse. As I show in a later section, this became a problem when pressures on industrial profits increased in the 1990s.

County Guidance and Assistance in Arranging Capital and Credit

During the 1980s, not only did Zouping's townships and villages keep a tight grip on their contracted enterprises, but county government also used its administrative power and resources to try to ensure successful development of the collective sector. The county issued plans for the development and production of collectively owned enterprises, particularly those at the township level. The Commune Enterprise Management Bureau *(shedui qiye guanliju)* was transformed into the Rural Enterprise Management Bureau *(xiangzhen qiye guanli ju)* and was given responsibility for planning and supervising the development of all types of rural enterprises—township, village, joint, and private—in the county. The day-to-day work and the direct supervision was given to the bureau's subordinate organization in each of the seventeen townships, known as the township economic commission *(xiang jingji weiyuan wei).*[33]

The small staff of each township economic commission, usually five to seven people, was charged with overseeing the targets' implementation, directing township enterprises, and overseeing the village-level enterprises as well as the private and joint household enterprises within each township.[34] To monitor implementation, the county called all of its seventeen economic commissions to monthly meetings to discuss the production situation in their respective township enterprises, to give recognition for jobs well done, and to correct problems where necessary. In addition, meetings were regularly scheduled every three months, and annual meetings were held as well. Each township economic commission received production as well as fiscal targets, including those for output and profits. But unlike during the Maoist period, townships that met their targets received monetary bonuses as well as plaques.[35]

To ensure that township and village governments could successfully carry out the county's plans for rural industrialization, the county made available the full range of its services. Because these enterprises were owned by townships and villages, the county could easily justify such help as part of its administrative duty to assist its subordinate levels of administration. If the county's resources were insufficient, it could intercede with higher-ranking jurisdictions when necessary. Within county government, aside from the Rural Enterprise Management Bureau, other bureaus and agencies—including the Finance Bureau, the Tax Bureau, and the Agricultural Bank—have a special section or person in charge of rural enterprise. Each office is capable of providing different types of assistance and lobbying other agencies on behalf of enterprises. The Tax Bureau, for example, can give tax reductions. New enterprises routinely receive tax exemptions. But each year the county also provides additional allowances for various other situations, such as technological renovation and new product lines. Table 2.2 shows the total amounts of the tax exemptions and the number of enterprises affected. During the height of the retrenchment period in 1989, the amount reached 2.8 million yuan.[36]

But assistance to collectively owned enterprises was not given out equally. If that was the case, the limited resources of the county would not have had much impact. For example, total tax breaks of

2.8 million yuan would have meant little if spread out among large numbers of enterprises. But of that amount, one of Zouping township's enterprises received 800,000 yuan.[37] Which firm received assistance depended in large part on its past performance and perceived future prospects. Officials were not always right in their evaluations, as problems in the 1990s suggest. But Zouping created *competition* for *preferential treatment*. Resources were channeled and advantages given to those enterprises deemed the most capable or showed the most promise of generating benefits for the community. Over the course of the 1980s, banks and bureaus increasingly allocated resources and provided assistance based on the merit or potential of an enterprise to generate revenues.

Zouping rated firms based on past performance. The ratings determined the level of services and assistance that an enterprise could receive from the government and its affiliated institutions. Some ratings were bureau-specific. For example, Zouping's material supply

Table 2.2 Zouping township and village enterprise tax exemptions, 1980–1989

Year	No. of enterprises subject to exemption	Exemption (million yuan)	Exemption as % of township and village enterprise taxes
1980	38	0.58	10.8
1981	42	0.59	7.8
1982	45	0.70	4.0
1983	48	0.85	4.3
1984	87	1.30	8.1
1985	93	1.60	6.5
1986	118	1.84	7.6
1987	121	2.12	8.5
1988	123	2.42	6.1
1989	124	2.80	6.3

Source: Interviews with county agencies.

bureau had key-point industries *(zhongdian)*. These industries had priority in getting supplies and had the best chance of receiving the lowest-priced inputs. For example, Dongguan's forging plant is such a key-point industry. In 1988 it received its inputs at prices that were 3 to 5 percent less than what other buyers paid.[38]

Even in the early 1990s such ratings still had meaning because the range of materials available under county control has grown with the market. In 1980 the Zouping County material supply bureau consisted of only two subsidiary companies, employing a total of 131 people. By 1989 it had expanded its operations to employ 241 people, handling total sales of 98.6 million yuan through ten trading companies. The material supply bureau was able to offer an impressive array of supplies obtained through various sources, including trade with Russia across the Heilongjiang border. In addition to the county-level material supply bureau, other government bureaus, such as the township enterprise management bureau, have set up material supply companies.[39]

From the mid-1980s to 1992, credit ratings were among the most important. Beginning around 1983–1984, the Rural Enterprise Management Bureau, along with the Agricultural Bank, annually rated enterprises to determine the fixed capital credit and level of service available from the local bank or savings cooperative.[40] This allowed the banks to know which enterprises were creditworthy and deemed important by local officials and therefore should be accorded the quickest approval for loans within their prescribed credit limits. Once a factory was in the red, it lost its credit rating. This system remained in effect until the early 1990s, when a growing number of township and village enterprises started to incur difficulties and could not repay their debts.[41]

Bank Loans. The county government cannot directly control the flow of bank loans, but county officials can indirectly affect who gets a loan. This was particularly important for rural enterprises, especially for village enterprises, which often found it difficult to get credit. Only after a village has established a reputation and has shown itself to be successful can it hope to obtain an official loan. This may explain why most village industry, especially in the early years, was funded from internal sources: there was simply no alternative. This was the case for most villages in poorer, less industrialized townships such as Sunzhen.[42] In 1987, 30 percent of Sunzhen's agricultural bank branch loans went to township and village enterprises, but of this amount only 10 percent went to village enterprises.[43]

County officials and agencies directly lobbied banks to grant loans to favored township or village enterprises. This lobbying can come from leading county cadres or cadres from such agencies as the Rural Enterprise Management Bureau, the Finance Bureau, and the Tax Bureau. Before the practice was banned in the late 1980s, the county Tax Bureau could help an enterprise secure a loan by allowing it to repay the loan before taxes were assessed (*shuiqian huankuan*), thus providing greater assurance to the bank that the loan would be repaid.

In addition, county officials increased the opportunities for enterprises to obtain loans. Originally, in Zouping, as in other rural counties, enterprises could only take loans from the Agricultural Bank at the county level or from the Savings and Loan Cooperatives or branch offices of the Agricultural Bank, known as *yingyesuo*, at the township level. Zouping County officials allowed local enterprises to circumvent regulations that limited them to certain financial institutions. By the early 1990s, both state and rural collective enterprises were dealing with whatever bank would give them loans and offered the best service and terms.[44]

By the late 1980s, branches of the Agricultural, Industrial-Commercial, and Construction banks increasingly vied for business, including that of the rural enterprises. The Construction Bank was particularly aggressive in competing for business. Despite the regulation that stated that the Agricultural Bank was to be the source of rural industrial loans, in 1988 the Construction Bank provided 15 million yuan in loans to the county's rural enterprises. The largest of these loans, 3 million yuan, went to a village enterprise.[45] By 1990 the county Construction Bank was the source of about 15 percent of the total loans to the county's rural enterprises, totaling approximately 75 million yuan.[46] All Zouping township–owned enterprises received loans from the Construction Bank, as did a number of township-owned enterprises in other townships.[47]

Such borrowing by local enterprises at other than their assigned financial institutions required approval of the local branch of the People's Bank. But such approval was usually given. When local officials are forced to choose between protecting local interests and strictly adhering to central policies, the choice is clear. As the head of one of the specialized banks explained, "The local People's Bank approves most requests for an enterprise to change banks. If it does not, the enterprise will fail because it will not get the needed funds. *What is most important is to support the enterprise. So the People's Bank has no choice but to approve.* As Marx said: 'one must proceed according to conditions'" (emphasis added).[48]

Other situations have allowed local officials to provide credit to key enterprises, despite restrictions imposed by the upper levels. For example, some of Zouping's collective rural enterprises received short-term loans from the Agricultural Bank during periods of very tight credit, such as 1988–1990, when the central authorities tried to enforce a credit freeze to slow inflation.[49] It is difficult to know where these funds actually came from, but if the experience of other counties reported in the press is any indication, it is quite possible that this money was borrowed on a short-term basis from funds that were originally earmarked for other uses.[50]

Zouping's officials, however, have been politically prudent and sensitive to the continued institutional constraints on their activities. Bank officials, like others at the local level, cannot afford to flaunt central regulations openly. In the early 1990s, a county-level Agricultural Bank official explained that rural enterprises shopped for banks, even though according to the regulations they should have an account at only one bank. To comply with regulations, an enterprise would maintain its basic account (*jiben jianghu*) at the officially designated bank but then open a secondary/supplementary account (*fuju jianghu*) at another bank for special projects.[51]

For example, the county brewery was assigned to the Industrial-Commercial Bank. When it needed a large loan to expand production, it first did go there. The bank was sympathetic and gave the factory 5 million yuan in circulation funds, but it failed to secure upper-level approval to increase the factory's credit limit to fund the expansion. The brewery then turned to the Construction Bank, which offered it a larger loan.[52] But while the brewery started its account at the Construction Bank, it continued to maintain an account at the Industrial-Commercial Bank.[53] In other instances regulations overlapped, so that an agency such as the Land Management Bureau *(tudi guanliju)*, which should have had its account at the Agricultural Bank, could legitimately do business at the Construction Bank because the bureau handles projects in basic construction, which fall under the jurisdiction of the Construction Bank. By the mid-1990s, such bureaucratic maneuvering was no longer necessary. The specialized banks, such as the Agricultural Bank, were commercialized, and regulations were relaxed to allow enterprises to conduct business with the bank that provided them with the best service and credit.

Bureaucratic Loans and Grants. Over the course of the 1980s, as recurrent retrenchment policies tightened credit to rural enterprises, Zouping County officials went beyond lobbying banks and trying to bend the rules to establish credit sources exempt from the centrally mandated restrictions attached to official bank loans. The first step was to directly grant loans to enterprises through the township's or village's bureaus and commissions. The amounts available in the different agencies varied, as did the size of the loans given. The loans were generally small and meant to see an enterprise through particularly difficult periods. Sometimes these funds were given as seed money for new projects.

The county Finance Bureau had various sources of support that it doled out on a case-by-case basis. One was the "agricultural support revolving fund" *(zhinong jiuzhuanjin)*, funded by the county, prefecture, and province.[54] The bureau also had an "agricultural development fund" *(nongye fazhan zijin)* that had 3 million yuan in 1990.[55] Both of these funds included money for township and village enterprises. The "finance support fund" *(caizheng fuchi zijin)* was specifically for the support of collective enterprises. Between 1981 and 1987, a total of 2 million yuan worth of loans was given from this fund, which was supported by allocations from the prefecture and the province. The volume of loans increased annually from 40,000 yuan in 1981 to 640,000 yuan in 1987. The number of enterprises that received loans increased from two in 1981 to twenty-two in 1987.[56]

The funds were doled out selectively. Collective enterprises applied to their township finance office (caizhengsuo) and waited for the decisions of the county Finance Bureau. Enterprises usually had one or two years to repay the loan. If the loan was repaid on time, no interest was charged, only a use fee. If the loan repayment was delinquent, then a low interest was charged.[57] These loans had a further advantage in that because the loan was transacted through the county branch of the Agricultural Bank, enterprises were allowed to repay these loans before their earnings were assessed for taxes.[58]

Zouping's Tax Bureau had similar short-term loan funds (fuchi zijin) generated by taxes collected from both private and collective rural enterprises.[59] Between 1984 and 1987, the Tax Bureau gave approximately 400,000 yuan to about 60 enterprises.[60] As with the Finance Bureau funds, the amounts and the number of enterprises being helped were increasing. One example from 1989, in the midst of the retrenchment, shows that the Tax Bureau handed out 470,000 yuan to about 20 enterprises; the largest loan was 50,000 yuan.[61]

Nongovernmental Bank Loans and Credit Associations

The second step the county took to provide alternative sources of credit was to establish local savings and loan institutions outside the central banking system to fund local development.[62] The process began during the 1988–1990 retrenchment, spreading to all townships in the county by the mid-1990s. The first nonbank credit association was set up in 1988 in Changshan township. Called a financial service center (jinrong fuwu suo), it made credit available to collective enterprises and private entrepreneurs. A township official explained that the service center had been set up in response to the difficulties and red tape involved in securing loans at the local credit cooperative. In contrast, the financial service center's loan application procedure was fairly simple, and approval was quick. For large loans over 20,000 yuan, a financial management committee (jinrong suo guanli weiyuan hui) was set up to approve the applications. Changshan's official pointed out that these funds were not spent for education or health; the financial service center provided funds specifically for use in the development of rural enterprises and agriculture.[63] He proudly stated that this source of funds allowed his township to survive the 1988–1990 retrenchment. Changshan's ten enterprises all borrowed from this fund during the retrenchment period. By May 1990, Changshan's financial service center had granted 300 loans. As of June 1990, deducting the outstanding loans, the center still had about 2 million yuan available.

Changshan's financial service center was welcomed not only in the township but in surrounding areas as well. Unlike savings and loan cooperatives, there is no residence requirement for those who use the service. This allows villages from other townships to take loans. One of the largest loans given by the Changshan financial service center was to a village in Zouping township, which borrowed 1.8 million yuan in March 1990 for use in a textile factory. The village was charged an interest rate of 15.8 percent and was given one year to repay the loan.

Market and Technical Assistance

The county has also been an invaluable source for technical expertise, which is probably one of the most sought-after inputs for rural industry. Factory managers and local officials alike list this as one of the most difficult problems facing rural industry. When a village enterprise needs help, it has the advantage of being able to call on the county bureaucracy.[64] The administrative bureaucracy is a free channel for information and resources for local industry. Officials are part of an information network embedded in the administrative hierarchy. The branches of the information grid automatically multiply the higher one goes in the bureaucracy. Zouping is fortunate in having former county officials who have succeeded in being promoted up the bureaucratic hierarchy. They facilitate access to these higher levels.[65] Using their bureaucratic positions and the contacts made through their routine administrative work, local officials can provide an array of essential services and disburse information to their local enterprises.

Study Tours. Local officials routinely use their bureaucratic position to provide firsthand information through the old practice of visiting successful models. Zouping's local-level officials, particularly those at the county level, take factory managers and township or village leaders to the most industrially developed areas, such as Jiangsu and Guangdong, and to famous national models to study management techniques as well as to explore what products can be made. Once they find a product, they use their connections to learn how to copy or to adapt the project for their locality.

In recent years, Zouping's officials have organized or have been included in trips abroad to sign contracts, buy machinery, and search for new products. While abroad, officials scour the stores in search of products that their localities can produce or export. Heads of successful villages have been included in these delegations. Regardless of whether a party secretary or a factory manager is a member of such delegations, local-level government officials are well versed in the production processes and technological needs of their key industries. The degree of attention paid by local officials to their important industries was evident in the well-informed technical questions that Zouping's county magistrate (who later became the first party secretary) asked when I accompanied him on a tour of the Samuel Adams Brewery in Boston.[66]

Meetings. To get market and technical information gathered by officials out to its townships and villages quickly and effectively, the county can call official meetings. These may be countywide or more localized meetings, with only selected townships and villages invited. For example, when Zouping County officials discover a product that they think is particularly profitable and suited to local conditions, they convene special meetings to bring it to the attention of their townships and villages. Zouping's Rural Enterprise Management Bureau organized such a meeting to promote the production of chemical products. The bureau convened the meeting in Linchi township, which was used as a model. The bureau had a Linchi township official chair the meeting, which was attended by relevant representatives of villages that already had chemical plants, as well as those village that had an interest in starting such ventures. The county held similar meetings to promote rug making; again, these were held at the township level. The idea to produce rugs stemmed from a township that had been subcontracting production for a Tianjin carpet company since 1986. Once the township started making rugs, a number of private entrepreneurs started to subcontract for the township-owned carpet factory. Taizi township by the mid-1990s was exporting rugs to the United States.[67]

Requests for Assistance. In other instances, a township or a village comes up with an idea for an enterprise or product and then seeks the help of the county officials to carry out the project. Local officials shepherd the project through the bureaucratic maze of licensing and gaining approvals. It is not uncommon for local officials to take factory managers or village party secretaries to the provincial capital or even to Beijing when developing a project, to get funding or approval. This is a routine part of the work of the county Rural Enterprise Management Bureau. Cadres in this bureau are always on trips to the prefecture, even to Beijing, on behalf of specific enterprises. When they are in the county, they often visit the townships and villages personally. A diary of one official from the Zouping County Rural Enterprise Management Bureau shows that during a one-month period in May 1988, he made six trips to Ji'nan, the provincial capital; one trip to Beijing; three trips to other townships; and six trips to various villages.

If the technical assistance needed is beyond the scope of county officials, they can help enterprises to get in touch with outside experts. For example, Xiwang village in Handian township wanted to produce a highly marketable type of cornstarch by-product. The village first came across the product in a trade magazine, but it knew nothing about the technology or expertise involved. The village party secretary, who was a representative to the provincial People's Congress, had heard more about this product while attending the People's Congress in Ji'nan. He discovered that the Wuxi Light Industrial Research Institute was the source of this product. The village party secretary then pursued his connections in the county, enlisting the support of various county officials, including the county magistrate. The project was turned over to the Rural Enterprise

Management Bureau. One of the vice bureau heads, who often took the lead in searching out relevant technology, knew about the product and had good connections in Wuxi, having gone there a number times on official business. He then took the village official to Wuxi to negotiate with the research institute. Together they convinced the research institute that the village, with the help of the county, would be capable of producing the product. A deal was concluded whereby the village paid technical fees to the research institute in return for equipment and on-site training of staff by technical experts.[68]

The Limits of the Collective-Sector Strategy

Through local planning and guidance combined with the corporate management of assets and resources, Zouping County successfully developed collectively owned enterprises. The combination of internal sources of collective funding and additional funds from the county made township and village enterprises economically feasible, even in the face of limited credit from the state banking system. Their success was facilitated by the gaps in production left by the large, state-owned enterprises. The pent-up demand provided a niche for these small, low-technology enterprises. Using relatively backward and inexpensive technology, enterprising local officials could make a success of these enterprises in a growing market.

By the 1990s, however, the national economic environment for rural industry had changed. Beginning with the recession of 1988, tight credit has made loans expensive and difficult to obtain. Rising competition from the expansion of rural enterprises nationwide has increased competitive pressures on rural firms. Increased market competition has steadily driven down average profit levels of rural industry nationwide.[69] The success of this sector in entering the export market necessitated higher production and technological standards—all of which required higher input costs and reduced profits. The low cost of the technology—a factor that initially allowed these enterprises to grow rapidly in the 1980s—has in the 1990s taken its toll as the market has grown and standards have increased.[70]

Consolidation through Selective Leasing and Privatization

It was never true that all collective enterprises succeeded. As indicated earlier, Zouping officials used a principle of internal competition in deciding which collectively owned enterprises would get capital, loans, and other kinds of assistance. Local officials have always had to set priorities for future development, and this has meant leaving the weaker and less promising enterprises behind and in some cases closing them, leasing them out, or selling them outright. All these options have existed from the early days of reform. In a competitive environment, some enterprises must fail, and as increasing competitive pressures bear on the profitability of local collective enterprises, officials have had to respond. They have done so in Zouping in two ways: by leasing or selling problematic enterprises more often than before, and by placing increased emphasis on new, private enterprises as sources of revenue and employment growth. The result has been a rapid evolution of Zouping industry toward a mixed economy in which private enterprise now plays an increasingly important role.

The costs of this development are different for the county, townships, and villages. The county government, which previously had lobbied banks to provide collectively owned enterprises with favorable loans, is no longer in a position to do so. This situation is made more difficult for those county officials who might still want to cling to the path of collective development because the banks have become increasingly conscious of profits. Over the course of the reforms, they have become commercial entities rather than simply an administrative arm of the government. They are now highly concerned about debt repayment.

The closures of some township and village enterprises have left the county's banks holding substantial amounts of bad debt. In the county as a whole in 1996, approximately sixty township and village enterprises had outstanding loans totaling around 40 million yuan that the banks were dubious about ever recovering. Of the total amount, approximately 20 million yuan was owed by thirty enterprises that had already closed. Not surprisingly, government banks to which these loans are owed are increasingly seeing township and village enterprises as liabilities that need to be restructured or closed.[71] The banks stopped giving financial ratings to township and village enterprises in 1992, after a number of failures occurred in 1991.

Local banks are adamantly in favor of tightening responsibility and accountability. The Agricultural Bank, the major lender for rural enterprises, is a strong advocate of privatizing township and village enterprises. In the view of one leading official, too many loans to township and village enterprises were improperly guaranteed, many by the township economic commissions. In the 1980s, particularly before 1988 and the retrenchment, the ability of enterprises to rely on the local corporate state allowed enterprises to develop rapidly. In a prolonged economic downturn, however, when large numbers of factories incur debt with little or no profits, neither the factory nor the corporate parent will have sufficient funds to repay debts. The problem for the banks is that it is also difficult to know which party bears ultimate responsibility for the repayment of these debts.[72]

Villages and townships also have begun to reassess the costs of maintaining direct control of their collective enterprises. While the contracting system allowed villages broad intervention, it also required extensive monitoring and problem solving. It is not surprising that village or township leaders would decide to rid themselves of some of their burden, particularly the unprofitable firms. Some villages are considering selling some of their less successful collectively owned enterprises to unburden themselves of problems and to better focus their energies and resources. At minimum, they are more interested in leasing out those enterprises that are problematic. Dongguan has not yet sold any enterprises, but in 1994 it leased out four—all fairly small and problem-ridden.[73] In recent years, villages such as Dongguan have begun to formalize the corporate character of their operations. Industrialized villages have changed their names to industrial corporations, and those that are large enough have become industrial conglomerates (jituan).[74]

While villages are in a position to lease or even sell some assets, the county's calculations decide which sector will receive the preferential treatment and will thereby be likely to grow more quickly. The pressures on Zouping's collective sector, along with changes in the fiscal system in 1994, has prompted the county to take a number of steps aimed at increasing efficiency of the remaining enterprises and to reconsider its attitude toward the private sector as well as to look beyond industry to other ways of developing the county's economy.[75]

New forms of management have been encouraged as a means of rectifying the problems in the collective industrial sector. Instead of mainly relying on contracting, authorities are pushing leasing, shareholding *(gufenzhi)*, and formation of conglomerates *(jituan)*.[76] Those enterprises that simply are not functional are to be declared bankrupt *(pochan)* and sold at auction *(paimai)*.[77] Auctioning enterprises began in 1994 with the sale of a small factory in Changshan township. By the end of 1995, a total seventeen enterprises had been sold—all township-owned. The sales have spread over nine of Zouping's seventeen townships. Linchi township has led the sale of township-owned enterprises: by the summer of 1996, it had sold the majority (eight) of its township-owned enterprises.[78] Zouping township ranks second, with the sale of two enterprises.[79] So far, few village enterprises have been sold.[80] Officials in charge of rural industry admit that the environment is now more difficult for township and village enterprises, but they also claim that for those that survive, the profit rate is higher. No figures were given, but improved performance was attributed to the formation of conglomerates, improvements in management, and county efforts to help these enterprises upgrade technical personnel by assigning more than one hundred vocational-school graduates to various enterprises.[81]

Encouraging New Private Enterprises

The interests of the county now have expanded beyond those of the townships and especially of village officials. The county government's revenues do not hinge on township and village enterprises, but for the townships and villages, they are crucial. The changed political and economic contexts have made the private sector a viable option and one that the county has come to realize is not only not threatening but actually a lucrative source of revenues. Between 1984 and 1988, taxes from the private sector hovered around 16 percent of total nonagricultural taxes. By 1994, its contribution had increased to almost one-quarter of total nonagricultural taxes. After more than a decade of development and experience, the county now sees the benefits of diversification, with a thriving private sector. The private sector provides an attractive alternative that not only yields increasing tax revenues but assumes *all* the risks of entrepreneurship and the burden of management.

By the mid-1990s, Zouping's corporatist system had altered its initial development strategy and adapted itself to encompass the private sector. Yet the activist role of local governments remains. A symbiotic relationship has emerged between key private entrepreneurs and the local officials from whom the entrepreneurs seek assistance.[82] Most of the types of assistance that were provided to the collectively owned township and village enterprises can be adapted or extended to the private sector as well. Townships or villages are unlikely to provide private enterprises with the same type of corporate funding through the redistribution of government funds. But the county certainly can provide credit assistance to the private sector, including the lobbying of banks. The county's decision to cut the bureaucratic loans and to enlarge the number and types of credit associations to serve all types of enterprises allows for its more diversified development strategy.

The mid-1990s saw a proliferation of township credit associations such as the one established in Changshan in the late 1980s. By 1996, every township had its own credit association, now called *jijinhui*. One difference with the newer township credit associations is that they are limited to serving enterprises within their own township, unlike Changshan's.[83] These associations directly compete with the credit cooperatives in each township, trying to lure more funds by offering higher interest rates on deposits than the official state institutions.

In addition to the township institutions are specialized credit associations, such as the Individual Entrepreneurs and Private Business Economic Fund *(geti siying jingji jijin hui)*, which serves private enterprise. The county government itself has created its own credit company, the County Finance Investment Company *(caizheng touzi gongsi)*. Loans from these credit institutions are more costly than loans from either the banks or the credit cooperatives, but these new institutions provide increasing amounts of credit to local enterprises, especially those desiring smaller, short-term loans. Deposits are attracted by offering higher savings interest rates than those given by the state banks. Zouping township's credit association was established in 1992, with an initial fund of approximately 100,000 yuan, half of which came from the township government. By 1993, it had increased its funds to 5 million yuan. In 1994, its loans totaled 15 million yuan and increased to 20 million by 1995.[84]

Equally, if not more important, local governments are in a good position to extend to the private sector technical advice and market information—a relatively costless service that the county can provide as part of its bureaucratic duties to any enterprise that can bring in new revenue. Technical assistance is important for the private firms in the early stages of their business, when their resources are limited, as it was for collectively owned township and village enterprises. For example, one tile-maker–turned–steelmaker succeeded because he could call upon the county Rural Enterprise Management Bureau for assistance. He discovered a profitable product, but he lacked the technical knowledge that would allow him to produce that product. After he approached the county, local officials helped him to contact consultants in Shanghai.[85] A scrap metal collector started his own factory, but only with assistance from county and township officials. In this case, the entrepreneur was from an area that had a long tradition of making small metal tools, but he needed help from Zouping County officials securing land and the necessary licenses, as well as technical personnel to bring his products up to acceptable standards.

The county's promotion of the private sector in the 1990s is a shift from its original development strategy, but it is not a renunciation of its earlier course. Statistics kept in the mid-1980s show that there have always been large numbers of legally registered small individual entrepreneurs in the county. What the county did in the mid-1990s was simply to provide this sector with preferential access to those resources that would allow the best of these firms to grow and to help new businesses become established, the way that the county helped the collective sector in the 1980s.

Beginning in 1994–1995, the county instituted preferential policies to encourage the development of large private firms *(siying qiye)*.
Local officials have promised to provide assistance in a number of
ways, from facilitating approvals and the granting of licenses to
helping with markets.[86] To further spur interest, private businesspeople who pay over 10,000 yuan in taxes have been allowed to change
their household status and be exempt from rural household obligations such as performing corvee labor *(yiwu gong)* and paying fees
to their village. If the taxes paid by a private businessperson are
sufficiently high, the exemptions and change in household registration can be extended to an entire family.[87] This sector has responded
positively. The number of large private firms grew from 69 in 1990
to 528 in 1995.[88]

Compared with areas such as Wenzhou, which have relied heavily
on private enterprise from the early 1980s,[89] Zouping's private sector
is still small and backward, but it is now growing rapidly. Before
1994, little evidence exists to suggest that local authorities allowed
privately owned enterprises to call themselves collectively owned.
The exceptions seem to be cases where a private entrepreneur enters
into a partnership with a village. For example, a village enterprise
used the investment of an individual, and then the village contributes to this initial investment to form a village-owned factory. The
individual investor becomes the factory manager and holds the contract for the factory.[90] After 1994, however, the county seems to be
joining areas such as Guangdong, which allows privately owned firms
to take full and direct advantage of the preferential taxes and credit
policies available to collectively owned enterprises.[91] According to
one official, approximately 10 to 20 percent of Zouping's officially
registered collective enterprises in recent years have in fact been
private.[92]

Conclusions

We have long known that China does not simply have one development model. Local state corporatism is but one strategy of development that arose out of a particular set of circumstances. Zouping's
experience shows that this development strategy is itself dynamic

and has evolved within one locality. Zouping's flexibility and adapt-ability is the key to the county's continuing growth. Zouping's econ-omy is now qualitatively different from what it was in the 1980s. The county has shown an impressive ability to face problems and adopt development strategies that are timely and suited to changing politi-cal and economic conditions. The role of the state has evolved with each phase of local development. It is when this evolution stops that we should expect to see stagnation rather than growth in a county such as Zouping.

Zouping's growth in the 1980s was not due to the expansion of the private sector or to covert private-sector activity. That did not begin until the 1990s. The county's growth proceeded through an evolutionary process that began with the growth of publicly owned township and village enterprises using the inherited institutions of the Maoist period—the bureaucratic networks and the collective structure that survived intact despite the decollectivization of agri-culture. This was a public-sector strategy in which the mix of private and public enterprise, and the forms of governance of public enter-prise, evolved gradually. Privatization began on a significant scale only after more than a decade of rapid public-sector growth, and even then, it proceeded only gradually.

The county decision in the 1990s to diversify its development strategy and to promote the private sector retains much of the characteristics of the growth seen in the 1980s. While not funded through corporate investment by townships and villages, this en-deavor is not laissez-faire capitalism. It is the extension of the county's preferential treatment to a sector that had heretofore been left to its own resources. Taken as a whole, Zouping's development is illustrative of the gradual transition from the socialist system to-ward a mixed economy. It is a situation in which institutional change has been slow in the face of a rapidly growing economy.

ANDREW G. WALDER

3 | The County Government as an Industrial Corporation

Shortly before arriving in Zouping County to conduct research on planning and financial reforms in county-owned industry, I had completed a similar investigation in a number of China's larger cities—Beijing, Shenyang, Tianjin, and others. Conventional wisdom at that time held that China's state-owned urban enterprises enjoyed too little autonomy in decision making, and that municipal governments intervened too intrusively in the conduct of business in state firms. My own research appeared to reflect this conventional wisdom, as I was able to uncover, in the course of interviews with enterprise managers and government officials, myriad ways in which enterprise autonomy granted on paper was undercut by the financial and taxation practices of local officials.[1]

Conventional wisdom also held that in stark contrast to tightly supervised urban state firms, the smaller firms of rural jurisdictions, largely outside the traditional framework of input-output planning, faced much stiffer market competition and enjoyed greater enterprise autonomy, and that this explained their more rapid growth of output and productivity. After beginning the same course of interviews in Zouping County, however, I realized almost immediately that the top political officials of the county intervened far more directly in the business affairs of their enterprises than their counterparts in the largest cities, yet in the years since my first visit, the enterprises that have been most closely supervised have enjoyed astonishingly rapid rates of growth. The purpose of this chapter is to illustrate and elaborate this initially counterintuitive finding—that smaller bureaucracy means a more direct government intervention that has done little to harm firm competitiveness—and to unravel some of its implications.

In the years since 1988, of course—and only partly owing to research conducted in Zouping County—it has become widely accepted that village and township governments have played a very active role in the management of rural industry. Many authors have since labeled this close degree of government economic intervention a form of "corporatism," or have likened village and township governments to economic corporations.[2] It therefore will come as no surprise that rural county governments also share this characteristic.

There remain large disagreements about exactly what arrangements this "corporation" analogy is meant to convey, how widespread these arrangements are, and whether such corporatism is merely a passing phase of the early stages of the transition to a market economy. In the hands of some authors, local "corporatism" means direct involvement of government officials in all major business decisions and enterprise managers who are paid government employees.[3] Other authors use the same term to convey a much looser association between government and industry, where local officials step back to assume a less intrusive regulatory role over public firms that are increasingly autonomous and in fact becoming "privatized" in a covert way through contracting and leasing out to individual entrepreneurs.[4] Where the first authors emphasize the widespread and relatively stable nature of the corporate management of economic assets, the latter emphasize their impermanence in the face of a relentless process of hidden privatization.

While a study of one county cannot adjudicate among competing generalizations about rural China as a whole, it can adjudicate among them in the context of a single place. As I have attempted to do for Zouping County, I have found that it is difficult to characterize a single government jurisdiction as fitting one or another model of government–enterprise relations, as the models vary widely among firms within a single jurisdiction. In Zouping, as I shall describe shortly, county officials are deeply involved in all the major decisions of some enterprises, and they are eager to divest themselves of any responsibility toward others. Over the past decade, they have maintained and even expanded the sector of firms with which they are intimately involved, even as rapid growth in other industries ensures that the proportionate size of this sector has declined. During the same period, county cadres have sought to release increasing numbers of firms outside of this core from their control—and responsibility.

This case study of one county therefore can inform our study of other areas by reformulating the questions we ask. Zouping has convinced me that instead of trying to gauge which generalization fits how many regions of China, we should offer explanatory propositions about *why* regions will vary. And before we compare regions against some ideal-typical model of government-industry relations, we should start with the assumption that there are wide local variations in the governance of individual enterprises, and we should offer propositions that explain this variation. Let me begin, then, with my conclusions, which are in the form of two propositions about such variation: the first within a region, and the second between regions.

Rural governments intervene selectively in local enterprises according to the economic stakes involved, and they maintain tight control over the largest and most important. They will intervene most closely in the operations of those public enterprises whose operations have the greatest impact—positive or negative—on local tax revenues. They will intervene less extensively in the affairs of the smaller enterprises and will in fact try to divest themselves of responsibility for the ones that are least profitable or are judged to have the least growth potential. Large enterprises that have poor business prospects, by contrast, will tend to be reorganized under close government supervision. Since the early 1980s, Zouping County officials have maintained and expanded a core of dominant enterprises under their direct control. At the same time, they have implemented various contracting schemes designed to give the managers of smaller and less profitable public enterprises greater autonomy and responsibility. This process moves forward as cadre dominance of local industry is solidified. In fact, in Zouping, the more the county government sheds itself of less essential enterprises, the better it can monitor the important ones.

Rural jurisdictions in which there are relatively few large enterprises will be those in which local cadres exercise dominant control over local industry. In jurisdictions with more enterprises or where the size distribution is relatively even, it will be more difficult for local cadres to dominate in a local economy. County cadres in Zouping dominate local industry because there are only forty-seven county enterprises, the four largest of which produced 70 percent of the county's entire output in 1992. The task of monitoring a handful of key enterprises is a relatively small one. Were Zouping to have four or five times as many enterprises and a less skewed distribution, it would be more difficult for cadres to monitor firms and exercise the same kind of dominating control.

In the remainder of this chapter I illustrate the evidence and reasoning that leads me to offer these propositions, and I also address the paradox implied in the first paragraph of this chapter: If close government supervision of public enterprise is deemed so harmful, how is it that rural public firms, where such supervision is even tighter, seem to fare much better?

Zouping County's Industrial Base

Compared with the massive industrial bases of the large cities where I had previously done research, that of Zouping has two strikingly different features. The first is its small scale, which leads to much closer and more intimate relationships between government and enterprise. The second, closely linked to the first, is the remarkable outward-oriented nature of local industrial production, which is a stark contrast with the internally oriented input-output planning of the major cities.

Scale

Like many other rural Chinese regions, especially those along the coast, Zouping has industrialized very rapidly in the last decade. Such growth came later than in the more celebrated rural regions of southern Jiangsu and coastal Guangdong, but it has nonetheless been striking. In 1980, gross value of industrial output was only 67 million yuan, less than half the output value of agriculture. Not until 1987 did output of industry surpass that of agriculture, but it took off during the ensuing five years.[5] From 1986 to 1993, sustained real growth in agricultural output occurred only in livestock, fisheries, and forestry (see Table 1.1). During the same period, industrial output grew more than five-fold in real terms (see Table 1.2).

By 1993, 63.5 percent of the county's total industrial output was still produced by public enterprises owned and operated by county, township, and village governments. During the takeoff period after 1987, the output of public industry grew 147 percent in real terms, while the output of private and cooperative industry grew even more rapidly, by 607 percent (calculated from Table 3.1).[6] While this period of rapid growth saw a steady decline in the public sector's share of output, from 83 to 64 percent, the public sector still dominates industrial production and continues to grow rapidly in absolute terms.

Table 3.1. Zouping County industry, output, and number of firms by type, 1988 and 1993

	1988		1993	
Jurisdiction	Gross output (millions yuan)	No. firms	Gross output (millions yuan)	No. firms
County	212.6 (44.1%)	42	380.9 (24.4%)	68
State	96.0 [20.0%]	20	229.7 [14.7%]	31
Collective	116.6 [24.1%]	22	151.2 [9.7%]	37
Township	52.0 (10.8%)	99	500.2 (32.0%)	259
Village-run	136.9 (28.4%)	405	110.3 (7.1%)	320
Cooperative	18.0 (3.7%)	637	97.7 (6.3%)	637
Individual	62.5 (13.0%)	3,339	471.5 (30.2%)	5,030
Total	482.0 (100%)	4,522	1,561 (100%)	6,314

Source: Table 1.2. Output figures are expressed in constant 1980 yuan. Brackets indicate percentages that are breakdowns of the total for county's percentage as a whole; percentages in parentheses total 100%.

Industry in the county is highly concentrated, and the main difference between public and private (including cooperative) sectors is in scale of production. The private sector's 36 percent share of production is generated by more than 5,000 enterprises with average annual production of 100,000 yuan per firm. The public sector's 64 percent share of output is produced by only 647 enterprises, and the scale of production varies greatly by government jurisdiction. Village- and township-run enterprises average 1 million yuan a year in production, while county-run enterprises average 5.6 million yuan (calculated from Table 3.1).

If we return more concretely to the corporate organization of public industrial enterprise in the county, we find that each of the 647 enterprises is lodged clearly under the ownership and control of a specific government jurisdiction. The 320 village-run enterprises are spread across 859 villages; a majority of villages clearly have no public industry (there is an average of more than five private household enterprises per village). At the next higher level of government, the township, there are 259 public enterprises spread across seventeen townships and towns, an average of fifteen apiece, generating an average of almost 30 million yuan in production (Table 3.1).

At the top of this hierarchy is the county government itself—the subject of this chapter. In 1993, the county owned and operated sixty-eight enterprises that had a total annual output of 381 million yuan, thirteen times that of the average township (of these sixty-eight enterprises, thirty-one are classified as "state" and thirty-seven "collective," but that legal distinction has little bearing on issues of ownership and control—they are all treated as county-owned enterprises).

The argument of this chapter is built around an implicit contrast with the industrial systems of the large urban jurisdictions in China. Just as the county's own industrial base dwarfs that of any single township or village, a county is in turn dwarfed by the massive industrial bases of the large cities. A city government such as Tianjin's presides over a massive industrial system of more than 5,000 firms. These firms cover virtually the entire range of product markets; they are organized into dozens of specialized industrial bureaus and corporations and are overseen by several layers of bureaucracy.[7] Zouping, and all other county governments, by contrast, has a much smaller, more specialized industrial base, and it faces vastly different incentives, fiscal constraints, and information and coordination problems. The lower the industrial jurisdiction, the clearer the incentives, the more immediate the fiscal constraints, and the easier it is for government to exercise effective control over its industrial assets.

Public enterprise in rural China is not an ownership form fundamentally different from that in the large cities; it is neither a hybrid property form nor freer from government control.[8] The differences between the effectiveness of public enterprise in urban and rural areas are due to the incentive and informational correlates of corporate scale. As I work through this argument by implicitly contrasting Zouping County's industrial system with those of the larger cities I have studied, keep in mind that any contrast at the county level will be more striking still at the township and village levels.

Outward Orientation

The small scale and simple structure of the county's industrial base dictate an outward orientation. The large and comprehensive industrial bases of large cities ensure that large proportions of output for local industry shall be required as an input for other local industries. In years past, these relationships took the form of input-output planning, where the vast majority of the inputs and outputs for local firms were designated by planners who specified customers and sources of supply in annual production plans, which, for the city as a whole, were in fact a massive internal balancing operation. The proportion of outputs and inputs designated in local plans has declined steadily during the reforms, and it now occupies only a minority of industrial transactions in most sectors, yet local supply and sales problems still tend to be internally oriented in large jurisdictions.[9]

By contrast, local sourcing for supply and sales has never been a possibility in Zouping County. Most industrial output is tied to the processing of agricultural products; the main industries are the brewing of beer and the distilling of liquor, the processing of raw cotton and cottonseed oil, and the production of cotton yarn and cloth. Local demand cannot possibly support the levels of output in these enterprises. Beer and liquor must be marketed to commercial agencies and retail outlets far beyond the county boundaries; cottonseed oil, ginned cotton, and cotton yarn and cloth similarly must be marketed to large-scale commercial or industrial operations that supply retail outlets or other industrial enterprises. One of the key functions of county government in this industrial system is to seek out and solidify marketing outlets for the county's rapidly growing production. In this sense, a county-level industrial system is of necessity far more driven by considerations of marketing, and far less driven by considerations of internal balance, than the large urban jurisdictions. This outward orientation, coupled with the smaller and more intimate scale of the local industrial base, makes public industry a very different animal in small county jurisdictions.

The County's Financial Stake in Industry

What do county officials get out of such a small industrial system? What incentives would drive them to play such an active role in the development of local public industry? The answer, in a word, is revenue. China's tax system, as all fiscal systems based originally on the Soviet model, relies heavily on volume of industrial output, only secondarily on corporate profits, and not at all on individual income. A county government's budgetary revenues are derived mainly from its own industrial enterprises. Sixty-five percent of Zouping's 1992 budgetary revenues were from taxes on industry alone (the total for industrial and commercial taxes less the business tax [Table 3.2]). The county's own enterprises accounted for virtually all of this revenue because the township and village governments collect revenue separately from their own enterprises.

The county also earned extrabudgetary revenues that were larger than the total amount of budgetary revenues (Table 3.2). These are earnings of enterprises, institutions, and administrative offices that are not taxable and that therefore are off budget (and are not subject to tax-sharing agreements with higher levels of government).

Many of these funds are also generated by industry, the most important categories being various ad hoc administrative surcharges and fees levied by the county and depreciation funds for industrial enterprises. The county's statistics are not as precise on this subject as they are for budgetary revenues, but no less than 55 percent of extrabudgetary income is from the county's state enterprises alone.[10] It is not possible to determine how much of the remaining income is due to various other surcharges and levies on the collective enterprises under the county. This close link between revenue and industry, combined with the rapid industrialization of the county, implies a large increase in the revenues that local party officials have at their disposal. Total revenues of the county government (budgetary and

Table 3.2 Sources of county revenue, 1988 and 1992 (in millions yuan)

Source	1988	1992
Taxes on industry and commerce		
Product tax	2.6	8.3
Value-added tax	4.8	11.9
Business tax	8.1	16.3
Collective enterprise income tax	6.9	9.3
State enterprise income tax	4.8	5.3
Other taxes	1.0	6.0
Total taxes on industry and commerce	28.2	57.1
Agricultural taxes	3.7	5.6
Other net income	.67	3.1
Budgetary subsidies from upper levels	7.0	0
Total budgetary income	39.6	65.8
Subsidies for special projects	0	12.2
Insurance funds and other items	0	3.8
Total budgetary income plus subsidies	39.6	81.8
Extrabudgetary revenue	51.1	76.2
Total County Revenues	92.0	158.0

Source: Zouping tongji nianjian 1988, 381, 385; *Zouping tongji nianjian 1992*, 263, 267. Figures are expressed in current yuan.

extrabudgetary) increased in real terms more than four-fold from 1980 to 1992 (Table 1.4). This increase is the direct result of the fiscal contracting system installed in the mid-1980s and the industrial boom that followed.

Such financial incentives exist for government officials in all jurisdictions in China, but these incentives are felt with much greater intensity by officials in formerly stagnant rural regions such as Zouping. This is a county that had no registered motor vehicles for civilian transportation purposes until the 1970s. The first five trucks appeared in 1970, the first sedan in 1971, the first passenger vans in 1976. The entire county had less than sixty miles of paved roads as late as 1977. The surge in government revenues experienced in the 1980s supported a massive capital construction campaign that remade the face of the county seat. A new network of paved highways crossed the county (tripling paved mileage by 1987), the main street grid of the county seat was relaid, sewer lines were put in, and the streets lined with sidewalks and planted with trees. The county's electrical power grid was extended, tripling power usage in the 1980s.[11] At least two new guest houses with restaurants were established for the county government, a fleet of new foreign or joint-venture–produced automobiles was acquired for official use, and new office buildings were erected.

In Zouping, as in other industrializing rural regions in China, the development of industry has an enormous impact on government revenues. These financial incentives for government are felt with much greater intensity in the more rural jurisdictions, because revenues increase at a faster rate than in regions already dominated by industry.[12] Zouping's county government is a clear illustration of this general rule.

The County's Limited Nonfinancial Interests in Industry

While the intensity of local officials' financial incentives regarding industry is greater than in larger and more industrialized urban jurisdictions, their nonfinancial interests in industry are at the same time much smaller. These nonfinancial interests in enterprises have long been seen as the main barrier to efficiency in public enterprises in planned economies because they constrain government in bargaining with firms and lead to a soft budget constraint. Because urban government jurisdictions depend heavily on industry for maintaining employment, for providing citizens with welfare and housing, and for providing scarce inputs for other industrial enterprises in the locality, the governments' ability to enforce financial discipline on firms is weakened.

While these are still major constraints facing the reform of the larger urban enterprises, it is striking how small these same constraints are in a rural jurisdiction such as Zouping. Consider first the question of employment: the county's entire industrial base in 1988 employed a total of only 13,121 people out of an adult population in the county of some 300,000. Many of these workers are from families that run private enterprises or that are still engaged in farming. This point was driven home during a research visit in 1988 that coincided with the county's June wheat harvest. During the harvest I visited some one-third of the county's enterprises. All of them except one were either closed or operating at reduced levels in order to allow workers to help their families bring in the harvest. The only enterprise to remain open, the Zouping County Cotton Textile Mill, was also the only of the county's enterprises to have any of the characteristics associated with an urban work unit, with a large percentage of its 3,186 employees living in the factory compound and enjoying extensive benefits. The 10,000 employees of the remaining forty-six county enterprises in 1988 lived, like most residents of China's rural towns, in privately owned homes and received few if any of the benefits of the employees of the large textile mill. Only at this textile mill are the county government's nonfinancial interests in employment and welfare provision similar to those characteristic of most urban enterprises.

Just as the county government is less constrained by concerns about employment and welfare, it does not need the products of any of its enterprises to solve supply problems for local industry. As explained earlier, virtually all of the county's products are marketed outside county boundaries. The only industries that produce typical shortage commodities are a small coal mine (output: 6 million yuan), a new copper mine (14 million yuan), a cement plant (5.4

million yuan), the cotton processing plants, and a lumber mill (1.7 million yuan). And there is no demand for copper ore in any of the county's industries. The county government therefore almost never finds itself constrained by an interest in the physical output of an enterprise as an input for other enterprises that it owns, thereby minimizing yet another nonfinancial interest to which soft budget constraints are commonly attributed.

The Budget Constraint on County Government

General discussions of the soft budget constraint on public firms in redistributive economies often assume weak budget constraints on government. Government budget constraints are softened to the extent that they can engage in deficit financing (by increasing the money supply or foreign and domestic borrowing), something un-available to subnational governments, and to the extent that a government jurisdiction with a large and diversified industrial base can increase its extraction of revenue from profitable firms to subsidize underperforming ones. In two ways, Zouping illustrates clearly how the budget constraints on lower-level jurisdictions are considerably harder than those of higher levels of government.

First, as Zouping has industrialized rapidly and its revenue base has expanded, the net flow of revenues between it and the next higher level of government, Huimin prefecture, has reversed. In 1988, Zouping received a 7 million yuan subsidy from the prefecture, equal to 21 percent of locally collected budgetary revenues, in order to cover its budgetary expenditures that year (calculated from Table 3.2). As a revenue-poor rural area, Zouping was for decades a drain on the provincial budget. These subsidies were designed to cover necessary services, not to provide the county with the means to industrialize. As the county's revenues grew with industrial growth, the budgetary subsidies disappeared, and by 1992, instead of receiving a subsidy, Zouping paid 3.5 million yuan in revenues to the prefecture, an amount equal to 5 percent of its budgetary revenue that year.[13] Zouping now received total subsidies of 12.2 million yuan from the province for "special projects," but this was not to cover local expenditures as in years past (see Table 3.2). Instead, it covered part of the local costs of provincewide infrastructure projects such as the new Ji'nan–Qingdao highway and the Yellow River flood control project. Zouping's net contribution to the provincial budget will likely increase as its industrialization drive continues.

The net flow of revenues between the county and the prefecture is governed by a financial agreement set annually in advance. The agreement contains incentives for the county to expand its revenue base by keeping larger amounts of revenues above projected amounts, but it also sets a floor on the minimum payments to be made to the prefecture. Unless the county suffers a natural disaster that tangibly affects its economy, it cannot expect a reduction in the minimum revenue remittances. The county must first slash its expenditures, especially its large capital construction budget, to live within its means. Only after it has cut such discretionary expenditures from its budget—and they are sizable at present—will the matter of reduced payments to the prefecture be discussed. Revenue shortfalls therefore entail high and immediate constraints in the form of opportunity costs for local officials (here we are speaking of the understanding and expectations of county officials I have interviewed, as no such shortfall has occurred in recent years).

Budget constraints are more immediate in a jurisdiction with such a small industrial base in a second way. The analysis of soft budget constraints in redistributive economies has always rested on the assumption of a massive process of redistribution of surpluses from profitable enterprises to the unprofitable. To the extent that the industrial base of a jurisdiction is large and diversified, such a balancing process can operate to soften budget constraints. But to the extent that the industrial base of a jurisdiction is small and specialized, such balancing processes are less feasible. In Tianjin, with thousands of firms operating in virtually all industrial markets, such redistributive processes can operate on a massive scale and provide a considerable budgetary cushion for the system as a whole. In Zouping, however, with only four dozen firms, all but a handful of which produce for consumer markets, and mostly in two markets (alcoholic beverages and cotton textiles), any slackening of sales will affect the industrial base as a whole and immediately reduce county revenues. The budget constraints on the county "corporation" therefore resemble more closely that of a small and relatively specialized conglomerate operating in a market economy than the redistributive bureaucracy envisaged in our theories about socialist economies (the same argument evidently applies with even greater force to townships and villages with a handful of enterprises).

Government Control over Industry: The Effects of Scale and Concentration

Up to this point I have focused on the ways in which the financial incentives and budgetary constraints that affect the economic behavior of rural government officials differ from those found in the larger corporate structures of the large cities. In this section and the next I turn from incentives and constraints to questions of agency and control. The smaller scale of rural industrial "corporations" not only provides clearer and stronger incentives for government officials, but it also allows these officials more effectively to exercise government ownership rights as they monitor and discipline the performance of their assets. As we shall see, top government officials in these lower jurisdictions are able to play a much more direct and effective role in the operations of public enterprises than anything imaginable in the large cities.

Let us assume, for the moment, that the mayor of Tianjin and Zouping's county magistrate are equally interested in superior financial performance of their industrial enterprises (although in fact the financial incentives and constraints are more intense at the county level). Both in the number of firms to monitor and in the number of levels of bureaucracy between the executive and the enterprise, problems of information and control are much smaller at the county level. The mayor of Tianjin is the ultimate principal of a huge multidivisional corporation that numbers 2,000 state and 3,700 collective industrial enterprises.[14] These plants are sorted into two dozen groups by product line, each of which is overseen by an industrial bureau (called "corporation" after the mid-1980s). These bureaus are the production divisions of the corporate structure. Many of these industrial bureaus are themselves so large that they are in turn subdivided into subbureaus (or "companies") that oversee smaller numbers of firms. In addition to these industrial bureaus, a city the size of Tianjin also employs a number of "specialized" bureaus that are the equivalent of offices in a corporate headquarters. The mayor's office will deal with enterprises and bureaus through a wide number of these specialized bureaus: taxation, finance, planning, price, labor and personnel, and others. Reports are passed up through these layers of bureaucracy, and directives are passed downward.

There are therefore at least three layers of bureaucracy between the mayor's office and the enterprises. Major decisions, such as capital investment loans, require many rounds of meetings between officials from the enterprise, the various bureaus, and representatives of the mayor's office. The ultimate principal at the top of the corporation is quite distant from the industrial assets that fund the budget.[15]

In Zouping, by contrast, the total number of county enterprises is roughly equal to the total number of economic bureaus in Tianjin. The county magistrate, assisted by a vice magistrate who oversees industry and public finance, works through one layer of bureaucracy. The most important enterprises in the county (textiles, alcoholic beverages, machinery, and mining), roughly half of the total, are grouped under the economic commission, whose staff of five or six officials work to implement development plans and monitor enterprise operations for the magistrate's office. Other significant enterprises are overseen by the Supply and Marketing Cooperative (especially the six lucrative cotton- and cottonseed oil-processing plants), and between one and five of the remaining smaller enterprises are overseen by each of several other offices: for example, the Light Industrial Office (towels, hardware, paper boxes), the Construction Commission (cement, plumbing, wallboard), the Grain Bureau (flour mill and animal feed), the Commercial Bureau (ice cream), and the Agricultural Bureau (tractor repair).

The task of monitoring county industry, however, is even simpler than these raw numbers imply, because output is concentrated in a small number of large firms, and the generation of revenues is still more concentrated. The ten largest county enterprises in 1992 alone generated almost 91 percent of the combined amount of profits earned and taxes paid by county industry,[16] and the top *four* enterprises generated almost 75 percent (calculated from Table 3.3). We have seen earlier that revenues from county industry generate no less than 65 percent of total budgetary revenues. If we assume that the ratio of taxes paid to realized profit is roughly equal across enterprises, then the top ten enterprises probably contribute roughly 60 percent of the county budgetary revenues, and the "big four" close to 50 percent. In financial terms, the task of the county government is to monitor and supervise a group of four to ten industrial enterprises that provide the majority of their current revenues and that have been the main engine of revenue growth since 1980.

Table 3.3   Zouping County's top ten revenue-generating enterprises, 1992

Enterprise	Realized profits and taxes (millions)	Percent of county total	No. of employees
Zouping Brewery	26.6	38.3	868
Zouping Oil and Cotton No. 5	12.7	18.3	1,626
Zouping Cotton Textiles	6.6	9.5	3,186
Shandong Fangong Distillery	5.4	7.8	396
Zouping Copper Mine	3.0	4.3	723
Zouping Electric Co.	2.6	3.0	250
Zouping Oil and Cotton No. 6	2.1	3.1	202
Zouping Pesticides	2.0	2.9	146
Zouping Oil and Cotton No. 2	1.4	2.0	202
Zouping Oil and Cotton No. 4	0.7	1.0	281
Total for top 10	63.1	90.9	7,880
Total for other 37	5.6	9.1	5,301
Total for all county enterprises	68.7	100	13,181

Source: Zouping tongji nianjian 1992, 128, 158–159. Profits and taxes are reported in current yuan.

Information and Monitoring Problems for Government

One can easily infer the intense interest of county officials in the operations of these key enterprises, and the strong incentives they have to monitor closely enterprise performance. In fact, this intense interest has translated into an observable pattern of deep involvement in, if not unilateral making of, all major business decisions of these firms. In my interviews in county offices and in ten of these enterprises, I gained the distinct impression that much of the entrepreneurial function in these larger enterprises is in fact performed by county officials. County officials take the lead in finding market opportunities, especially in pushing their firms to export, and in lining up partners for such ventures at the prefectural and provincial government, and among overseas businesspeople. They also are fully responsible for lining up investment funds for major projects: they control investment funds from local public finance, especially extrabudgetary funds, and determine access to local bank loans. When major funding must be obtained from outside the county, they take the lead in lining up opportunities and have been aggressive in using tax breaks to subsidize repayment.

The intimate involvement of county officials in the county's industrial enterprises is nowhere as clear as in the history and operations of the Zouping County Brewery. In 1992 this was by far the most important enterprise in the county, with realized profits and taxes of 27 million yuan, more than twice that of the next largest enterprise and almost 40 percent of the total for county industry as a whole (Table 3.3). The brewery turned out its first product only in 1984, after county officials decided two years before to close down an unprofitable chemical fertilizer factory and convert it into a brewery. They sent several technicians to apprentice at the Beijing Brewery, known nationally for its Five Star and Beijing brands. After major capital investments arranged by the county, the brewery began turning out its leading brand, Amber (hupo). In an effort to improve taste, county officials arranged to purchase higher-quality grain from Zhejiang and Jiangsu provinces and to import hops from Canada and Australia. They improved pumping capacity from a local mountain spring. They imported a new bottling line from Romania (a decision they would later regret and rectify). In the mid-1980s, their brew took third prize in a provincial competition and established a firm niche in the Shandong market, selling largely to county commercial companies and individual shops.

When I visited the brewery in 1988, it was in the midst of full-throttle growth. With the help of large tax breaks that enabled them to invest in new capacity and repay loans taken out to do so (they had paid no taxes to the county government for a number of years), they had just retired the debt on their first major capital investment project, which put their annual capacity at 18,000 tons and made an annual surplus of what would normally be called "realized profits and taxes" of 4.6 million yuan, except that all revenues that would have gone to the county government as taxes were remitted instead to banks to repay loans. They were just embarking on a much larger capital investment project designed to increase output to 50,000 tons and, with an eye on broader national and international markets, to improve their bottling and pasteurization processes. By 1992, with this project completed, the brewery had increased its realized profits and taxes by a factor of six. Where in 1987 the brewery's realized profits and taxes were less than half that of the county's former industrial giant, the Cotton Textile Mill, in 1992 the plant generated more than four times that of the Textile Mill and roughly 40 percent of the total for county industry. Again, if we assume that the brewery contributes a ratio of taxes to its profits that are not lower than the county average, that would mean that the brewery accounted for some one-fourth of the county's budgetary revenues in 1992.

County officials are not so deeply involved in this entrepreneurial fashion in all of their enterprises. Indeed, the opportunities for entrepreneurship are not the same in all product lines. County officials have also spearheaded a successful effort to reorganize the county distillery, improve the quality of its products, add a line of bottled spring water, set up a foreign joint venture, and push into the export market. In a smaller and largely unsuccessful venture, they revamped a clothing factory by purchasing capital equipment from Germany in an effort to produce blue jeans for export.

Yet the county's six lucrative cottonseed-oil and cotton-processing mills, which process the local cotton crop into ginned cotton for industrial markets and cottonseed oil for sale to state commercial agencies, have not captured local officials' attention in the same fashion. The technology is relatively standard, the markets are large but also simple, the opportunity for export very small, and the opportunity for growth limited to the size of the local crop. Similarly, the large cotton textile mill, an older plant (circa 1977) that produces cotton yarn and cloth for export primarily through contracts with a provincial government import-export corporation, offers fewer entrepreneurial opportunities. County officials scrutinize closely the operations of these other enterprises and are deeply involved in all plans to invest in plant capacity and work hard to assemble funding for the projects of which they approve, but they have not taken the lead in these enterprises in the way that they have for the brewery and distillery.

The focus of official attention on the brewery sometimes led me to the impression, in meetings with two successive county magistrates, that I was talking to a beer company executive rather than a government official. At my first meeting with the county magistrate in 1988, I was served the local brew at lunch and, after complimenting its taste, found myself drawn into an extended discussion of marketing opportunities for the beer abroad. The magistrate explained that the taste did not travel well, for they had not yet installed a pasteurization process, but that pasteurization had its drawbacks, for it might dull the taste. This problem would have to be resolved before they could export, first to Hong Kong and eventually the United States. He also explained that they had made a serious blunder early on: they had imported bottling equipment from Romania that was not of export quality and that, moreover, used half-liter bottles that were inappropriate for export markets where twelve-ounce bottles and six-pack cartons are the norm. He expressed a keen interest in the U.S. market and suggested that I set up a Boston distributorship (I foolishly declined). This impression of county officials as beer executives was reinforced during a 1993 visit to Boston by the magistrate's successor, during which he engaged a brewer guide at the Samuel Adams Brewery in an extended and spirited discussion of malts and hops, fermentation rates and temperatures, and other technical details of the brewing process.

While this degree of official involvement is not matched in the other local enterprises, county officials do subject the sales and financial figures of all of the county's firms to intense and continuous scrutiny. I found little evidence of the kind of bargaining over investment and output that characterizes government-enterprise relationships in the larger cities.[17] In large cities, industrial bureaus usually bargain on behalf of their enterprises, and they are motivated to capture more investment and better terms for their small industrial empires, often distorting information about enterprise performance in the course of continuing rounds of bargaining with specialized bureaus. There is no equivalent bureaucratic layer, and no equivalent problem, in Zouping industry. The economic commission (or its equivalent) is unambiguously an agent of top county officials; these officials are intensely interested in the financial performance of the enterprise and have little tolerance for losses. If a firm is losing money, the county officials have little difficulty determining quickly the reasons for this and deciding whether to revamp the enterprise through further investment (as with the blue jeans factory) or to close it down (as with the chemical fertilizer plant that became the site and equipment provider for the new brewery).

While officials kept a tight rein over their key sources of revenue, it was already evident by 1988 that they were willing to experiment with the smaller and less profitable enterprises in ways that allowed them far greater autonomy and at the same time relieved county officials of the burden of overseeing their operations in detail. In 1987 and 1988, small and troubled operations such as the Zouping Machinery Plant, which had specialized in the unprofitable manufacture of threshing machines, implemented a new contract system for managers. Plant director positions were opened up to competitive bidding, and alternative bids from individuals inside or outside the firm were assessed. The candidates made their bids by presenting to a management committee of the economic commission a three-year plan for production, sales, and revenues. The candidates were interviewed by the committee, and selection was based on the committee's judgment of the soundness of the proposal and the abilities (not promises) of the candidate. The sales and financial targets laid down in the candidate's bid then served as the basis for a three-year management contract. Bonuses are paid based on fulfillment of the agreed-on targets, and failure to meet the contracted targets is cause for termination of the contract at the end of the term.

Much greater rewards, and also greater risks, were attached to these contracts than was true for the standard wage and bonus arrangements in the larger firms. Managers were permitted to triple or quadruple their salaries if they overfulfilled their tax quotas by certain amounts. At the same time, however, these managers were made to put up collateral against underfulfillment of tax payments. Refrigerators, homes, and savings accounts were all designated as collateral under these contracts. Admittedly, these were items of small value, and the officials in charge of these schemes saw this, along with their unwillingness to expropriate a manager of his home, as weak points in the new system. But the signal was clear: the managers were to suffer the consequences of poor performance, even if their collateral could not come close to covering their obligations.

I got the clear impression, both from the way that this system was implemented in the smaller firms with poor prospects, and in many conversations with the economic commission officials who served as my hosts and guides during my research, that county officials were eager to rid themselves of the burdens of these small firms in order to concentrate on more important and more lucrative sources of revenue. Even in a highly "corporatist" jurisdiction as is Zouping, one could observe small firms—more trouble to county officials than they were worth—gradually being spun off in various contracting arrangements, while the county officials continued to concentrate their attention on the key public enterprises. During the years of our observation of Zouping, this process of spinning off control of firms through contracts, dubbed "hidden privatization" by some authors, did nothing to alter the county officials' firm control over the majority of industrial output. Only if subsequent growth rates in these spun-off firms were to surpass those of the core firms for a sustained period would this process alter local cadres' dominance of industry. Owing largely to the frenetic growth of the brewery and distillery, and secondarily to the expansion of the cotton-processing plants, such a process has yet to get under way in Zouping.

Conclusion: Why Rural Industry Is Different

The main thrust of this chapter is a counterintuitive point about the sources of dynamism in rural public enterprise, presented through a series of contrasts between small rural industrial systems and large urban ones. As observed in Zouping County, the main difference between urban and rural public industry is not that rural industry is somehow freer from "state" interference, or that it is a "semi-private" or hybrid entity that combines the characteristics of public and private ownership. To be sure, Zouping's county industries compete vigorously in product markets, but they are nonetheless government owned and operated in exactly the same sense as are the state enterprises of the large cities. The differences have to do with the correlates of corporate scale, all of which affect the variables commonly understood to soften budget constraints and weaken the financial performance of government-owned and -operated industry. In the smaller and more specialized industrial bases of rural government jurisdictions, the financial incentives and budget constraints of governments are stronger, and the capacity of government to monitor and discipline performance is also stronger. Zouping is very different from the larger urban jurisdictions because its financial incentives are much stronger, its fiscal constraints are much tighter, and it is able to monitor more closely the performance of the managers hired to operate the assets.

I do not mean to suggest that these differences in industrial organization and the related incentive and agency issues are responsible for all differences between urban and rural industry. I write here only of a contrast between publicly owned and operated industrial enterprises at different levels of government. Clearly, not all rural enterprises are publicly owned and operated, and in Zouping, as elsewhere in rural China, the private and cooperative sector is the most rapidly growing of them all (see Tables 1.2 and 3.1).

While I have emphasized the image of a tightly integrated industrial corporation in which top political officials are intimately involved in key decisions of their firms, note that this image becomes less applicable as one moves away from the key enterprises—especially the rapidly growing Zouping Brewery. County officials are not so intimately involved in decisions affecting the giant cotton textile mill, and they are even less concerned about, and involved in, the key decisions of the smaller and less promising public firms in their jurisdiction. Yet even in the more loosely held enterprises in this "corporation," the county headquarters is actively involved in hiring managers or setting terms of contracts, and assisting in the myriad ways described by Oi in the previous chapter. In Zouping, firms are monitored closely according to an enterprise's impact on local revenues—what constitutes the "profit" for the de facto owners.

Even in Zouping, where county officials have played such an important role in industrial organization, we still find nascent processes that others have described as "informal privatization." Clearly the county seeks to become less involved in the affairs of the less consequential firms with poor prospects. Local officials are happy to delegate autonomy to these firms to cut their losses and redirect their attention to the brewery and other promising larger concerns. If one's measure of informal privatization is the number of enterprises that are gradually loosened from tight government supervision, it is easy to exaggerate the pace of this trend: for every brewery and cotton mill, there are many firms like the agricultural machinery or hand-held electric tools plant. In terms of output and profit, however, the county government appears in recent years to have consolidated its hold over the key industrial assets, which up to the present time have grown rapidly.

This case study of one county industrial system therefore suggests a series of observations about future efforts to characterize these processes in rural China as a whole. The first is that it is now essential to specify exactly what role local government plays with regard to *which* enterprises that are under its jurisdiction. Do other jurisdictions exhibit the same variegated pattern as Zouping, where a small number of large and profitable firms are held very tightly, while the smaller and less profitable ones are gradually allowed freer rein? In jurisdictions with larger industrial bases and with many more enterprises than Zouping, or where firms are not so heavily concentrated in size, will the problem of monitoring firms lead governments to delegate more autonomy to larger numbers than in Zouping? And over time, do those firms on which local governments concentrate their attention grow rapidly, or are their growth rates outpaced by the smaller firms held less closely, or by the private sector or foreign firms outside the traditional public sector? Zouping cannot answer these questions, but it has helped us to define them more clearly. Not all corporations are alike—not in Japan, not in the United States, and not, we may safely assume, in the new public-sector entities that have emerged in China's rural market economy.

4 | Fengjia: A Village in Transition

China's reform era began with the dismantling of collective agriculture in the poorer rural regions of Sichuan and Anhui provinces in 1979. As it spread, this shift to family farming led to substantial and steady increases in agricultural output. Even more significant during this early period was the exponential growth of "sideline industries." Private initiatives were officially lauded as the key to success, further legitimizing the subsequent dismantling of the rural collectives and the urban reform in 1984.[1]

The winds of change, however, were slow to reach Fengjia, a village situated in the northern corn belt of Zouping County. Shandong has been slower to embrace reform than other coastal provinces.[2] What accounts for this slow response to reform opportunities is hard to pinpoint. Some suggest that peasants enjoyed more secure living conditions in Shandong and that they did not crave change. Or perhaps a conservative provincial bureaucracy has slowed reform initiatives. Or perhaps, as local people are prone to suggest, people of Shandong are more conservative in personality and hence less willing to break with the past.

Whatever its causes, the late arrival of reform in Fengjia allowed us to witness this dramatic change in detail when we began fieldwork there in the summer of 1987. Barely a year before our arrival, the village government (formally called production brigade) had completed the final phase of the Production Responsibility System by allocating and leasing farmland to individual households. Along with farmland division, in January 1987, collectively owned draft animals—chiefly cattle, mules, and horses—were also evenly distributed among village families. Several collective enterprises were leased out to private operations. Peasant families had regained their roles as the *chef d'entreprise* of agricultural production, management, and consumption.[3]

Along with the increased family roles in production, the village government was also changed, in accordance with national guidelines. The brigade government, dominated by the party secretary of the local Communist Party branch, was to be reorganized into three separate offices in order to maintain the functional separation between the party and the administration on the one hand, and between administration and economic affairs on the other. A new mode of production was established in Fengjia. Our research began at this critical juncture and permitted us to document this unfolding process and identify factors that will eventually have a long-term bearing on village life. Several questions could be raised: To what extent has the village genuinely complied with this reform policy? To what extent has this policy affected overall productivity in this village? What have been the major sociocultural factors, both within and without this village, that affected its current development? What have been the changed and unchanged aspects in Fengjia social life when compared with its collective past? In other words, how have villagers reacted, individually and collectively, to this new opportunity? To what extent has this production method brought about changes in family labor allocation, work patterns, and interpersonal relationships? How will this newly reestablished familial mode of production affect villagers' articulation with external markets, as well as their perception of women's status?

In this chapter we try to answer some of these questions. In order to draw a more comprehensive picture of Fengjia's recent transition, we begin with a brief historical account of the village, plus basic demographic and production data prior to the recent reform. In the chapter's second section, we describe both continuity and change in Fengjia as it implemented the Production Responsibility System. In the next section we analyze the impact these changes have had on Fengjia's economic activity and sociocultural life. The conclusion is to extrapolate from this study several general observations about Chinese rural society and their significance in China studies. Because some of the phenomena that we discuss here are still emerging, our findings should be looked on as tentative and suggestive rather than conclusive.

The History of a Single-Surname Village

It would be presumptuous to suggest that Fengjia is typical of Zouping County's 858 villages. The only thing we can safely say about Fengjia, in comparison with other natural villages in Zouping, is that it does not stand out as either too large or too small in terms of population size. Like many other villages in Zouping, the name Fengjia means the village of the Feng (surname) families (*jia*)—a natural village composed of a dominant surname group. The Fengs, who constituted over 70 percent of the 295 families in 1989, used to have an elaborate kinship organization called the lineage, with a shared ancestral shrine, burial grounds, and written genealogy.[4] The other large surname groups are the Zhangs, with thirty-five families (or 12 percent of the total), and the Lins, with twenty-one families (or 7 percent). The rest belong to numerous small surname groups, with between one and ten families. Most of these families were originally brought into this village by the Fengs as dependents or bonded servants.

Villagers claimed that Fengjia was first settled by the Fengs during the Ming-Qing transition, or mid–seventeenth century, when this area was depopulated owing to dynastic transition and wars. These early Feng settlers were from neighboring Shanxi province, which was hilly and had low living standards. No reliable historical document, however, has been able to substantiate this claim. The fuzziness of this issue is further aggravated by the fact that the current Feng lineage actually is composed of two separate branches, the so-called Local-Resident Feng (*zaidi Feng*; the Fengs who were already here when the others came and who now consist of approximately 30 percent of all the Fengs) and the Late-Comer Feng (*wailai*

Feng; the Fengs who came from other places, and who consist of 70 percent of all Fengs). These two branches have now been incorporated into the same lineage, as seen in the genealogy book, probably through the fabrication of history by the smaller and weaker branch in order to benefit from this shared surname. The existing Feng genealogy book was complied in A.D. 1865 by a prominent member belonging to the sixteenth generation in the genealogy. According to this document, the founding ancestor of the lineage in Fengjia was a member of the ninth generation, who migrated from Zhangqiu township (approximately forty kilometers southwest of Fengjia) to this village. The current Fengjia party secretary, Feng Yongxi, belongs to the twenty-second generation in the genealogy. If we assume that it takes roughly twenty years to produce a new generation, we may speculate that the first Feng settled in this village around the 1720s (20 years x 13 generations = 260 years).

The prominence of the Fengs in this village can be seen in the fact that, before 1949, their lineage is the only one with a genealogy, ancestral shrine, and corporate trust land. It was also the Fengs who produced most titleholders during the Qing Dynasty—that is, those who passed civil or military examinations sponsored by the government and received honorary official titles. Furthermore, before 1949, village custom had it that during the Chinese New Year all villagers participated in ritual worships at the village temple of Guangong (the patron god of the military as well as of merchants), located on the eastern fringe of the village, and then at the Feng ancestral shrine on the western fringe of the village. This was an important marker of the Feng lineage dominance. Ancestral worship in the Chinese cultural context involves complex rights and obligations between the deceased and the worshipers.[5] By paying homage to the Feng ancestors in this New Year rite, the non-Fengs were ritually acknowledging the Feng lineage as their benefactors so that they would be protected by the Fengs as if they were lineage members.

The dominance of the Feng lineage has probably been the single most important factor affecting this village's recent history. A village dominated by a highly organized, consanguineal kin group can easily mobilize the community for concerted actions. Internal dissensions can be subtly dissuaded and muted. Individuals representing the collective interest, with the show of force from the community, can broker with external authorities for certain policy implementations that the government favors. In return, the authorities channel resources to the community for its loyalty. This two-way, reciprocal favoritism further strengthens the position of the dominant group or its broker to achieve an even higher level of internal cohesion and homogeneity. It is through this realization that we might be able to explain the unique course of development in Fengjia in this century, ultimately leading to the current reform.

In the early 1930s, when Liang Shuming, one of the most prominent reformers in China, began his rural construction experiment in Zouping County, sponsored by the notorious warlord Han Fuqu,[6] Fengjia embraced this movement by tearing down the village Guangong temple and by converting the Feng ancestral shrine into the village elementary school. This could not have been done without the consent of the lineage elders. During the Second Sino-Japanese War (1937–1945), Fengjia was the headquarters of the Sixth Regiment, a degenerated Nationalist army unit that was later transformed into a local militia to resist the Japanese occupation army *as well as* the Communist guerrillas. During this period, more than thirty villagers enlisted in the Sixth Regiment. Again, we doubt that the Sixth Regiment would have chosen Fengjia as its headquarters without the active cooperation of the Feng lineage. In brief, during the Nationalist era, this village actively cultivated patronage with the authorities in various projects.

It was thus probably not a coincidence that, in 1946, when Fengjia was taken by the Communist guerrillas, Feng Yongxi, age fifteen (born 1931) and the most favored great-grandson of the last prominent titleholder, was sent off to Ji'nan, the capital of Shandong, that was still under Nationalist control. He spent the next two years there as an apprentice making mirror frames. Ji'nan was taken by the Communists in 1948, and Feng Yongxi went as far south as Xuzhou (in Jiangsu province) during this period, apparently with the retreating Nationalists. He returned to Fengjia in 1950, joined the village militia in 1951, and in 1952, at age twenty-one, became the head of the village militia. In this capacity, Feng Yongxi led village youth to participate in the county government's flood prevention projects along the Yellow River. He joined the party in 1955 and has controlled Fengjia since then. Feng Yongxi's position in this dominant village lineage can be seen in the Feng genealogy book when it was revised in 1942, at the urging of the last prominent degree holder. Among the young Fengs born after 1930, Feng Yongxi was the only one in the twenty-second generation whose name was recorded in the genealogy book.

What we are suggesting here is that despite the dramatic upheavals in rural China during this century, a dominant local group, specifically a kin-based lineage, could more or less preserve its power through the selection and backing of one of its more talented members as the local head. A unified village can successfully curry favors with government authorities by carrying out specific tasks that are deemed important. In return, tangible benefits may be funneled to the group to bolster its position. In this sense, Feng Yongxi can be looked on as representing the collective interests of the old Feng lineage, and he has been successful in crafting and charting the village's course of development in perpetuating the Feng lineage dominance. These two factors—namely, the degree of village-level cohesion and the ability of its representative to maintain control—are probably the two most important clues to understanding the kaleidoscopic development paths among China's multitude of villages.

Economy and Living Standards, 1949–1986

Living conditions have improved quite significantly in Fengjia since 1949. The restructuring of rural social institutions by the Communist government—such as the land reform (1949–1951), collectivization (1953–1957), and the establishment of the People's Commune (1958–1978)—certainly have had substantial impacts. Even more important, however, is improved agricultural productivity. The penetration of the party-state in economic spheres down to the village level permits the establishment of a unified, homogeneous agricultural regime. Scientific experiments, cropping technology, seed varieties, and machine-powered farm equipment trickled down to rural villages. The reverse flows contained agricultural "surpluses" in the form of taxation-in-kind and procurement quotas. In between political campaigns, the village population increased. The living standard also improved, albeit slowly at first. The village government keeps records on many aspects of the village since 1949. A synopsis of these records can identify several general trends in Fengjia, and the magnitude of change.

Table 4.1 indicates several trends in Fengjia since 1949. The first one is the population increase, except for the 1957–1960 period when the famine caused by the failed Great Leap Forward reduced the net population by 10.6 percent (from 809 in 1957 to 723 in 1960). Along with population increases, there has been the reduc-

Table 4.1. Population, farmland, and mechanical power in Fengjia, 1949–1986

| Year | No. families | No. people | Farm land (mu) | | Tractor units/hp | Combust engine unit/hp | Elec. engine unit/hp |
			Total	Irrigated			
1949	170	700	3,100	—	—	—	—
1955	180	740	3,100	—	—	—	—
1957	183	809	3,100	—	—	—	—
1960	185	723	2,950	—	—	—	—
1965	193	861	2,869	585	—	—	—
1970	217	1,001	2,752	1,140	—	5/60	—
1975	235	1,069	2,624	1,034	3/140	20/212	—
1980	263	1,099	2,537	1,202	7/302	34/393	32/201
1981	283	1,119	2,537	1,202	7/302	34/393	34/222
1982	285	1,124	2,537	2,123	7/302	32/388	46/332
1983	285	1,124	2,537	2,123	—	—	—
1984	285	1,127	2,537	2,123	3/112	27/677	125/670
1985	273	1,126	2,600	2,600	3/112	27/678	125/670
1986	282	1,116	2,600	2,600	11/246	38/717	162/860

Source: Fengjia Village Government Accounting Ledgers, 1987.

tion of farm land as housing, roads, and other public construction cut into the village land pool.[7] Another significant trend is the increase in the number of irrigated fields since 1964. This trend continued until 1985, when all village farmland was irrigated. Technological improvements have been the major counterbalancing factor to ensure continuously improving Fengjia living standards, despite the significant population increase and farmland reduction. Similarly, the introduction of combustion engines (for tillage and irrigation), tractors (for plowing and harvesting), and electric engines (for both irrigation and power machinery in factories) all point to the increased productive capability in Fengjia during the past two or three decades.

Another way to examine the villagers' changing material well-being since 1949 is to look at their agricultural productivity, including the net outputs for wheat (as their daily staple and cash crop), cotton (cash crop), and animals (mainly cattle, horses, and mules as draft animals and pigs to meet government procurement of pork).

Again, we can identify several trends from Table 4.2. First is the significant increase in wheat production since 1971. Unit production increased from 181 jin (one jin equals one-half kilogram) per mu (fifteen mu equal one hectare) in 1971, an all-time high, to 386 jin/mu in 1972, a 112 percent increase in a year, to 672 jin/mu in 1973, another significant 74 percent increase from the preceding year. Unit production of wheat has been maintained at between 800 and 1000 jin/mu since then. The total village wheat production increased by ten times between 1970 and 1976. This phenomenal growth has had two major impacts on village life. The first one is the replacement of the so-called harsh grains (*culiang*, including *gaoliang*, sweet potatoes, and corn) in villagers' diets with wheat flour. For peasants in northern China, having three meals in wheat flour is the equivalent of living in heaven. While there is no quantifiable data to support this point, our impression in our conversations with the villagers is that they are quite content with their current living conditions. The second impact of this development is that the village income level increased significantly as the crop output increased.

What contributed to this "Green Revolution" in Fengjia in the

Table 4.2 Yearly agricultural production in Fengjia, 1949–1986

Year	Wheat production			Cotton production			No. draft animals	No. pigs
	Unit sown	Unit prod. jin/mu	Total jin	Unit sown	Unit prod.	Total jin		
1949	767	92	70,564	1,440	33	47,420	86	36
1955	745	107	79,715	1,450	51	73,950	101	93
1957	750	121	90,750	1,450	53	76,850	117	89
1960	326	11	3,586	1,450	9	13,050	68	47
1962	745	46	34,260	1,450	9	13,050	68	41
1963	813	93	75,609	1,017	32	32,544	52	43
1965	871	119	103,963	1,374	48	65,702	54	31
1966	732	104	74,680	853	34.4	29,345	67	142
1967	810	160	130,300	1,080	57	61,300	75	148
1968	827	106	87,437	1,170	39	43,190	84	91
1969	825	169	139,852	1,204	76	91,228	102	28
1970	813	125	101,514	1,216	89	108,277	102	104
1971	909	181	164,805	1,220	106	128,622	102	180
1972	920	386	355,171	1,220	62	75,077	109	109
1973	922	672	619,853	1,370	106	146,102	110	176
1974	920	835	769,189	1,370	65	88,464	112	328
1975	1,020	946.5	976,010	1,370	110	150,194	117	425
1976	993	1,011	1,011,000	1,370	46.4	63,546	125	645
1977	1,000	1,007	1,007,051	1,350	80	106,711	132	703
1978	1,000	1,070	1,073,243	1,350	74.6	99,078	134	721
1979	1,093	936	1,022,673	1,350	132.3	178,556	148	695
1980	1,093	875	956,180	1,350	201.6	271,576	152	433
1981	1,093	1,037	1,133,093	1,350	155	209,520	153	91
1982	1,042	917	955,859	1,400	158.2	221,422	155	32
1983	1,042	807	840,972	1,400	164	229,581	156	15
1984	1,042	910	948,454	1,400	189.6	265,471	158	572
1985	1,043	930	969,990	1,180	161	190,000	155	1,135
1986	1,323	967	1,280,000	1,021	193.5	197,553	235	500

Source: Fengjia Village Government Accounting Ledgers, 1987.

early 1970s? The villagers credit an agronomist, sent from the Shandong Academy of Agricultural Sciences to perform farm labor in Fengjia, with introducing to the villagers modern soil survey and soil analysis techniques, as well as new seeds and fertilizer. Furthermore, the construction and completion in the early 1970s of an irrigation canal that provides adequate irrigation water to fields has also been credited for this increase.[8] As a consequence of this collaboration, the Shandong Academy of Agricultural Sciences has continuously used Fengjia as an experimental site for new crop varieties. It has also designated Fengjia as a supplier of wheat seeds. The price differential between wheat sold as staple and seeds is enormous. For instance, in summer 1991, one jin of wheat sold for 0.36 yuan in the grain market. The same amount can be sold for one yuan as seed.

This technological breakthrough in wheat production, however, was not duplicated in cotton production, although its unit production has also increased steadily since the early 1970s. The production figures for wheat and cotton from 1976 onward seemed to indicate that winter wheat and cotton are "environmentally appropriate" or "economically complementary." In years when the village enjoyed bumper wheat harvests, cotton production remained stable. On the other hand, when wheat production declined, high cotton yields made up for part of the deficit. The negative correlations between these two crops over the years seems to indicate that the selection of winter wheat and cotton as the main crops was probably not coincidental or accidental.

The second trend in Fengjia since 1949 is the steady increase in the number of draft animals and pigs. As cattle, mules, and pigs rely somewhat on agricultural residues, the increased agricultural production permitted villagers to raise more animals. More draft animals help the villagers with farmwork and provide transportation. Increased hog production permitted the villagers to have more pork in their diet and to sell more pork to government procurement programs, thus giving them more income. The dramatic decline in the number of hogs between 1980 and 1981 (from 433 to 91 heads at year-end) was due to the decentralization effort introduced in 1981 to turn collectively run pigpens into household operations. The village government sold most of the pigs it owned and declared

that individual households could keep their own pigs in their courtyards. This move signified the first step in agricultural decentralization in Fengjia.

In late 1986 or early 1987, as Fengjia prepared to divide the land
according to the Production Responsibility System, the village had a
population of 1,116 in 282 families, with an average of 3.96 persons
per family. The total farmland was 2,600 mu (or about 173.3 hec-
tares), although the village government withheld an undetermined
amount of "flexible land" for discretionary use. Roughly half of the
farmland (1,323 mu) was used for winter wheat/summer corn production, and the remaining half for cotton (1,021 mu), peanuts (303
mu), vegetables (36 mu), and an apple orchard (27 mu). Agriculture
contributed more than two-thirds of the collective net income
(827,820 yuan out of a total 1,230,801 yuan) in 1986.

The remainder of the income came from sideline industries that
included four factories, a bakery (making steamed buns), a grocery
store, a clinic, a construction team, and a transportation team. The
four factories included the peanut-oil–pressing factory that was built
in 1963 and employed thirty workers. The popsicle factory built in
1982 employed thirty-five seasonal workers, mainly between May and
August. The small flour mill was built in 1982 and employed ten
workers. And, finally, the starch factory was built in 1983 and employed thirty-nine workers. The collective also owned four tractors
used mainly for plowing, seven harvesters for harvesting, and four
automobiles that served transportation needs. Per capita net income at the end of 1986 was 1,103 yuan, above the national average
in that year.

Rural Reform and Its Implementation, 1986–1993

Zouping County began to implement the Production Responsibility
System in 1983. The system's most radical form, called *dabaogan* (big
contract work), was for the brigade to divide all farmland within its
control and lease it to members of the community on a per capita
basis. All other collective property, such as productive enterprises,
farm implements, animals, and transportation vehicles, was also divided or leased out for private operations. Along with the bene-

fits came obligations. All taxes and government procurement were also divided among villagers according to their contract rights. In Zouping, however, the county government did not enforce the implementation of this *dabaogan* in all villages. A county-level official estimated that, by mid-1987, about one-half of Zouping's 858 villages had adopted this *dabaogan* policy. The other half took a second approach, a sort of a compromise between decentralization and collective ownership. This was the so-called Dual Management System *(shuangceng jingying)*, which Fengjia adopted in 1986.

Dual management divided the village economy into two sectors: the agricultural and the nonagricultural. The latter included both collective and sideline industries. In practice, dual management turned the agricultural sector back to peasant households, in accordance with the spirit of the Production Responsibility System, while keeping the nonagricultural enterprises, often the more profitable ones, in the hands of the village government. Cynics may consider this dual management system a cop-out by rural cadres who tried to preserve their power and privilege by keeping the profitable non-farm sector in their hands. The argument for dual management, however, is that some of these sideline industries have such a large capital investment or employ so many workers that they cannot easily be turned into private hands. This was precisely what Party Secretary Feng Yongxi said when he explained why Fengjia's reform had taken this particular path.

The Farm Sector

In 1986, all 2,600 mu of farmland on the books in Fengjia was divided among 1,116 villagers on an equal basis. This turned out to be 2.3 mu per person, or 9.2 mu (or about 1.51 acres) for a family of four. No written contract was signed between village families and the government. The village government promised that this arrangement (that is, the amount of land each family received) would be reviewed and adjusted every three years to reflect the changing family compositions, such as a daughter-in-law marrying into the family, the birth of a child, or the death of a parent. The government procurement quota of wheat from Fengjia in 1987—a

total of 240,000 jin out of the village's approximately 1 million jin
harvested (or about 92 jin per mu of leased land)—was to be split
equally among all villagers according to the amount of land leased.
Government procurement was definitely a financial burden for the
peasants. They sold the wheat at 0.23 yuan per jin to the government, as opposed to the free-market price of 0.36 yuan per jin that
year. In other words, the hidden tax in the form of government
procurement is about 11.96 yuan per mu of leased land. The land
tax of 8,600 yuan (or about 3.31 yuan per mu), however, was not
transferred to village families as was customary in other villages. The
village government paid this sum out of its operating budget.

In dividing the farmland, specific attention was given to the variability of land quality and the variability of planted crops. Andrew
Kipnis describes these multiple concerns:

> Land was divided into two types based on the two major crop
> rotations. On "cotton land," cotton, usually intercropped with
> mung beans, was harvested once a year; on "wheat" or "corn" land
> (depending on the time of year), winter wheat and summer corn
> were alternated to yield two harvests a year. Each of the two types
> of land was further subdivided into good and bad land. In all, each
> household was allocated slightly over one mu each of wheat/corn
> land and cotton land (a total of 2.3 mu) per head.[9]

Thus an average family of four in Fengjia receives 9.2 mu (or 1.51
acres) farmland from the collective as its private operating land. This
9.2 mu is most likely to be divided into four tracts: a few rows of good
cotton field to the northwest of the village; a few rows of good
wheat/corn field to the northeast of the village; another few rows of
low-quality cotton field to the southeast of the village; and, finally, a
few rows of poor wheat/corn field to the southwest of the village.
Each family marks its land from its neighbors with slightly higher or
wider earth bunds. A casual observer may not notice such subtle
landmarks.

Even though the village government divided up farmland among
villagers as their privately leased property, the main farmwork is still
managed by the collective. The village government owns many farm
machines. With open and flat fields in this part of North China, it

would be far more advantageous to maintain mechanized farming—especially in such labor-intensive tasks as plowing, harvesting, irrigation, and pest control—than to have each family manage its own land. To carry out these essential tasks, the village government maintains four farm operation units, established during the collective era, under its administration:

1. The machinery unit is composed of twelve persons who operate four tractors for plowing and seven harvesters for harvesting, the two most labor-demanding tasks. These twelve individuals are also responsible for maintaining these machines.
2. The irrigation unit has twenty-two persons—a unit head and twenty-one workers—who operate and maintain the twenty-one electric water pumps owned by the collective.
3. The technology unit has five persons who provide technical assistance to villagers about the timing and quantity of chemical fertilizers or pesticides to apply to the fields and how to select crop varieties.
4. The supply unit consists of five persons responsible for receiving supplies from the government distribution agents, such as chemical fertilizers, coal, gasoline, pesticides, and seeds, and for distributing them to individual families.

The preservation of these four collective farm operation units appears to have dual implications for the villagers. On the positive side, they minimize the amount of work each family must undertake. These work units charge farmers for performing these essential tasks, such as irrigating one mu of land with well water for two yuan, while irrigating the same land with water from an irrigation canal for one yuan. The level of mechanization in Fengjia was not affected by decollectivization.

The downside of these collective operations, however, is stifled individual initiative. Because mechanization implies that ideally all adjacent farmland should be plowed, planted, irrigated, and harvested uniformly, the village government in essence still dictates the villagers' farm operations, especially with regard to the major crops of wheat and cotton. What to grow and when to grow it are largely decisions made by these village-level leaders. The land titles that villagers gained after the implementation of the Production Responsibility System contained merely rights to take care of the fields after the major work was done, as well as to plant the intercropping of corn after the winter wheat harvest and to plant mung beans, peanuts, and sesame seeds between cotton rows.

Besides farmland, Fengjia also has 36 mu of vegetable gardens leased out to a dozen village families for a total sum of 28,000 yuan per year. A similar arrangement was made for the apple orchard. It was leased out to seven families for an annual fee of 14,500 yuan, plus 10,000 jin of apples to be distributed to all families.

Several collectively owned livestock operations in Fengjia have been leased to individual households since 1981. The village chicken coops and pigsty were abandoned in that year, and village families were allowed to raise their own chickens and pigs. In the 1987 division, collectively owned draft animals—mainly cows, mules, and horses—were divided among villagers on a per capita basis. The 235 draft animals owned by the collective in early 1987 were appraised and then divided on a per capita basis among the 1,116 villagers. Thus a family of five may receive an adult mule with an assessed value of 400 yuan. After receiving this mule, the family responsible for its upkeep has exclusive rights to use it in farmwork or hauling.

In sum, we may conclude that this privatization effort under the Production Responsibility System in the agricultural sector in Fengjia is probably more significant on paper than in reality. Under the so-called Dual Management System, the former brigade government still micromanages agricultural production for most village families, especially in deciding crop varieties, acreage to be planted, and planting time, as well as the actual work. It is true that village families now lease their assigned land from the collective as private operations. It is also true that villagers no longer depend on the collective for their farm remuneration in the form of work points. Theoretically, they can sell their agricultural surpluses whenever they want and to whomever offers the best prices. The reality is far from the ideal, however. Almost all cotton produced in 1986 (177,200 jin out of a total production of 197,553 jin) was sold to the state procurement agency through the village government. The corn was sold to the village-run starch factory. And, finally, the surplus wheat was sold to the government as seed grain through the village government. Thus the village government not only manages and controls most of the farm production input factors in Fengjia (such as rationed chemical fertilizer, pesticide, gasoline, plant seeds, and machinery), but it also manages most of the villagers' marketing channels that directly affect their financial remuneration.

The Nonfarm Sector

In the nonfarm sector, the implementation of the Production Responsibility System also initiated the leasing out of selected collective enterprises, although its extent was curtailed by the Dual Management System. The brigade government leased out collective enterprises that were small in capital or in number of employees. A comparison of the 1985 and 1986 village accounting ledgers (Table 4.3) show the number of collective enterprises and the differences in profits generated in these two years.

Of the nine collective enterprises in 1986, only three were leased out for private operation: the flour mill, the bakery, and the grocery store. They were all small-scale, with no more than ten regular employees. They were also service-oriented, with small amounts of capital investment. The other enterprises with heavy capital investment or a large number of workers are in the hands of the village government. The only exception is the village clinic. The clinic, with its three barefoot doctors, did not (or was not allowed to) become private, not because of its high profit margin but because of the strategic importance of public health in the collective well-being.

The dramatic increase in gross earnings for the oil-pressing factory (mainly processing peanuts) in 1986 does not reflect the real situation. The village government invested heavily in that year to renovate and expand the entire factory. This improved facility increased the total volume of peanuts processed, but the total operating expenses increased dramatically owing to the much larger amount of peanuts purchased and peanut oil sold. But the net profit showed only a modest increase.

Party secretary Feng Yongxi was quite explicit about why he had insisted on maintaining collective enterprises while swimming against the national decollectivization trend:

> The government slogan since the Third Plenum of the Eleventh Party Congress has been *gaige kaifang, gongtong fuyu* (reform and opening up, and shared prosperity). What is the best way to maintain shared prosperity? Not through giving away profit-making enterprises to a few individuals. In controlling these large enterprises, the village government is able to use the profits to support villagewide social welfare programs. Furthermore, the village government can assign high-income work to families that have greater financial need. In so doing, we are ensuring that prosperity will be shared by all villagers!

Table 4.3 Gross income from village enterprises, 1985 and 1986

	1985 Gross income (yuan)	1986 Gross income (yuan)	Difference (yuan)	No. workers
Starch factory	488,708	931,700	442,992	39
Popsicle factory	53,000	47,104	5,896	35[a]
Oil pressing	60,000	2,169,347	2,109,347	30
Flour mill[b]	38,000	—	—	10
Bakery[b]	14,000	—	—	5
Grocery store[b]	22,500	—	—	5
Construction	32,954	67,205	34,251	?[c]
Transportation	87,332	95,317	7,985	?[c]
Clinic	10,825	—	—	3
Total	807,319	3,310,673	2,503,345	129

Source: Fengjia Village Government Accounting Ledgers, 1987.
    a. Seasonal workers in the months of May, June, July, and August. Closed in 1989.
    b. Facility leased out for private operation. Total receipts for the three are undifferentiated in account ledgers.
    c. Work on seasonal, part-time, and piecemeal basis.

Village Government Reform

According to the guidelines of the Production Responsibility System, the abolition of the commune system was to be accompanied by the restructuring of the village government. The brigade government— a comprehensive organization that encompasses almost all aspects of village life, including economic production, distribution, consumption, education, health care, ideology, and public security—is to be divided into three separate branches: the Communist Party Branch Committee *(dangzhibu)*, the Village Committee *(cunmin wei-yuanhui)*, and the Enterprise Management Committee *(qiye guanli weiyuanhui)*. The Party Branch Committee is the advocate of Communist ideology and supervises village administration to ensure that party policy is executed properly. The Village Committee is the administrative unit that carries out day-to-day management of public affairs, such as household registration, public security, distribution of rationed goods, and implementation of government policies and procurement goals. Finally, the Enterprise Management Committee is to manage collectively owned production facilities, such as leasing out the apple orchard or vegetable garden, or operating the factories.

Ideally, these three branches of the government should be composed of three different sets of people. With clearly defined functions and responsibilities, these three organs should be able to maintain some kind of system of checks and balances. The purposes of this government reform are clear. The first one is to prevent the concentration of power in the hands of a local official, usually the party secretary. The separation of the party from the administration *(dangzheng fengli)* and the separation of the administration from the economy *(zhengqi fengli)* is aimed at building a more "rational" (in the Weberian sense of the word) government structure to eliminate abuses at the local level. The second goal of this reform is for the government to refrain from micromanaging every single household's economic affairs as it did under the brigade system. Under this reform, each peasant family should have autonomy in agricultural production and marketing, as long as it fulfills all contractual obligations, such as government procurement quotas and land taxes.

With a compartmentalized government system, the peasant households should also have leeway to develop private initiatives.

This government reform in Fengjia, again, is less than comprehensive. The Village Committee is composed of six members: the chairman of the committee (who also doubles as the village mayor), two vice chairs (one drives the village automobile; the other supervises collective enterprises), and three team heads. These three team heads are elected from the three teams (now called village small units) that make up the village. These three team heads also have their specific assignments within the Village Committee: one is in charge of security, one oversees civilian affairs, and one (usually a woman) is in charge of education, health, and women's affairs.

Theoretically, all committee members are chosen by villagers through free and open elections held once every three years. The real problem is to ensure that the elections at both the small-unit and village levels will produce six committee members who match exactly these functional specifications. It is here that the party secretary, who is not a member of the Village Committee, intervenes and plays the pivotal role in identifying the six candidates for the election, orchestrating the election, and appointing committee members to various posts. Theoretically, the Village Committee is to be elected by popular vote, thus representing the entire village in administration.

In Fengjia, however, the committee served as Party Secretary Feng Yongxi's personal deputies in running village affairs. The current village mayor, Zhang Lin, was handpicked by Feng Yongxi to be his successor. Because he is a certified agronomist, Zhang Lin is content to watch over agricultural production in the village. One of the two vice chairs of the Village Committee drives Party Secretary Feng to numerous meetings that he regularly attends. The other vice chair regularly reports to Feng Yongxi all major incidents in village enterprises. All of these committee members are considered to have full-time jobs, and they draw 120 yuan per month for their work.

The Communist Party Branch in Fengjia had thirty members in 1987. The party secretary, Feng Yongxi, was appointed by the higher-level party offices. Unless he commits gross errors—such as taking the wrong side in a political campaign or outrageously abusing his power—the higher authorities will not easily remove him from office. The post of the party secretary is thus much more secure than the village mayor, whose tenure lasts for three years.

The Party Branch Committee has five regular members: the party secretary (Feng Yongxi), two vice secretaries (Zhang Lin, who is also the head of the Village Committee, and the automobile driver, who is also one of the two vice chairs of the Village Committee), and two other members. One of the two members is Fengjia's plumber-cum-electrician, responsible for the village's running-water system and its electricity. He is also a member of the Village Committee. The last party committee member is the manager of the village starch factory. He is not a member of the Village Committee, but the importance of the starch factory for employment and in the marketing of corn is such that he is looked on as a real power holder in Fengjia. All five of these members receive regular salaries from the village for their work, probably comparable to the Village Committee members, but we were unable to determine the actual amount.

Fengjia, however, has never set up an Enterprise Management Committee. The collective economic affairs are instead managed by the Village Committee and the Party Branch Committee, with half of their memberships overlapping. Because the Village Committee chair, Zhang Lin, is the vice secretary of the Party Branch Committee and is a subordinate of Feng Yongxi, we can clearly see who wields the real power in Fengjia. Feng Yongxi is nonapologetic about this less-than-genuine political reform. One point he raised is that the national government has never made it clear whether the Village Committee is the villagewide assembly representing local autonomy or the lowest-level government office carrying out administrative responsibilities. The national government has never enacted laws to define the organization and function of the village-level government. And while the national government promotes the separation of party and administration, as well as that of administration and economy, the official doctrine is that the Communist party still occupies the leadership position in this revolutionary transition period. He saw no contradictions between the government's current reform drive and the practices implemented in Fengjia.

Sociocultural Changes

Rural reform implemented in Fengjia, and perhaps throughout much of the North China Plain, is not as comprehensive and thorough as that in the southern provinces of Fujian and Guangdong.[10] Despite the lack of a broad restructuring of its political-economic organizations in Fengjia, we may still discern several tangible changes, especially in areas of family organization and intrafamilial relationships, economic diversification, and sociocultural life within the village.

The most significant sociocultural change appears to be within the family unit. Village families regained land titles through leases with the village government. The farm family has been recognized as the operating and managing unit of agriculture. A certain level of economic autonomy has been reestablished. In major farm operation activities, however, the village government is still very much in charge of important decisions, such as the timing of plowing and irrigation, the choice of crop varieties, and the marketing of farm produce, especially for the major crops of cotton and wheat. In the secondary agricultural production areas, however, the village families do have increased decision-making power. These decisions include whether to raise fowl, pigs, or draft animals in their courtyards; the amount of intercropping for mung beans, soybeans, or sesame seeds to be planted in a season; and the amount of time to be spent in the fields.

Furthermore, villagers are also responsible for selling their "surplus" produce either in nearby periodic markets or to itinerant merchants who trade goods with villagers on a barter system. In the summer months in Fengjia it is common to see itinerant merchants on their bicycles or donkey carts trading fresh fruit—peaches, plums, or watermelons—with villagers for their wheat. As the *chef d'entreprise* of the family economy, villagers have increased interest in markets and information. The level of agricultural commercialization has increased as a consequence. Villagers who contracted vegetable gardens now have to find their own buyers in nearby periodic markets. Apple orchard operators contact wholesalers in large cities as far south as Shanghai or Nanjing in order to sell their crops.

Even more important in this period of change is the impact on intrafamilial relationships, specifically in two areas. Under the Production Responsibility System, every villager receives 2.3 mu leased land from the village government, regardless of that person's age and gender. Earlier, village elderly who had retired from farmwork used to depend on their sons for old-age support. They helped their son(s) by taking care of the grandchildren or cooking for them during busy seasons. But now these aged parents have gained additional economic value because they also receive leased farmland—still the most important income source in Fengjia. This has obviously strengthened their position within the family: their presence increases family landholdings.

The importance of this land title for the elderly can be seen in formal family divisions. During family division, it is quite common for all the sons to divide their parents' leased land. They will, in return, pledge to provide a certain amount of cash, grain (mostly wheat), and coal (for winter heating) to their parents on an annual basis. If, for any reason, only one of the sons farms all the parental leased land, he will then be responsible for a much larger share of parental support, sometimes double that of his siblings. It is understood that the family will have to relinquish this portion of the leased land when the aged parents pass away. Until then, their land titles are looked on as personal assets that can be used by their sons.

The second impact of this Production Responsibility System on the intrafamilial relationship, contrary to conventional speculation, is the rising importance of women in these newly reformulated farm families. In 1986 Fengjia had 550 adult laborers, about one-half men and one-half women. Of the adult male laborers, 179 had nonfarm employment: 129 worked in various collective enterprises, and 50 were involved in a collective work unit, as tractor operators, irrigation pump operators, and salaried officials of the village government and the Party Branch Committee (except for one female official who was responsible for women's work). Because few women are employed in nonfarm trades, they have been the principal source of farm labor in Fengjia.

Major changes have occurred with respect to women's participation in labor under the current reform. Before 1986, the village government organized women to perform farm tasks for the collective. They earned work points to augment their husbands' wages or salaries. Their economic contributions were recognized only marginally because the return from farming was pooled together, managed by the village government, and distributed to households. When the farmland returned to village families after 1986, women became the principal source of farm labor within each family. It is quite common to see village women go to the fields at four or five on summer mornings and spend the rest of the day there weeding, trimming, or fertilizing their crops. In their absence, the parents-in-law or husbands take on the responsibility of child care and cooking. When the women go home for meals, they may also breast-feed their nursing babies. Other than that, they have delegated most child care responsibilities to their husbands, parents-in-law, or other mother surrogates. They have become the chief providers and managers of the family estates as well as an important source of income. This new status is well recognized by both their husbands and parents-in-law.

The increased economic importance of the elderly, plus the reliance on female labor in agriculture, leads to one conclusion: the advantages of the traditional extended family—a phenomenon also seen in southern China.[11] The complementarity between the aged parents in child care and landholding and the women in farm management is self evident. An extended family can accommodate a much higher level of division of labor than that of a nuclear family. As the village economy gradually diversifies, the benefits of an extended family will certainly be an incentive for its development, as Myron Cohen discovered in Taiwan.[12]

Economic Diversification

The privatization of agriculture in Fengjia certainly enhances the economic autonomy of the farm family, as well as the commercialization of agriculture. The main thrust of economic diversification—job creation—has not, however, come from individual families but rather from the collective. In 1989, the village government converted the popsicle factory into a cotton textile factory. Cotton from Fengjia and surrounding villages is processed into yarn and then shipped to textile mills in large cities. Because cotton is a government monopoly, the decision to build this cotton gin was certainly made not by the village government alone but by regional authorities.

The tangible benefits of the cotton gin are many. First of all, it creates about a dozen semi-professional jobs (managers, foremen, truck drivers, mechanics, night watchmen) for village men and approximately seventy semi-skilled jobs for village young women and girls. The establishment of the cotton gin provides the first major opportunity for Fengjia women to be engaged in nonfarm jobs. Besides increasing wages, this cotton gin also generates processing fees for the village coffers. Furthermore, villagers no longer need to ship their cotton to government purchasing agents. In return for this service of processing government-purchased cotton, the village government is in a position to demand additional electricity, gasoline, coal, and other consumer goods rationed by government distribution agents.

Two related questions can be raised in this context. The first one is, Could any enterprising person or several individuals with sufficient capital in Fengjia have established this cotton gin? The answer is most likely no, for several reasons. The initial capital investment for this facility was certainly beyond the capacity of most villagers. Furthermore, the factory site, the processed cotton, and other production inputs (for example, electricity, fuel, workers) are all public goods. Individuals operating privately owned production facilities have limited access to these public goods. In other words, in an area where the government procurement agencies still control many scarce resources—in this case cotton—individuals have fewer opportunities to develop private initiatives.

The second question we may ask in this context is, Why did the authorities grant permission to build this cotton gin in Fengjia and not in any other village? This was certainly based on several practical considerations. As a unified community, Fengjia was in a better position to mobilize the villagers for a common goal than would be an internally divided community. In other words, as a cohesive lineage community, Fengjia was better prepared to serve as a "model village" than the others. Its track record merits this observation.

Since 1987, Fengjia has been willing to collaborate with external authorities in experimenting with new cropping technologies, as well as in accepting the presence of American researchers.

Conclusion

The reform movement that has swept through much of rural China began to appear in Fengjia in 1986–1987. The increases in village-wide and per capita production can be seen in Table 4.4. Although most of these changes appear to be superficial, this halfhearted reform should not be interpreted as the result of one or a few malfeasant local officials who stalled the central government's benevolent plan to liberate the oppressed peasants in order to preserve their own personal power. The real situation is far more complicated. Several factors contributed to this unique path of development in Fengjia. The reluctance—or perhaps we should say the resistance—to dismantling completely the overreaching collective organizations probably came not only from the party secretary and local officials but also from the villagers as well.

First, the Green Revolution that drastically improved agricultural productivity occurred in the early 1970s in Fengjia. Decentralizing collective agriculture would not bring about substantial increases in the farm sector. In other words, in an agricultural regime that is already overly capitalized and overly labor-intensive, the familial mode of production promises virtually no additional benefits. Pre-

Table 4.4 Increases in per capita and gross domestic product in Fengjia, 1970–1988

Year	Per capita (yuan)	Gross domestic product
1970	113	154,000
1975	152	431,000
1980	500	1,130,000
1988	1,167	4,540,000

Source: Fengjia Village Government Ledgers, 1991.

serving certain mechanized collective agricultural operations permits village men to continue their nonfarm employment. It also allows village women to manage the farm while their husbands work in nonfarm jobs. In Fengjia, as well as in other more prosperous regions, the real economic growth comes not from sustained growth in the farm sector, but rather from the development of nonfarm trades. Furthermore, Fengjia also has its special seed-sale arrangement, which probably could not be preserved under complete household farming.

The second reason for the lack of comprehensive reform in Fengjia is related to its unique character. As a village dominated by a lineage with a skillful leader, Fengjia has been rather successful in dealing with external authorities. With the backing of a cohesive community, Party Secretary Feng Yongxi has successfully brokered deals with various government offices. The willingness of Fengjia to play the role of a "model village" certainly gives credence to government policies. In return, the external authorities reciprocate with tangible benefits to the village. The role played by Feng Yongxi is thus not that of an autocratic ruler relying exclusively on coercive force for the villagers' compliance but rather that of an authoritative administrator who commands a following from the villagers while doling out practical benefits as compensation.

Through his connections with the Shandong Academy of Agricultural Sciences, Feng Yongxi turned this village into an experimental region for new crop varieties. In return, the Shandong Academy of Agricultural Sciences has made Fengjia the supplier of wheat seeds. This designation increased the value of wheat from 0.36 yuan per jin to one yuan per jin in the summer of 1991, almost a three-fold increase. The monetary gain was enormous, and all villagers enjoyed this windfall. Another example of Feng's leadership is the cotton gin. It was established in Fengjia because Feng could better accommodate the needs of higher-level authorities. This capacity was built on Fengjia's domination by a single lineage and on Feng Yongxi as the undisputed leader of that lineage.

This patron-client relationship exists not only between Fengjia and external authorities but also within the village. Through his connections with county and prefecture officials, Feng Yongxi has been rather successful in finding factory employment for village children of top-level officials, including the mayor and the manager of the starch factory, who is also member of the Party Branch Committee. These factories are located in urban areas. Youngsters employed there are thus able to change their residence classifications in the household registration system from "farm" to "nonfarm," the most highly desired social mobility among Chinese peasants.

In other words, in our analyses of reform politics in Fengjia, what we are seeing is not a one-way, top-down coercive command process, nor a bottom-up, grassroots-level demand for change. Neither is Feng Yongxi an agent of the party-state to execute unpopular policies, nor are the villagers the victims of the capricious whims of the party-state. They are all accomplices in a sociopolitical "game" to maximize personal well-being.

In his study of Chinese urban work units, Andrew Walder identifies two operating principles that ensure management authority and policy implementation: principled particularism and organized dependence.[13] The former refers to the use of favoritism and awards, both material and nonmaterial, by higher-level authorities to ensure the loyalty of the subordinates. The latter refers to the protection and benefits provided by the work units that continuously reinforce workers' reliance on their units to satisfy their needs. In her analysis of rural cadre power in China, Jean Oi further suggests a "clientelist" model in which the dominant relationship "assumes considerably more flexibility, subjectivity, and personal sentiment in the exercise of control that may or may not result in effective policy implementation. From the clientelist perspective, authority is routinely exercised through allocating opportunities, goods, and resources over which the elite have monopolistic control and on which the nonelite depend."[14] Our findings in Fengjia show that the power hierarchy in the rural bureaucracy is lubricated by the chain of reciprocal favoritism that is jealously scrutinized by all parties. A successful operator is one who can command the support of all followers, deliver the goods requested by superiors, and receive favors to enhance the followers' well-being.

Our findings in Fengjia support both Walder's notion of "Communist neo-traditionalism" and Oi's view of the "clientelist model" of power domination that is prevalent in contemporary China. While we agree with their descriptive models, we suggest that Fengjia's successful adaptation strategies in coping with China's tortuous modern history seem to derive from local cultural traditions established before Communist rule. Fengjia was a willing participant in social reform programs during the warlord regime in Shandong in the early 1930s, a sponsor of the Nationalist resistance army against the Japanese in the 1940s, and a successful agricultural experimentation model from the 1970s onward. The regimentation of the Communist party-state and the success of the party-state in penetrating the rural villages have made these operational principles more apparent, as a longitudinal study in a Hebei village also makes this point apparent.[15]

The success of Fengjia rests on an overwhelmingly dominant lineage and a skillful village leader. The internal cohesion is looked on favorably by external political authorities who are eager to identify local "models" for policy demonstrations. Without a doubt, Fengjia villagers have benefited from such political clientelism. The negative side of this village-based uniformity, however, is stifled individual initiatives. There has been no private enterprise other than those small-scale operations released by the village government during the reform period, such as the flour mill, the bakery, and the grocery store. A few villagers have become itinerant merchants in nearby market towns or villages. They have kept low profiles within the village and are reluctant to divulge their activities, as if they are ashamed of them. Apparently, in the balance between public well-being and individual concerns in Fengjia, the former takes precedence over the latter.

As the familial mode of production reestablishes itself as the focus of the rural economy, Fengjia women have taken on increasing responsibility for farmwork. With the dismantling of the rural collective organizations and the reemergence of family farm operations, will there be a revival of the stereotypical patriarchal family that is characterized by a tyrannical father (vis-à-vis the children), an abusive mother-in-law (vis-à-vis the daughter-in-law), and a violent and oppressive husband (vis-à-vis the wife)? Will women be reduced to second-class citizenship again? Our initial impression is that the traditional extended family has become popular during the reform era because it offers tangible benefits, such as land titles for the aged parents and a fine-tuned familial division of labor in an increasingly diversified economy. But does that imply a simple return to the past as the villagers are now permitted to exercise more personal choice?

By our speculation, probably not. Village life today is qualitatively different from that of the preliberation era. The pivotal role played by Fengjia women has made them indispensable partners in this new family-farm operation. The involvement of young women in factory jobs will further enhance their self-esteem and autonomy. What we see in Fengjia is thus not a simple revival of the old, nor a new creation based on Marxist-Maoist orthodoxy, but a synthesis of both.

TERRY SICULAR

5 | Establishing Markets: The Process of Commercialization in Agriculture

Since the late 1970s, the Chinese government has taken major steps to open up domestic markets and promote the development of commerce and trade. Policies implemented during the reform period have included reducing the scope of commercial planning, eliminating state commercial monopolies, and permitting individuals, collectives, and enterprises to buy and sell at mutually acceptable, market-based prices. The effects of such measures are evident in the busy commercial districts of China's cities and in the lively market fairs throughout the countryside.

The depth and nature of this commercial development are not well understood. In particular, questions exist concerning the extent to which China's commercial reforms have promoted the development of competitive, efficient, and widely accessible markets. Even though the government has lifted restrictions on trade, simply announcing such measures does not ensure that markets will emerge. The infrastructure, institutions, and economic attitudes necessary for competitive, efficient markets may require time to develop and need to be actively nurtured. Even though planning has been reduced, the government continues to set prices and plan procurement and sales for key products. The procurement quotas and ration programs that remain could still heavily influence production, commercial participation, and market outcomes. Even though state monopolies on most products have been eased, the preexisting system of state commercial enterprises and agencies largely remains in place. In such circumstances new market entrants may be at a competitive disadvantage, and so the reforms could lead to the development of imperfect monopsonistic or monopolistic markets.

With an eye toward gaining insights into these questions, this chapter examines commerce in agricultural products in Zouping County. County-level statistics and household survey data collected in Zouping permit a detailed look at commercial development in the county. The county-level data used here are official statistics and in most cases are comparable to the sorts of nationwide statistics published by the State Statistical Bureau in provincial and national statistical yearbooks. The household survey data were collected in 1991 through an independent survey of 257 households in 16 villages in the county. Households were selected by means of a stratified random sample. Members of the Zouping County Statistical Bureau's Rural Survey Team and trained accountants from the villages conducted the interviews using a specially designed questionnaire. Each household was asked detailed questions about its economic and commercial activities in the calendar year 1990.

Five broad conclusions emerge from analysis of the Zouping data. First, commerce in Zouping has grown substantially and has penetrated deeply into the rural economy. Second, the reforms have led to the development of increasingly complex commercial activities and relationships. In this context, familiar terms such as "state," "plan," and "market" must be reevaluated. In the following text I examine these terms and suggest definitions appropriate for the current environment.

Third, the state continues to play an important role in the commercial sphere. In Zouping, state-owned commercial enterprises and the supply and marketing co-op system still handle a large share of retail sales and of agricultural purchases from farmers. The state dominates trade in wheat and cotton. Fourth, although the government continues to set quotas for procurement of wheat and cotton, the extent of truly "planned" trade is not entirely clear. In the case of wheat, beyond-quota deliveries to the state at negotiated prices may not be voluntary. In the case of cotton, underfulfillment of quotas is so widespread that farmers are apparently no longer constrained, or perhaps only weakly constrained, by the plan.

Fifth and last, state interventions in rural markets have a discernible impact on household incomes. Estimates based on the 1990 survey data suggest that state procurement of these products at planned prices reduced the incomes of Zouping farm households by nearly 15 percent. The implicit subsidy associated with state supplies of inputs at low prices offset this income reduction only slightly. The net burden of purchases and sales at planned prices varied widely among households; on balance, they appear to have increased slightly the degree of income inequality.

Are these conclusions specific to Zouping? Is Zouping at all representative? In some sense no locality in rural China is representative—rural China is simply too diverse. While Zouping is not representative, evidence suggests that it is unexceptional (Table 5.1). Official statistics show that county gross domestic product (GDP) per

Table 5.1 Basic economic data, Zouping County, 1988–1992

	1988	1989	1990	1991	1992
Population	660,489	664,281	670,571	673,127	671,644
GDP per capita	986	1,096	1,280	1,577	1,775
(% of national average)	(78%)	(77%)	(83%)	(91%)	(87%)
Rate of growth (constant prices)					
Net material product	19.5	10.7	7.8	18.3	13.8
GDP	n.a.	9.0	16.6	24.4	11.4
Structure of GDP (%)					
Agriculture[a]	61	58	54	49	32
Industry and construction	22	24	25	30	43
Services	17	18	21	21	25
Rural household net income per capita	532	627	702	750	747
(% of national average)	(98%)	(104%)	(111%)	(106%)	(95%)

Sources: State Statistical Bureau, *Zhongguo tongji nianjian* (Statistical Yearbook of China [Beijing: Zhongguo tongji chubanshe, 1993, and earlier years]); interviews, Zouping County.

a. The low share of agriculture in 1992 is probably aberrant and reflects unusually poor agricultural performance that year. In 1992, Zouping's net value of agricultural output fell by 20 percent in real terms.

capita in 1992 was 1,775 yuan, slightly below the national average.[1] Growth in Zouping's net material product *(guomin shouru)*, holding prices constant, has averaged 9 to 10 percent during the 1980s, compared with 9 percent for China as a whole.[2] Agriculture has maintained its dominant position in the local economy, but its relative importance has declined over time. Net per capita income of rural households in Zouping has risen from 532 yuan in 1988 to 747 yuan in 1992, close to the national average.[3] Data on commercialization discussed in the following analysis similarly indicate that Zouping is an "average" county. Thus study of Zouping can shed light on commercial development elsewhere in rural China.

An Overview of Commercial Reforms in Agriculture

Prior to 1978, state commerce dominated the exchange of major farm products in Zouping and in China more generally.[4] Cotton, grain, and vegetable oils were subject to unified procurement *(tongyi shougou)*, under which the government set plans for procurement and maintained a monopoly or near monopoly on domestic trade. For cotton, farmers could sell only to state procurement stations run by the Cotton and Hemp Bureau *(mianmaju)*, which was administratively under the National Federation of Supply and Marketing Co-ops. The government prohibited other individuals or organizations from engaging in cotton trade. Farm sales of grains and oil seeds went primarily to state procurement stations under the Ministry of Grain (later the Bureau of Grain).[5] After local delivery quotas had been met, farmers could sell additional amounts to the state at higher, above-quota prices. Provincial or county officials sometimes permitted farmers to sell certain varieties of grain and oil seeds to other buyers at market prices; however, the government only allowed such trade locally (within county borders) and on a small scale.

The government prohibited individuals and organizations other than the designated state agencies from specializing in commerce or engaging in the long-distance transport of farm products. Collective farms were required to sell their output through designated state channels, and so nonstate trade was effectively limited to those items such as hogs and vegetables produced by households outside the collective sphere. In the case of hogs, under the "one knife" *(yi ba dao)* policy, only agencies under the Ministry of Food could commercially slaughter hogs. Consequently, farmers could in fact sell hogs only through official channels. The combined effect of these and similar measures was to confine trade of farm products outside of official channels to small-scale and local exchange among rural residents.

Commercial policies began to change after 1978, when the government began to promote a policy of "multiple channels" for commerce. Beginning in 1981, individuals were permitted to establish small-scale commercial businesses to conduct trade in animal products, vegetables, minor crops, and light manufactures such as textiles and clothing. In 1982, the government eased restrictions on the trade of grain: long-distance trade in grain was permitted, and the government allowed individuals, noncommercial state agencies, enterprises, and collectives to buy and sell grain once the local grain quota had been met. Following these reforms, trade outside of the designated state channels began to grow. At this time the periodic market system, which historically had been an important channel for rural commerce, began to reemerge.

While government planning of procurement continued, the scope of planning was gradually reduced. In the early 1980s many products were dropped from the list of items subject to delivery quotas and ration sales. Grain remained subject to plan, but the government reduced the level of mandatory quotas. Reductions in planning combined with rapid growth in agricultural output expanded the scope for market exchange. State commercial agencies began to participate in market trade under the guise of "negotiated" procurement *(yijia shougou)*. The state increasingly purchased farm output at "negotiated" prices that were set administratively to follow trends in supply and demand. In principle, negotiated prices were to be set slightly below market prices, and sales to the state at these prices were voluntary.

Thus in the early 1980s, farmers wishing to sell beyond-plan output had several options. First, they could sell certain crops to the state at the guaranteed procurement price for above-quota deliveries (for grain and oil seeds, this price was 50 percent higher than the quota price; for cotton, it was 30 percent higher). Second, they could sell to the state at negotiated prices. Third, they could sell through newly emerging unofficial channels at market prices.

Commercial reforms took a major step forward in 1984–1985, when the central government announced it would abolish unified procurement for grain and oil seeds and would gradually eliminate planned procurement for other farm products. Quota procurement of grain was to be replaced by procurement using voluntary advance contracts with farmers (*hetong dinggou*). The government announced that for any procurement beyond the contracted amounts, it would buy from farmers at negotiated prices.

Concurrently, the government eased restrictions on trade outside of official state channels. Exchange of grain through unofficial channels was now allowed even during the procurement season. The government dropped its monopoly on cotton. Indeed, for all but a few key products such as grain and cotton, the government announced its intention to eliminate gradually state commerce and to allow trade to flow entirely through market channels.[6]

The 1984–1985 reforms were never fully implemented, and the ensuing years saw some reversal of the trend toward commercial liberalization. In 1987, the central government announced that grain contracts with the state were mandatory. In the same year the government reinstated its monopoly on cotton. Mandatory production targets, which had been abolished in 1985, were revived so as to ensure fulfillment of commercial plans. Despite these measures, trade outside of official channels was still permitted for most products and continued to grow. During the late 1980s, then, government policies preserved a mix of plan and market and also a mix of state and nonstate commerce.

Efforts to reform the commercial system once again picked up steam in the early 1990s. In 1992, the central government announced its intention to liberalize rural markets further and to reduce direct government interventions. Specific measures to accomplish this goal varied from place to place. For example, by June 1993, all provinces but Gansu, Hainan, and Tibet had dropped grain rationing. Most provinces, however, continued to enforce mandatory delivery quotas for grain. In the fall of 1992, the central government announced an experimental policy eliminating the state cotton monopoly in selected provinces, including Shandong. Beginning with the 1993 cotton harvest, these provinces were to eliminate mandatory production targets, adopt more flexible pricing policies, and permit beyond-target cotton to be sold on the market.[7] The announced reforms in cotton marketing were held in check after cotton production dropped precipitously in 1993. With the reemergence of inflation in late 1993 and 1994, further commercial reforms were delayed.

The Expansion of Agricultural Commerce in Zouping

Both county-level statistics and household survey data reveal that the reforms have led to extensive commercial development in Zouping. Moreover, commercial activity has become increasingly varied and complex. Commercial reforms in Zouping County appear to have more or less followed central policies, although with some lag in the early 1980s. For example, the county government began to permit specialized traders and long-distance transport in grain only in 1984, two years after the central government announcement. Zouping was in step with central directives when trade in grain and cotton was liberalized in 1985, and it was in step when grain deliveries became mandatory again in 1986–1987. Mandatory grain quotas for farmers have since remained in place, as they have in most other parts of China.

Zouping reinstated the cotton monopoly in 1987 (although the monopoly was only strictly enforced in parts of the county targeted for cotton production and procurement), and in 1990 the county also revived mandatory sown-area targets for cotton. Ration sales of grain were eliminated relatively early, in mid-1992. In 1993, the county dropped mandatory cotton targets and took steps to liberalize cotton trade in line with the provincewide policies.

Zouping's commercial development has been rapid. Between 1980 and 1992, retail sales in Zouping (including both agricultural and nonagricultural products, unadjusted for inflation) grew at an average annual rate of 15.5 percent, slightly exceeding the growth in county net material product.[8] This rate of increase was close to the national and provincial averages.[9] By the late 1980s and early 1990s, the level of retail sales was equivalent in value to between 40 and 50 percent of county GDP (Table 5.2).[10] Rapid increases in the number of commercial businesses accompanied this growth in trade volume. In 1980, Zouping had 1,041 commercial businesses, of which 97 were "individual" or private. In 1993, Zouping had 7,465 registered commercial retail enterprises, of which 7,270 were "individual" and 104 were wholesale enterprises, of which 75 were "individual."

If commercialization is defined as the extent to which households engage in purchases and sales rather than producing for their own consumption, then available data suggest that commercialization has penetrated quite far into Zouping's rural economy (Table 5.2). By the early 1990s, residents in rural Zouping supplied only one-third of their total consumption self-sufficiently. Well over half of rural

Table 5.2 Indicators of the level of commercialization in Zouping, 1988–1992

	1988	1989	1990	1991	1992
Social retail sales as a percent of county GDP	52	52	49	43	42
Percent of consumption of rural residents that is self-supplied	41	49[a]	33	33	33
Percent of rural economic income from sales of products	55	60	60	61	68
Percent of rural agricultural income from sales of agricultural products	51	50	50	60	69
Output value of agricultural commodities as a percent of gross value of agricultural output	58	66	62	60	63
By product grain	42	42	37	38	41
economic crops	80	73	74	81	95
fruits and vegetables	64	65	64	74	73
livestock products	87	91	78	74	90

Source: Interviews, Zouping County.

a. This proportion is above normal: in 1989, the absolute level of consumption purchases was substantially lower than that in either the preceding or subsequent year.

economic income and a similar share of the gross value of agricultural output were derived from sales of products. While comparable statistics do not exist for earlier years, available data suggest that the degree of commercialization has increased. In 1980, for example, only 32 percent of gross collective income from all sources (including sideline activities) was derived from sales of output.

The survey data provide additional, more detailed evidence of the extent of commercialization in rural Zouping. Observers of village life in China have sometimes viewed farm households as being self-sufficient. This perception perhaps arises because households produce much of the food that they consume. The Zouping household survey data confirm that households produce a significant share of the food that they consume; nevertheless, grain is the only major food item that is predominately self-supplied. For other foods and farm products, households rely heavily on commercial exchange (see Table 5.3).

In addition, the surveyed households devoted a large proportion of family time and resources to production of goods and services

Table 5.3 Farm household purchases of farm products in Zouping, 1990

Item	Quantity purchased (catties)	Purchases as a percent of consumption[a]	Percent of households buying	Percent of households producing[b]
Wheat	31	2.6	8	100
Corn	282	4.1	9	99
Vegetable oils	45	n.a.	74	85
Pork	51	99	100	30
Poultry	3.7	53	32	74
Eggs	18	30	43	74
Vegetables	n.a.	n.a.	93	22

Source: Farm household survey, Zouping County, 1991.

a. For corn, this is calculated as purchases divided by the sum of family consumption and animal feed. For other products, the denominator is family consumption, which is the primary use.

b. For oils, includes households producing cotton (which yields oil-bearing cottonseed). The production of other oil crops such as peanut and sesame is less common.

for sale. Most agricultural output was sold: more than 60 percent of the gross value of household agricultural output was marketed (see Table 5.4). Certain farm products—for instance, cotton, hogs, and fruit—were produced almost entirely for sale. Other farm products—vegetables, poultry and eggs, and grain—were produced both for home consumption and for sale.

The household survey data indicate that the only farm product produced primarily for self-consumption was wheat. Only 28 percent of wheat produced is sold, and almost all retained wheat is used for human consumption. Corn, the other major grain produced in Zouping, is produced primarily for the market. Half of the corn produced is sold, more than 40 percent is used for animal feed, and less than 10 percent is consumed as food. Because households sell many of the animals and eggs they produce, most retained corn is therefore marketed indirectly in the form of livestock products.

Slightly more than half of the surveyed households (52 percent) reported nonagricultural income from a family business or from

Table 5.4 Farm household sales of farm products in Zouping, 1990

Item	Quantity	% of Output
Total sales of agricultural products (yuan)[a]	3,372	61
Grain (catties)	2,834	42
Wheat	947	28
Corn	1,745	51
Cotton (catties)	312	93
Meat hogs (head)	0.42	100
Poultry (birds)	5.03	59
Eggs (catties)	344	46
Vegetables (catties)	622	52
Fruit (catties)[b]	556	83

Source: Farm household survey, Zouping County, 1991.

a. Total sales as a percent of output is calculated using household gross value of agricultural output in the denominator.

b. Fruit includes watermelon.

off-farm wage employment (including employment as cadres [Table 5.5]). Income from family businesses is largely derived from the sale of goods and services, and so it reflects commercial involvement. Wage employment is by definition a commercial activity, as it is the sale of labor services. Families reporting sideline or wage income on average derived 40 percent of their total income from nonagricultural sources. One in five of the sample households earned more than half of its income from nonagricultural sources (Table 5.6).

Commercial participation requires the development of infrastructure and institutions that support commercial activity. Since the late 1970s, the county and township governments have invested in transportation and communications infrastructure, with the result that

Table 5.5 Farm household income and its composition in Zouping, 1990

Average household income, total	4,741 yuan
Average household income, per capita	1,167 yuan

Composition of household income (%)		Households earning this type of income (%)
Agriculture[a]	78	100
crops	94	n.a.
animal husbandry	7	n.a.
fruit	−1	n.a.
Nonagriculture	22	52
wages	53	49
household business income	19	18
from government or collective	2	13
other	26	n.a.

Source: Farm household survey, Zouping County, 1991.

Note: These incomes are calculated using data from the independent survey of 257 households. The numbers here differ from official statistics in Table 5.1, based on the State Statistical Bureau survey because (1) the definition of income is different, (2) the sample is different, and (3) households' willingness to report earnings may differ between this survey and the official survey.

a. Excludes the one household in the sample that had negative total income in 1990. This household experienced negative income because it invested in fruit and animal production in 1990 in expectation of future returns.

the total network of surfaced roads in the county more than doubled from 194 kilometers in 1980 to 539 kilometers in 1993. During the same period, the number of automobiles and trucks registered in the county rose from 250 to 2,500, the number of long-distance telephone lines increased from 6 to 160, and the number of telephones more than doubled.

An important institution facilitating Zouping's commercial development during the reform period has been the rural market fair or periodic market.[11] Zouping's periodic market system has experienced a remarkable revival. The number of periodic marketplaces increased from thirty-one in 1979–1980 to ninety-three in 1992. In the early 1980s, periodic markets usually were reestablished at traditional marketplaces; from the mid-1980s onward, markets increasingly emerged at new locations. The largest periodic markets are well-attended, drawing more than 10,000 people on market days. Increases in the number of periodic marketplaces understates the expansion in trade through this channel, as the average volume of trade at each market has risen dramatically. The total volume of transactions at periodic markets grew at an average rate of 25 percent a year between 1988 and 1992, outpacing inflation by a substantial margin. Indeed, retail sales at periodic markets have grown more rapidly than total retail sales in the county. By 1992, they were equivalent to one-quarter of total retail sales for the county (see Table 5.7).

Table 5.6 Distribution of farm households by share of income from nonagricultural business and wages in Zouping, 1990

Wage and business income as a % of total household income	Number of households	% of households
= 0	101	40
> 0	154	60
> 25	107	42
> 50	57	22
> 75	15	6

Source: Farm household survey, Zouping County, 1991.

Table 5.7 Trade at periodic markets in Zouping, 1988–1992

	1988	1989	1990	1991	1992
I. Number of periodic marketplaces	62	62	64	78	93
A. Of which the average number of people attending is					
1. greater than 10,000	16	16	16	18	18
2. between 3,000 and 10,000	15	15	17	26	36
3. fewer than 3,000	31	31	31	34	39
B. Wholesale markets for farm products	2	2	2	3	12
II. Retail sales volume on periodic markets as a % of total social retail sales (percent)	16.7	16.3	22.0	23.0	26.0
III. Total volume of transactions (million yuan)	54.31	61.94	80.85	103.48	130.58
A. On wholesale markets (%)	6.1	6.0	5.0	3.6	6.9
B. Composition by product category (%)	100.0	100.0	100.0	100.0	100.0
1. Grain	10.4	14.7	10.1	7.0	7.1
2. Meat, poultry, eggs, and fish	27.5	26.1	26.0	26.3	24.4
3. Oils and oil seeds	3.4	3.3	3.9	2.9	3.0
4. Fruit and vegetables	17.0	16.7	16.6	23.8	19.4
5. Livestock[a]	13.1	9.1	6.9	9.3	8.2
6. Manufactures	20.2	21.3	29.4	21.5	14.5
7. Other	8.4	8.8	7.1	9.2	23.4
C. Composition by seller	100.0	100.0	100.0	100.0	100.0
1. Farmers	31.4	34.6	39.7	48.6	37.0
2. Private merchants	40.0	39.6	34.4	35.1	38.3
3. State commerce and supply and marketing coops	14.5	9.2	8.4	7.8	9.9
4. Other collective units	7.6	8.0	7.5	5.4	8.1
5. Other	6.6	8.6	10.1	3.1	6.7
D. Composition by buyer	100.0	100.0	100.0	100.0	100.0
1. Rural residents	62.1	52.3	53.7	72.1	71.3
2. Urban residents	16.5	15.9	9.6	9.1	10.0
3. Private merchants	7.0	8.0	12.5	4.6	3.9
4. State commerce and supply and marketing coops	2.0	5.7	5.9	4.7	4.5
5. Administrative units, enterprises, schools, military, and other organizations	4.5	7.7	6.3	6.0	4.8
6. Other	8.0	10.4	12.1	3.6	5.5

Source: Interviews, Zouping County.

a. Includes large animals, and also hogs and poultry purchased for animal husbandry.

The revival of periodic markets is significant because these markets not only provide a locus for commercial exchange but also are an important avenue for entrepreneurial development. Selling at periodic markets requires minimal start-up costs and can be done on a small scale. Individuals and households that wish to set up a business can begin by selling their wares at one of the smaller township or village markets. Successful businesses can expand to several markets that meet on different days, can attend larger markets such as those in the county seat, and can ultimately graduate to a permanent establishment. The periodic markets thus provide an entry point and gradual path for the development of private enterprise.

Plan, Market, and State

Discussions of reform in China and other socialist countries often employ phrases such as "plan and market" or "state and market." Rural commerce in Zouping defies easy classification along these lines. In the reformed commercial environment, the lines between plan, market, and state are not always clear. Here I discuss these terms and suggest definitions appropriate for the reform environment.

Farmers in Zouping and elsewhere in China sell their products through a variety of channels, to a variety of buyers, and at a variety of prices. As mentioned earlier, periodic markets have become an increasingly important channel for exchange in rural Zouping. Many transactions, however, pass through other channels. Households sometimes take their products directly to the users, for example, by delivering corn directly to the township cornstarch factory or selling eggs door to door. Other times they sell their products to state-owned intermediaries or to private merchants.

Buyers of farm products are diverse. Aside from consumers and private merchants, buyers include governmental or quasi-governmental agencies within the state commercial system such as the Grain Company *(liangshi jituan gongsi)*, under the county Grain Bureau, and the Cotton and Hemp Company *(mianma gongsi)*, under the county Supply and Marketing Co-op. State commercial agencies from other localities sometimes come to Zouping to purchase farm products such as fruit and vegetables directly from farmers; they then ship the products back home. State-owned and collective factories that use farm products as inputs purchase directly from farmers, as do organizations such as schools, hospitals, and government administrative offices.

Transactions can be made under several pricing systems. State commercial agencies buy grain and cotton from farmers under plan at administratively set prices. These same agencies also buy (and sell) farm products outside of the plan at negotiated prices. While in principle, negotiated prices are supposed to follow trends in supply and demand, evidence reveals that at times they have deviated substantially from market prices. Other organizations and agencies, as well as consumers and private merchants, purchase farm products from farmers at mutually agreed-on prices determined by the market.

This multiplicity of commercial channels, agents, and prices in rural China confounds the usual "plan" versus "market" or "state" versus "market" classifications. If a farmer sells corn to a state-owned enterprise at a market price, is the sale through state or market channels? Is grain procurement by the state Grain Company at negotiated prices plan or market trade? Three features of the reform environment make such classification difficult. First, many government agencies and state-owned enterprises have become active market participants. They now buy and sell farm products outside of plan at prices that resemble market prices. The planned trade of these agencies is no longer divorced from the market, because the existence of market opportunities creates incentives to evade quotas, especially if planned prices deviate too far from market prices. To a greater or lesser extent, then, state agencies, like private and collective agents, must operate through or in accord with markets.

Second, for certain key products where a state agency is the dominant buyer (or seller), the position of the state agency appears similar to that of a monopsonistic (monopolistic) firm. Economists define a monopsonist buyer as a one that, by virtue of its size in the market, has the power to set prices to its advantage. Certain state agencies clearly dominate markets; for example, the county Cotton and Hemp Company has sole rights to purchase cotton from farmers—no other competitors are permitted to enter the market. The county Grain Bureau similarly dominates the market for wheat, but other, smaller buyers also exist. These agencies set prices in their respective markets. In their size and pricing behavior, then, these agencies resemble standard monopsonistic firms. This raises the question of whether their activities should be interpreted as "planned" trade, or simply as market trade in a monopsony setting.

Third, the "state" is not a single, undifferentiated entity.[12] Farmers sell grain to the grain procurement station under the county Grain Bureau, the designated state commercial agent for grain. They also sell grain to state-owned food-processing enterprises, state-run livestock farms, and state grain bureaus from other localities. These various state agents need not act in coordination; indeed, they are likely to be competitive. For these reasons, terms such as "plan," "market," and "state" require clarification.

In view of these considerations, the distinction between "state" and "nonstate" is no longer conceptually useful. A more relevant distinction is the one between purchases and sales by those government agencies that are officially designated to conduct trade for the products in question, and purchases and sales by other, nondesignated agents. State agencies officially designated to conduct commerce are charged with the task of carrying out the government's broader commercial policies and objectives. These are the agencies that conduct quota procurement and ration sales, that manage state storage facilities, that engage in open-market operations so as to stabilize markets, and that provide supplies for poverty and disaster relief. In some cases, these agencies are required to purchase as much output as farmers wish to sell at the government price. The officially designated commercial agencies may be concerned with profits and losses, but their behavior in the trade of designated products is to a large degree policy-driven and so differs from the behavior of market-oriented, profit-seeking enterprises.

While nondesignated state agencies and state-owned enterprises do not necessarily behave like profit-seeking agents, they are more likely to do so, especially in their independent commercial activities. Historically, these other government agencies and enterprises were required to trade through the official commercial agencies. The reforms have made possible independent trading outside of official channels. Generally speaking, noncommercial state enterprises and agencies use their independent trade as an avenue for making profits, and their commercial behavior is more profit- than policy-oriented.

In view of these differences, I use the term "designated agencies" to mean those government agencies that are officially charged with the task of carrying out commerce for the products in question. Trade in grain by designated commercial agencies would thus refer to purchases and sales of grain by the state Grain Company and its affiliated offices and agencies under the Grain Bureau. Trade in cotton by designated agencies would refer to purchases and sales of cotton by the Cotton and Hemp Company and its affiliated agencies within the Supply and Marketing Co-op system. State trade in meat and poultry products by designated agencies would refer to purchases and sales of such products by the state Food Company, also formally under the Supply and Marketing Co-op system.

Trade through "nondesignated" channels refers to purchase or sale of farm products by all other agents. Nondesignated trade would obviously include trade among private individuals. It would also include trade by collective enterprises and state agencies or enterprises when they are not the designated agents handling state commerce for the product in question. Independent purchases of farm products outside of official state commercial channels by a state-owned industrial enterprise, a school or hospital, the military, or even by an office in the government bureaucracy are therefore classified as nondesignated.

The term "market" should not be used in juxtaposition with the term "state," because "market" refers to the nature of the transaction, whereas "state" or "designated" refers to the type of agent participating in the transaction. Economists view "market" transactions as voluntary exchange of mutually agreed on quantities at mutually agreed on prices. "Market" prices reflect supply and demand, where "supply" is the quantity that producers are willing to provide at each price and "demand" is the quantity that consumers are willing to buy at each price.

Market trade need not take place in a perfectly competitive environment. As mentioned earlier, in some markets government agencies may have monopoly or monopsony power. Even so, exchange can be voluntary in nature, and prices can reflect supply and demand. For example, suppose that a state agency is a monopsonist and faces no competitors. Suppose further that while farmers cannot sell to other buyers, they can choose freely how much to sell to the state. In this setting the government agency must consider the farmers' response when setting its price. If it sets a higher price, farmers will be willing to sell more; if it sets a lower price, farmers will want to sell less. The state agency must take into account this trade-off between price and quantity. The price that ultimately prevails, then, reflects the preferences of both the buyer and the sellers. This price may be neither competitive nor efficient, but it is still a "market" price, and the transactions that take place are "market" trade.

In contrast, "planned" trade refers to transactions where participation is nonvoluntary or obligatory. Specifically, "planned" trade is trade where the quantity sold or purchased is subject to some constraint or coercion. Planned trade thus includes obligatory quota sales to the government and rationed purchases from the government. In the former instance, the government has imposed a minimum quantity of goods that must be delivered at the planned price; in the latter case, the government has imposed a maximum quantity that can be purchased at the planned price. "Planned prices" are the administratively set prices that apply to such trade.

Because planned trade so defined is carried out by the officially designated government commercial agencies mentioned earlier, it is a component of "state" trade. "State" trade, however, is not limited to planned transactions. If negotiated trade is truly voluntary, for example, then state purchases and sales at negotiated prices would be classified as market trade.[13]

Designated versus Nondesignated Commerce in Zouping

The issues discussed above naturally raise questions about the relative importance of designated versus nondesignated trade, and of planned versus market trade. Available data show that purchases and sales of products by officially designated, state-owned commercial agencies remains important. County-level statistics on the composition of retail sales in Zouping by type of seller appear in Table 5.8. These statistics include retail sales of both agricultural and nonagricultural products. In the early 1990s, designated, state-owned commercial enterprises and the Supply and Marketing Co-op system together accounted for nearly 60 percent of total retail sales, while other businesses accounted for about 40 percent of retail sales. Zouping was not unusual in this regard: national statistics show that in 1990 and 1991, state-owned commercial enterprises and Supply and Marketing Co-ops sold 55 percent of national social retail sales.[14]

County-level statistics show further that designated state agents (the Ministry of Commerce system, Supply and Marketing Co-ops, the Grain Bureau, and the Foreign Trade system) accounted for 67 percent of farm purchases in 1988 and 50 percent in 1992 (Table 5.9).[15] The official state commercial agencies have continued to monopolize trade in cotton and remain dominant buyers of grain, although their share of grain purchases has been falling. Meat and poultry are marketed both through designated and nondesignated channels. Interestingly, Table 5.9 shows that, for meat and poultry, purchases by agencies under the Ministry of Commerce have in-

Table 5.8 Composition of social retail sales in Zouping, 1988–1992

	(percentages)				
	Total social retail sales	State-owned commerce	Supply and marketing co-ops	Other collectives	Registered individual businesses	Farmer direct sales to urban residents
1988	100	24.6	38.0	13.9	20.5	3.0
1989	100	22.4	45.3	10.2	18.5	3.6
1990	100	27.2	34.2	16.3	19.2	3.1
1991	100	29.4	28.8	18.7	19.8	3.3
1992	100	34.3	24.6	18.4	19.6	3.1

Source: Interviews, Zouping County.

Note: Total social sales are given in Table 5.1. Note that these data do not include intrarural transactions, and that ration sales by the state are valued at lower prices than market sales.

Table 5.9 Zouping County purchases of agricultural products from farmers, 1988 and 1992

	Total purchases (million yuan)	Grain (tons)	Cotton (tons)	Meat hogs (head)	Poultry (birds)	Eggs (tons)	Apples (tons)
1988 Total Purchases	245.45	75,432	12,199	60,138	528,000	440	6,223
% purchased by							
Ministry of Commerce System	2	—	—	—	29	1	—
Supply and Marketing Coops	39	5	100	2	8	—	2
Grain Bureau	12	64	—	—	—	—	—
Foreign Trade System	14	—	—	—	5	—	—
Collective and private commerce, and direct purchases by urban consumers	24	10	—	68	78	95	98
Industrial, food, and construction enterprises, and other	9	20	—	2	10	5	—

creased in recent years. These data, however, are somewhat misleading, as they reflect the fact that in the early 1990s township-level procurement stations for these products were leased out to individuals (see notes to Table 5.9). Most other farm products are marketed primarily through nondesignated channels.

A major drawback of the official statistics is that they exclude intrarural exchange among farmers and so overstate the relative importance of designated trade. Although the data collected for our household survey do not suffer from this flaw, they provide little information on purchases of manufactures and exclude most urban and interregional exchange, in which spheres the official state commerce may play an important role. The survey data, then, also provide a partial picture: they show the relative importance of designated versus nondesignated channels in agricultural trade from the perspective of farmers.

Table 5.9 (continued)

	Total purchases (million yuan)	Grain (tons)	Cotton (tons)	Meat hogs (head)	Poultry (birds)	Eggs (tons)	Apples (tons)
1992 Total Purchases	282.61	70,044	10,335	58,123	557,500	1,228	1,811
% purchased by							
Ministry of Commerce System	2	—	—	66	43	2	—
Supply and Marketing Co-ops	34	3	100	1	4	—	5
Grain Bureau	11	51	—	—	—	—	—
Foreign Trade System	3	—	—	—	—	—	—
Collective and private commerce, and direct purchases by urban consumers	36	19	—	31	46	92	91
Industrial, food, and construction enterprises, and other	13	26	—	2	7	6	4

Source: Interviews, Zouping County.
Notes:
The data in this table exclude direct purchases by rural residents from farmers.
"—" indicates a share of less than 1 percent.
Grain is measured in units of "trade" (husked) grain.
The rise between 1988 and 1992 in purchases of hogs and poultry by the Ministry of Commerce system is slightly misleading. In that year the Food Company, which is the agency under this ministry that procures meat and poultry, contracted its township food procurement stations out to individuals. After these stations were contracted out, they became more active in the market. Under the contracting or lease approach, however, these stations should perhaps be considered "nonstate" or "quasi-state" units.

According to the survey data, households trade most farm products through nondesignated channels. Indeed, purchases of farm products from the state are minimal. The sample households appear to buy only wheat and corn from the state, and the quantities purchased are trivial—on average, three jin (one jin equals one-half kilogram) of wheat and six jin of corn.[16] Indeed, only fourteen households in the sample purchased any wheat or corn from the state, and these fourteen households all resided in the two surveyed villages that received subsidized grain allocations for disaster relief from the government.

It is possible that households purchase some vegetable oils from the state (the survey data do not allow a breakdown of oil purchases between state and nonstate sources). The presence of private suppliers of vegetable oil in the periodic markets and of collectively run oil-pressing factories, however, suggests that a significant portion of family oil consumption is purchased from nonstate sources. All other farm products purchased for family consumption are bought from nonstate agents—that is, all poultry, eggs, vegetables, fruit, and meat—and all grain other than wheat and corn are bought from either private or collective sellers.

In selling their products, the households also rely largely on non-designated, nonstate channels. All sales of livestock products, fruit, vegetables, and minor grains and oil seeds (excluding cottonseed) went to nonstate buyers. The only products sold to the state in any quantity were cotton (and some cottonseed), wheat, and corn. As a proportion of quantities sold, 100 percent of cotton, 65 percent of wheat, and 8 percent of corn were sold to the state.

Although few farm products were sold to the state, those products were the major crops. Households sold 40 percent of the total value of marketed agricultural output to designated state commercial agencies. Cotton was by far the most important item here: it accounted for one-third of all sales of farm products, and for more than 80 percent of the total value of sales to the state.

An interesting finding from the survey is that the only products that farmers sold to the designated agents in any quantity were those still subject to planned delivery quotas. Moreover, almost all these sales were in fulfillment of quotas. Only 4 percent of wheat sold to the state was beyond the contract at negotiated prices. Some households sold cotton beyond the plan, but under the cotton monopsony, households had no alternative avenue for disposal.[17]

Plan versus Market Trade in Zouping

The continued dominance of designated state trade in certain spheres and its close association with agricultural quotas suggest that planned trade remains important. In Zouping, the government continues to set delivery quotas for grain (wheat) and cotton. The issue of plan versus market is therefore relevant for these two crops, which I now discuss in some detail.

Planned trade, as defined earlier, is characterized by an obligatory quota or mandatory limit on the quantity exchanged. By this definition, what matters is not the presence of a quota per se but whether that quota is enforced and compulsory. The nominal presence of a "quota" or "target" does not necessarily mean that households are compelled to comply, nor does the absence of a quota or target mean that households are free of obligations. Thus planned trade should include sales to the designated state agents in the absence of a formal quota if those sales are compulsory.

Fieldwork in Zouping revealed that these distinctions are important. Examination of commerce for grain shows, for example, that farmers sell grain to the Grain Bureau at negotiated prices, and that negotiated prices are lower than market prices. Yet there is no apparent "quota" for deliveries to the state at negotiated prices. In contrast, the government sets delivery quotas for cotton, but those quotas are commonly underfulfilled. In the case of grain, then, the level of delivery quotas may understate the true importance of planning, while for cotton it may overstate the importance of planning. Indeed, for cotton, the state's position has increasingly come to resemble that of a monopsonist rather than that of a planner.

Plan versus Market for Grain

Planned trade remains important for grain, especially for wheat. Available evidence suggests that grain quotas are still mandatory and that a large share of grain marketed by farmers is sold under plan. For Zouping County as a whole, the level of the grain quota or delivery contract has been stable at 20,000 to 25,000 tons through most of the 1980s and early 1990s (see Table 5.10).[18] In recent years, state policies have required that farmers meet most, if not all, of the quota using wheat (Table 5.11). County-level statistics on grain deliveries suggest that grain contracts have been strictly enforced in Zouping. In the late 1980s and early 1990s, countywide deliveries at the planned quota or contract price exceeded the county contract

Table 5.10 Procurement of grain by the Grain Bureau in Zouping (metric tons), 1978–1993

| Year | Total procurement | Of which | | | Planned quota or contract | Planned quota as a % of output | Total procurement as a % of[b] | |
		At negotiated price	At above-quota bonus price	At quota or contract price			Grain output	Social purchases of grain[c]
1978	29,790	265	n.a.	n.a.	19,932	9.8	14.7	n.a.
1979	30,026[a]	170	11,654	n.a.	18,202	8.7	14.3	n.a.
1980	22,039[a]	321	3,517	n.a.	18,201	9.1	11.0	n.a.
1981	22,610[a]	600	0	n.a.	22,010	11.2	11.5	n.a.
1982	22,510[a]	500	0	n.a.	22,010	13.5	13.6	n.a.
1983	25,975[a]	3,810	0	n.a.	22,165	9.4	11.0	n.a.
1984	46,895[a]	4,500	20,295	22,100	22,100	8.5	18.1	n.a.
1985	30,750	4,385	—	27,500	26,510	9.4	10.9	n.a.
1986	47,121	23,503	—	23,618	24,000	7.1	13.9	n.a.
1987	47,700	19,833	—	27,867	22,650	6.9	14.6	n.a.
1988	41,395	18,829	—	22,566	22,650	6.8	12.4	63.6
1989	59,649	36,991	—	22,658	22,650	6.8	17.9	72.3
1990	55,123	31,242	—	23,881	22,650	6.2	15.2	53.6
1991	70,086	45,845	—	24,241	24,010	5.5	16.2	65.2
1992	70,210[a]	46,200	—	n.a.	24,010	6.0	17.4	51.1
1993	n.a.	n.a.	—	n.a.	22,700	n.a.	n.a.	n.a.

Source: Interviews, Zouping County.

a. Estimated as the sum of the quota plus procurement at above-quota and negotiated prices. Actual deliveries at quota prices may have differed slightly from the quota level.

b. Note that state procurement data are probably for the production year, while data for production and social purchases are for the calendar year.

c. Note that "social purchases" (*shehui shougou*) exclude intrarural exchange. See discussion in text.

Table 5.11 Procurement of wheat and corn by the Grain Bureau in Zouping (metric tons), 1985–1993

| | Wheat procurement | Of which | | Planned contract for wheat | Planned contract as a % of wheat output | Wheat procurement as % of output |
		At negotiated price	At contract price			
1985	29,598	2,098	27,500	22,275	15.3	20
1986	44,824	21,206	23,618	22,000	13.0	26
1987	34,652	11,968	22,684	20,000	13.8	24
1988	32,474	9,908	22,566	20,000	12.2	20
1989	46,115	23,457	22,658	20,000	11.5	27
1990	44,925	21,044	23,881	20,000	10.9	25
1991	53,227	28,986	24,241	22,000	10.1	25
1992	54,910[a]	30,900	n.a.	22,000	10.3	26
1993	n.a.	n.a.	n.a.	20,000	n.a.	n.a.

| | Corn procurement | Of which | | Corn procurement as % of output |
		At negotiated price	At contract price	
1985	2,287	2,287	0	2
1986	2,297	2,297	0	2
1987	7,865	7,865	0	5
1988	8,921	8,921	0	6
1989	13,534	13,534	0	9
1990	10,198	10,198	0	6
1991	16,859	16,859	0	9
1992	15,300	15,300	0	9

Source: Interviews, Zouping County.
a. Estimated as sum of wheat procurements at negotiated prices and the grain quota.

in all but one year, 1986. Even in that year, which was perhaps aberrant because of initial confusion over whether the new grain contracts were mandatory, the deliveries fell short of the quota by only 2 percent. The household survey data also show high compliance with grain quotas. Almost all households in the sample (94 percent) faced grain contract quotas, with the average quota equal to 191 kilograms. In the sample, every household that faced a grain quota fulfilled or overfulfilled its quota.[19]

This uniformly high degree of quota fulfillment suggests that grain quotas were mandatory and so truly constituted planned trade. Price data provide additional evidence supporting this conclusion. In Zouping, the planned prices paid for quota deliveries have been consistently lower than market prices, sometimes by a large margin. For ten of the thirteen years for which data are available, wheat market prices have exceeded the quota or contract price by 40 percent or more (see Table 5.12). Facing such a large price gap, farmers are unlikely to have fulfilled their quotas voluntarily.

Of course, the significance of this compliance depends in part on the magnitude of the quotas. Relative to total grain output, mandatory deliveries have declined over time. By the late 1980s/early 1990s, the county quota was equal to only about 6 or 7 percent of grain output. Compared with wheat output, which is perhaps a more appropriate yardstick, the quota has been less than 15 percent of total output (see Tables 5.10 and 5.11). The survey data are consistent with these county-level statistics: in 1990, the grain contract was on average equal to 13 percent of wheat production for surveyed households.

Because households retain a large share of the grain that they produce for their own use, quota levels should perhaps be compared not with total output but with marketed output. County-level statistics show that in the late 1980s and early 1990s, between 20 and 30 percent of all grain sold by farmers was sold to the Grain Bureau at contract prices. Similarly, the survey data show that 25 percent of all grain sold by households was sold to the Grain Bureau at the contract price. For wheat alone, the survey data reveal that 64 percent of wheat sold by households was sold at the contract price.[20] As a share of total trade in grain (and especially in wheat), then, planned trade in the form of quota deliveries is still substantial.

Farmers also sell grain beyond their quotas to the state at negotiated prices and on the market at market prices. The county Grain
Bureau buys both wheat and corn at negotiated prices. Since 1985,
negotiated procurement of grain has grown from less than 5,000
tons to more than 45,000 tons, so that by the early 1990s negotiated

Table 5.12 Grain prices in Zouping County, 1980–1993

	Wheat (yuan/kg)				Corn (yuan/kg)			
	A Contract or quota price	B Negotiated purchase price	C Periodic market price	C/A	A Contract or quota price	B Negotiated purchase price	C Periodic market price	C/A
1980	0.334	n.a.	0.56	1.68	0.234	n.a.	0.34	1.45
1981	0.334	n.a.	0.68	2.04	0.234	n.a.	0.34	1.45
1982	0.334	n.a.	0.68	2.04	0.234	n.a.	0.40	1.71
1983	0.334	n.a.	0.58	1.74	0.234	n.a.	0.38	1.62
1984	0.334	n.a.	0.57	1.71	0.234	n.a.	0.28	1.20
1985	0.452	n.a.	0.50	1.11	0.312	n.a.	0.30	0.96
1986	0.452	n.a.	0.54	1.20	0.312	n.a.	0.42	1.35
1987	0.482	n.a.	0.70	1.45	0.332	n.a.	0.40	1.21
1988	0.482	n.a.	0.84	1.74	0.332	n.a.	0.50	1.51
1989	0.516	n.a.	1.18	2.29	0.352	n.a.	0.72	2.05
1990	0.516	0.69	0.84	1.63	0.352	0.52	0.56	1.59
1991	0.516	0.68	0.75	1.45	0.352	0.52	0.47	1.34
1992	0.620–0.640[a]	0.67	0.76	1.23	0.480	0.58	0.62	1.29
1993	0.650[b]	n.a.	n.a.	n.a.	n.a.	n.a.	n.a.	n.a.

Source: Interviews, Zouping County.

a. Different sources gave slightly different values for the 1992 contract price.

b. Farmers also received a cash supplement for inputs of 0.09 yuan per kg wheat delivered under
contract, which, if added to the contract price, brings the total payment per kg wheat to 0.74 yuan.

Note: Quota prices are for standard-grade grain; market prices are average prices for all grades
traded.

grain procurement exceeded 10 percent of county grain output and was nearly twice as large as contract procurement. This growth in negotiated procurement reflects that grain output has been rising over time, while quotas have remained fairly constant.

If sales to the state at negotiated prices are voluntary, then these transactions should be classified as market sales. The recent expansion of negotiated procurement would then imply that the state now buys more grain through the market than under plan. In actuality, however, deliveries at negotiated prices may have been obligatory. According to some sources, the county Grain Bureau set quotas for procurement of grain at negotiated prices during the late 1980s. The extent to which these quotas were enforced at the household level is unclear.

Evidence on negotiated prices supports the conclusion that negotiated procurement was not fully voluntary (Figures 5.1 and 5.2). In

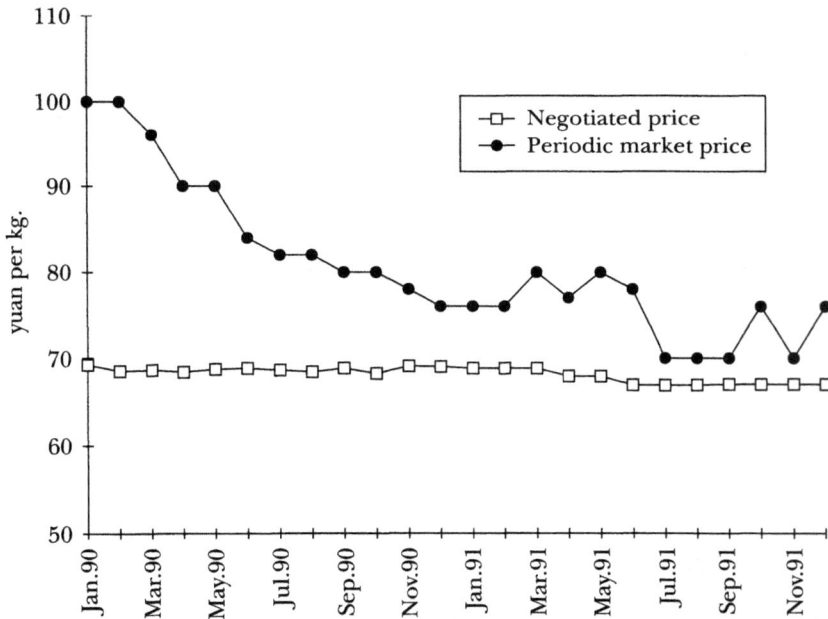

Figure 5.1 Monthly wheat prices, Zouping County, 1990–1991

1990 and 1991, the two years for which data are available, the negotiated purchase prices for wheat were uniformly lower than the periodic market prices. For corn, the negotiated price was substantially lower than the market price until October 1990, when market prices fell by one-third. For both wheat and corn, the negotiated prices remained virtually constant, while local market prices fluctuated substantially. Thus the gap between market and negotiated prices for wheat narrowed in 1991, but only because market prices declined. Because wheat and corn prices were high in 1988 and 1989 (Table 5.2), it is likely that the gap between market and negotiated prices was large prior to 1990.

Despite this price gap, state procurement of grain at negotiated prices rose substantially in the late 1980s and early 1990s. In 1989, negotiated procurements of wheat more than doubled, and negotiated procurements of corn rose more than 50 percent. These facts

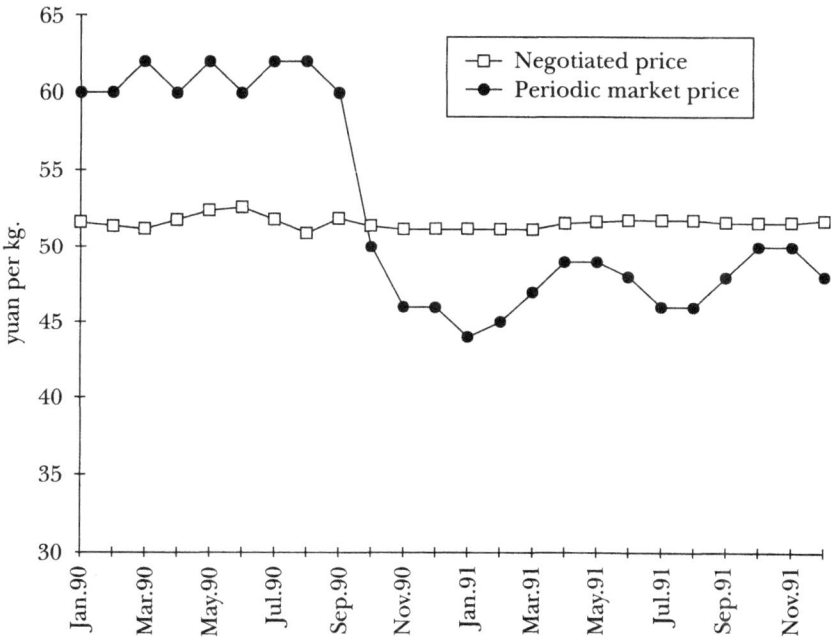

Figure 5.2 Monthly corn prices, Zouping County, 1990–1991

suggest either that deliveries to the state at negotiated prices were to some extent compulsory or that farmers did not have access to alternative buyers. It is possible, for example, that during these years the government restricted grain markets and limited grain purchases by nondesignated agents. If deliveries at negotiated prices were compulsory, then negotiated procurement would, like quota or contract procurement, be a form of planned trade. If not, then negotiated procurement should be viewed as a form of market trade, with the Grain Bureau attempting to set its price monopsonistically.

Sales of grain through nondesignated channels fall clearly into market sales. According to the county-level data in Table 5.9 (which exclude intrarural sales), between 30 and 50 percent of grain purchased from farmers during the late 1980s and early 1990s was bought by nondesignated agents. These buyers included private individuals and industrial and other enterprises. The survey data, which include intrarural sales, show that in 1990 farmers sold about 70 percent of grain to such buyers.

These statistics indicate that market trade in grain is now substantial in Zouping. At the least, market sales constitute one-third to one-half of grain sales. If negotiated procurement is considered as part of market trade, then by the 1990s the share of grain sold on the market exceeded 70 percent, and this expansion of market trade for grain reflected the growing involvement of designated state agencies as market players.

Plan versus Market for Cotton

All cotton is procured by the state at planned prices, and nominally there is no negotiated or market exchange. In reality, however, the force of planning for cotton is weak, and the level of deliveries appears to be a function less of the quota level than of the returns to cotton production. In Zouping, the county government has set mandatory targets for cotton procurement, and in some years also for the area in which the cotton is sown. Cotton production and procurement have consistently fallen short of the plan. The county-wide procurement target was 23,000 tons until 1991, when it was reduced slightly. Between 1985 and 1993, actual procurement was below the target in every year but 1987, when yields were above normal (see Table 5.13). On average, between 1985 and 1993, cotton deliveries were only 75 percent of the quota.

The household survey data reveal a similar lack of plan fulfillment. In 1990, 80 percent of the sample households faced delivery targets for cotton. On average, the amount of cotton each household delivered was equal to only 87 percent of its delivery target. More than half the households in the survey sample did not fulfill their cotton procurement targets; one-third of the households delivered less than 75 percent of their targets.[21] The widespread incidence of underfulfillment suggests that cotton plans were not uniformly or strictly enforced, and so they were not fully mandatory.

Plans were underfulfilled not because households withheld cotton from the state but because they produced too little cotton to meet the plan. Both aggregate county statistics and the household survey data show that the level of cotton deliveries depends largely on the quantity of cotton produced. County statistics show that the government has procured more than 90 percent of production in almost every year since 1979, and the correlation between production and procurement is 0.995. The surveyed households delivered 99 percent of the cotton they produced to the state in 1990, and the cross-section correlation between output and deliveries was 0.99.

The quantity produced in turn depends on the profitability of growing cotton relative to other crops. Local officials and farmers in Zouping said that farmers grow insufficient cotton to meet plan targets because returns to cotton were low. Cotton is a relatively high-cost crop that requires more labor and chemical inputs than grain and other crops. While costs of producing cotton are high, in the late 1980s and early 1990s its price fell relative to the prices of competing crops. In the late 1980s, market prices for most farm products increased substantially, but the state's planned price for cotton rose only modestly. Cotton production declined at this time. The planned price for cotton was increased in 1989 and 1990, and concurrently market prices for competing crops fell. Cotton production recovered, as did plan fulfillment, but in 1992 cotton resumed its decline.

One factor contributing to the downward trend in cotton produc-

Table 5.13 Cotton procurement by the State Cotton and Hemp Company in
Zouping, 1978–1993

| | Cotton output (tons) | Sown area (10,000 mu) | Yield (kilos/mu) | Procurement | | | |
				Procurement target (tons)	Actual procurement (tons)	Procurement as % of output	Procurement price (yuan/ton)
1978	3,040	23.82	13	n.a.	2,595	85	n.a.
1979	3,700	23.93	16	n.a.	3,324	90	2916/3790.8[a]
1980	12,425	28.24	44	n.a.	12,034	97	2916/3790.8[a]
1981	15,225	34.13	46	n.a.	14,997	96	2916/3790.8[a]
1982	15,728	43.86	36	n.a.	15,141	96	2916/3790.8[a]
1983	21,564	42.46	51	n.a.	20,326	94	3528.4
1984	35,150	47.91	73	n.a.	34,430	98	3615.8
1985	20,250	36.14	56	23,000	19,569	97	3528.4
1986	20,750	34.67	60	23,000	20,197	97	3440.8
1987	27,500	36.58	75	23,000	27,140	99	3528.4
1988	15,000	35.40	42	23,000	10,831	72	3928.4
1989	17,915	34.69	52	23,000	16,483	92	4728.4
1990	22,000	40.63	52	23,000	19,850	90	6000.0
1991	24,845	47.41	52	23,000	22,039	89	6000.0
1992	12,150[b]	42.94[b]	28	20,000	9,529	78	6000.0
1993	9,800	22.94	43	22,000	8,569	87	6600.0

Source: Interviews, Zouping County.

a. From 1979 through 1982, the base procurement price was 2,916 yuan; beyond-quota deliveries received a 30 percent bonus, or 3,790.8 yuan total.

b. Reportedly, drought and pest problems contributed to low output in 1992 and 1993. Harvested cotton area was only 84 percent of the area sown to cotton in 1992, and only 66 percent of the area sown in 1993.

tion is the uneven nature of the commercial reforms. The state monopsony on cotton persisted well into the 1990s, while the government opened up markets for most other farm products ten years earlier. During the past decade, markets for other products and opportunities for off-farm employment have developed and expanded. By 1990, then, the state faced indirect competition from products traded freely on the market, even though it had no direct competition in the cotton market. Thus if planned prices for cotton were too low, farmers diverted their energy and resources elsewhere.

This is not to say that cotton planning has been entirely ineffectual. Evidence suggests that in the absence of planning, farmers would produce less cotton. For example, in years when local officials have made extra efforts to monitor and enforce cotton plans, cotton area and output has expanded. Such was the case in 1990 and 1991, when mandatory cotton area targets were reintroduced and the planned procurement price was increased. In those years, cotton production and deliveries rose substantially. In contrast, after the announcement in the fall of 1992 of the liberalization of cotton marketing and the elimination of mandatory targets, the area in which cotton was sown fell by almost half, even though cotton prices remained unchanged (see Table 5.13).

The government has tried to address the problem of plan underfulfillment by setting penalties. For example, in Zouping, farmers are supposed to deliver 2.5 kilograms of grain at the planned price for each kilogram cotton delivery shortfall. In practice, this penalty is not enforced. Survey data for 1990 and 1991 show that despite widespread underfulfillment of the quota, no households paid this or any other penalty, and in 1992 the county government waived all penalties for cotton delivery shortfalls because of drought and insect problems. Application of the penalty is difficult because cotton yields are naturally variable, and the government cannot easily determine if yields are low owing to natural causes beyond the farmers' control, or if they are low owing to farmers' decisions to employ labor and other inputs elsewhere.

Why is the government able to enforce plans for grain but not for cotton? The difference between grain and cotton is perhaps due to the fact that farmers have reasons to produce grain regardless of the state-planned price and quota levels. Farmers produce grain beyond the quota because (1) they need additional grain for use as food and animal feed, and (2) beyond-quota grain can be sold on the market at higher prices. Consequently, both the government and the farmers know that even in years when the harvest is poor, the quantity of grain produced will exceed the quota by a large margin. In contrast, owing to the state monopsony and prohibitions on textile production by nondesignated agents, the only reason to produce cotton is for sale to the state. Farmers have little incentive to meet their cotton quotas unless the planned procurement price is high enough to make sales of cotton to the state relatively profitable. Ironically, the liberalization of commerce for grain appears to have helped promote plan fulfillment, whereas lack of liberalization for cotton has had the opposite effect.

Under these circumstances, state procurement of cotton does not fit well the definition of planned trade discussed earlier. The state's position in the market instead seems closer to that of a monopsonist. As in the case of monopsony, the government is the sole buyer of cotton; as in monopsony, it faces a trade-off between the price it pays and the quantity of cotton that farmers are willing to sell. Efforts to enforce targets and quotas perhaps change the level and slope of the supply curve, but the government is unable to dictate quantities.

The State, the Plan, and Household Incomes

Government interventions in both grain and cotton markets transfer income between farm households and the state. If the state can enforce plans, then it can implicitly tax producers by setting high delivery quotas and low prices. Even if the state cannot fully enforce plans, if it has monopsony power, it can implicitly tax producers by setting a low price. In this case, however, the government's ability to tax is reduced because farmers will respond to low prices by decreasing the quantities they supply. In either case, the amount of the implicit tax depends on (1) the quantity delivered to the government at the planned price and (2) the difference between the planned price and the market price that would prevail if markets were competitive. In this section I estimate the magnitude of the implicit taxes on grain and cotton and examine whether the net impact of these taxes is progressive or regressive.[22]

Estimating the magnitude of the implicit grain tax is simplified by the fact that grain is traded at market prices. Although the market price of grain could differ from the price that would prevail in the absence of any government interventions, it nevertheless captures the opportunity cost to farmers of selling grain under plan. Through most of the 1980s, planned prices for grain were lower than market prices (Table 5.12). The gap between plan and market prices, and thus the size of the implicit tax per unit grain, was largest in 1988–1989, when inflation had driven up market prices. In the early 1990s, a combination of factors reduced this unit tax: good harvests lowered market prices, and the government raised the contract or quota price. By 1992, the market price for wheat was only about 20 percent above the planned price. In 1993, the addition of the cash supplement for inputs of 0.09 yuan raised the quota price so that it was approximately equal to the market price. At this time, then, the implicit tax was effectively eliminated. After 1993, however, the tax reemerged as inflation caused the gap between state and market prices to widen.

Farmers also face an explicit tax on grain, the so-called agricultural tax (*nongye shui*). The agricultural tax is paid in kind using wheat. Farmers receive no payment for wheat delivered in fulfillment of the agricultural tax, and so the amount of tax paid per unit of wheat simply equals the prevailing market price.

Calculating the implicit tax for cotton is complicated by the fact that, owing to the monopsony policy, there is no observable market price. In principle, the amount of the tax per unit of cotton depends on the difference between the state's monopsony price and the hypothetical competitive market price. A common measure of the competitive market price is the import price—that is, the price that China pays for cotton imports on international markets. Available data show that in 1990 China paid, on average, U.S.$1.70 per kilogram of cotton imports, which, at the official exchange rate, translates to about nine yuan per kilogram. The state procurement price

was six yuan, 50 percent lower than the import price. This calculation implies that farmers paid a tax of about three yuan per kilogram
of cotton sold to the state.[23]

Multiplying unit taxes by quantities delivered gives estimates of the
total amount of the taxes associated with state interventions in the
grain and cotton markets. The results of these calculations are given
in Table 5.14. The grain quota and agricultural tax each reduced
average income of the surveyed households by about 2 percent. The
implicit cotton tax reduced average household income by about 10
percent. In total, these taxes averaged 583 yuan, equivalent to 14
percent of total household income or about 20 percent of household income from agriculture.

The implicit subsidies associated with planned sales of farm inputs
offset these taxes only slightly. The implicit subsidy on inputs is equal
to the quantity of rationed supplies times the difference between the
market and planned prices. In 1990, the surveyed households received planned sales of urea and diesel fuel at highly subsidized
prices: on average, the market price paid by surveyed households for
urea was double the planned price, and the market price for diesel
fuel was nearly triple the planned price. The quantities of inputs
that farmers received at subsidized prices, however, were small. Con-

Table 5.14 Implicit taxes and subsidies associated with planned procurement of
farm products in Zouping (yuan/household), 1990

	Average value (% of pretax income)		Minimum	Maximum	Gini index
Implicit taxes/subsidies					
Grain quota and agricultural tax	129	(3.7)	24	358	—
Cotton quota	454	(10.0)	0	2,697	—
Rationed inputs	58	(1.5)	0	434	—
Net implicit tax	525	(12.1)	−34	2,373	—
Per capita household income					
Without implicit taxes/subsidies	1277 (100)		16	5410	0.29
With implicit taxes/subsidies	1149 (90.0)		−6	5250	0.32

Source: Farm household survey, Zouping County, 1991.
Note: The calculations giving these estimates are explained in the text.

sequently, the value of the implicit input subsidies was equal to only 1.5 percent of household income. After subtracting these input subsidies, the net implicit tax paid by households was equal to 12 percent of their total income, or 15 percent of their agricultural income.

The burden of these implicit taxes and subsidies, especially for cotton, varied widely among households. The net tax (the sum of grain and cotton taxes minus implicit input subsidies) ranged from a net subsidy of 34 yuan to a net tax of 2,373 yuan. Within villages, the per capita tax level tended to be uniform, as the villages usually divided their cotton land, grain land, and delivery quotas among households on the basis of family size. Much of the difference in per capita taxes therefore reflected variation among villages.

On balance, these implicit taxes and subsidies slightly increased the degree of income inequality. The Gini coefficient for per capita household income in the absence of implicit taxes and subsidies was 0.29; with implicit taxes and subsidies, the Gini coefficient rises to 0.32. This increase indicates that the net tax on farm households arising from state commercial interventions was, on balance, slightly regressive.

The preceding calculations of implicit taxes and subsidies hold quantities constant. That is, the calculations assume that households would not alter their production or sales behavior if the government changed its quota and price policies. In reality, households *would* change their behavior if the procurement policies changed. By so doing, they could take better advantage of the liberalized commercial environment and so increase their incomes. For this reason, the true burden on households of state procurement policies exceeds the estimates shown in Table 5.14.

Conclusions

The experience of Zouping County reveals that China's economic reforms have cleared the way for extensive commercial development. The degree of commercialization in Zouping is relatively high and rising. Zouping's rural households participate actively in markets. Through exchange, households generate much of their income and satisfy most of their consumption needs. Furthermore, the sorts of institutions and infrastructure necessary for continued commercial development have emerged, as evidenced by the revival of periodic markets, the increased number of merchants and middlemen, and the improvements in roadway and communication networks.

With the reforms have come qualitative changes in the nature of the state and planning. Designated state commercial agencies now participate in markets and respond to market signals. Nondesignated state agencies and enterprises operate independently in the commercial sphere. Planned quotas and targets are in many cases no longer enforceable, or only partly enforceable. Such developments necessitate a reevaluation of what is meant by terms such as "state," "plan," and "market."

The relationship between plan and market, and between designated and nondesignated commercial agents, has evolved over time. The scope of planning has narrowed and that of markets widened. In the changed commercial environment, the official state commercial system has found alternate methods of maintaining market power. By defending their status as the dominant or sole buyers, state commercial agencies have retained their ability to buy certain farm products at relatively low prices. These new methods, like the old ones, transfer income from producers to the state.

Recent policy announcements indicate that the central government plans to reduce further the use of mandatory commercial planning. Even in the absence of active steps in this direction, the momentum of commercial development would probably continue to erode the effectiveness of mandatory plans. The balance between plan and market, then, is almost certain to shift further in the direction of markets.

The reduction and even elimination of planning does not, however, mean that the state will wither away. Even without planning, the state commercial system can make use of its status, size, and past experience to maintain dominance in key markets. Designated state agencies may therefore continue to set prices so as to earn extranormal profits or revenues. If so, they would in effect be behaving like monopsonists (or monopolists). Alternatively, the government could use its market power to pursue other political and economic objectives. For example, the Grain Bureau could place greater priority on maintaining price stability or on supplying grain to poor areas than on maximizing profits.

Whether the designated state agencies can maintain their market dominance in the long term depends on whether other actors emerge that can effectively compete. Private merchants and businesses typically must begin from small, relatively weak positions. Their ability to challenge the state commercial system effectively is questionable. A more likely threat is competition from nondesignated state agencies and enterprises and from state commercial agencies in other locations. For example, the Zouping Brewery, a county-level state enterprise, could decide to purchase grain for its own use directly from farmers or even to diversify into the grain business. Large textile factories or state cotton agencies from neighboring areas such as Zibo or Ji'nan could try to purchase directly from Zouping farmers and so bypass the Zouping County Cotton and Hemp Company.[24] Such agencies and enterprises are more likely to have the resources needed to challenge the monopsony of the county Grain Bureau or Cotton and Hemp Company. Thus the development of competitive, efficient, and accessible markets requires not only policies allowing private commerce but also measures promoting competition among state agencies and state enterprises.[25]

II | Distributional Consequences of Reform

SARAH COOK

6 | Work, Wealth, and Power in Agriculture: Do Political Connections Affect the Returns to Household Labor?

The rapid growth of China's rural economy during the past two decades has been accompanied by an increase in income inequality among rural households. New patterns of economic and social stratification are emerging within villages and townships as households adapt to the new market economy. Following the egalitarian distribution system of the collective era, some increase in the level of inequality was an inevitable and beneficial outcome of economic reform. The commercialization of the rural economy and the increasing dominance of the market as a mechanism for the allocation of resources creates new incentives, opportunities, and risks. As rural households become more dependent on commercial exchange, opportunities for economic enrichment increase, but households are also exposed to the greater risks and uncertainties associated with markets.[1] The differing abilities of households to take advantage of these opportunities or to protect themselves against risk inevitably fosters some degree of inequality.

Why certain households are able to take advantage of new opportunities while others get left behind is a question that is still largely unanswered, although various explanations have been proposed, including household composition and life-cycle effects, levels of human capital, location, social or kinship networks, and political status or connections.[2] While all these explanations contain some element of truth, the paucity of data at the household and village level means that little empirical work has been done to illuminate the mechanisms that differentiate the incomes of households. In this chapter, using a rich data base from Zouping County,[3] I argue that economic and social stratification in rural China are in large part determined by political status or connections, and that a key channel through which political factors affect household incomes is their impact on the productivity of household labor.

Labor is typically the most valuable productive asset for low-income rural households. The type of employment in which household members engage, and hence the returns to their labor, is thus an important determinant of income.[4] Although nonagricultural employment increased at an impressive rate during the 1980s, it was insufficient to absorb the large pool of surplus rural labor. Under these conditions of excess labor supply, and in the absence of adequate market mechanisms for allocating preferred jobs, nonmarket mechanisms arise to ration entry into such employment. Political status, as measured by government position, Communist party membership, and pre-1949 "class background,"[5] is hypothesised to be one of the most important such mechanisms.

In the following section, I review the debate on the role played by political elites during transition and identify potential channels through which cadres or officials might retain power. A description of rural labor market conditions in Zouping County illustrates one such channel, showing how market imperfections create conditions in which households are dependent on political connections for higher-paying employment. The results of an econometric analysis of household survey data support the argument that labor markets operate imperfectly and that individuals are constrained in leaving the agricultural sector. The marginal returns to labor in agriculture are well below those in other activities, while political connections—particularly party membership—have a positive effect on the returns to household labor. The final section discusses the implications of these results for the debate over whether political elites retain power during transition, and for changing patterns of economic and social stratification in rural China.

Political Elites in a Transitional Economy

In Maoist China, political status played a critical role in determining the economic opportunities and well-being of the Chinese people. Access to formal education, employment, and income, for example, depended largely on one's political characteristics. In the reform era, the importance of political relationships is less clear. A crucial question is how much power Communist party members and government officials retain during the transition from socialism to a more market-based economy.[6] Previously entrenched elites may adapt to the changing environment and use their power base to benefit from reform, or they may that find their skills are ill-suited to the emerging market economy and thus lose their power. The outcome of this process will in part determine the pattern of economic and social stratification in the reformed economy.

The thesis that rural cadres lose power during transition is most cogently presented by Victor Nee.[7] In his "Theory of Market Transition," Nee argues that a shift from redistribution to markets involves a change in sources of power and privilege, with direct producers gaining in power relative to redistributors (cadres). As market allocation replaces bureaucratic coordination, rural households should gain access to an increasing number of channels to acquire resources and to market goods and services, reducing their dependence on local officials. Cadres, who possess skills that become increasingly irrelevant in the market economy, should then lose power to previously disadvantaged groups. Economic stratification or a class structure along the lines of former political status should not emerge.[8]

By contrast, Jean Oi suggests that after initial opposition to the reforms, some cadres developed control over new sources of power and privilege and continued to play an important patronage role. Even if alternative channels for gaining access to scarce resources existed, she argues, the transaction costs associated with them would be high. Political connections would therefore provide cheaper access to important goods. Furthermore, new types of goods and services, such as enterprise licenses, which could only be obtained through bureaucratic channels, were becoming increasingly valuable in the liberalizing economy. Cadres and party members, starting out in positions of political advantage, should be able to adapt their skills to their new environment (as rural households had done) and thus gain economic as well as political power.[9]

This view appears to be supported by the slowdown of the "transition" process and of rural economic growth in the mid-1980s. The lack of political liberalization and the continuity of old political institutions prevented the direct transition from plan to market as cadres retained control over vital economic resources. Instead, a "hybrid" economy emerged with old (centrally planned) institutions coexisting alongside new (market) economic institutions. An alternative interpretation is proposed by Nee, who suggests that the reforms had not yet progressed far enough for cadre power to be reduced, while conceding that "emergent market transactions are embedded in social networks in which rural cadres hold pivotal positions"[10] and that, under conditions of partial reform, cadres retain the capacity to benefit from their political position.[11]

Recent studies suggest the need for a more refined conceptualization of the relationship between the local state and markets in order to understand how cadres and farmers respond to their changing environment. The notion of a direct transition from plan to market has been replaced by concern about more subtle and complex changes in the nature of institutions, ownership and property rights, and relations between state and market.[12] Oi's recent work exemplifies these new concerns. In her work on local state corporatism, Oi describes a system in which local government officials have incentives to act as economic players in the market.[13] At the same time, they are able to intervene to allocate resources as a bureaucracy; for example, they may redistribute profits among enterprises or retain extra revenues for social welfare expenditures.

New Sources of Elite Power in the Transitional Economy

The involvement of township and village governments in local economic development is one channel through which political elites have acquired new sources of power following decollectivization. To the extent that they can promote—and control some of the benefits of—economic growth, local officials have access to opportunities for personal gain as well as the capacity to affect the economic opportunities of rural households. Their role in enterprise management gives them an alternative to the private sector as a route for economic advancement. Their control over other economic and bureaucratic resources, including information, provides them with advantages in competing with, supporting, or entering the private sector. As township and village enterprises are frequently the primary employers of rural wage labor, local officials control an important instrument for affecting the distribution of income among rural households. Recent studies provide evidence of the important contribution that such off-farm employment makes to household incomes, as well as indicating that having a cadre in the family is correlated with success in running private household businesses.[14]

In the early years of reform and decollectivization, party members and cadres were in an advantageous position to gain access to collective assets. These assets, acquired when the household responsibility system was introduced, frequently provided the basis on which families became "specialized" households *(zhuanye hu)* and, in some cases, successful private entrepreneurs or "10,000-yuan households" *(wanyuan hu)*.[15] Similarly, in a study of a village enterprise in Sichuan, Yang Minchuan notes that cadres were given initial privileges in acquiring ownership shares in the enterprise.[16] These shares gave their owners the right to allocate jobs in the enterprise on the basis of kinship ties, regardless of village residence.

Other less direct channels exist through which political connections might affect household productivity and income. For example, if political status provides access to better education, and if education is rewarded in the labor market, then higher levels of education or human capital will act as another mechanism translating political status into higher incomes. Connections have also been noted between class background and economic status, with former "rich farmers" being more likely to undertake nonagricultural enterprises to supplement their agricultural income.[17] The fact that this formerly politically disadvantaged group appears better able to benefit from new economic opportunities may seem puzzling. Possible explanations offered for this phenomenon include skills acquired in earlier family enterprises or in adverse economic circumstances during political campaigns, or financial support from overseas relatives.[18]

A complete assessment of how those in positions of political authority respond to or benefit from transition would require a closer examination of the collective enterprise sector and the monetary and nonmonetary rewards to cadres, many of which may not be reflected in reported income. The focus of this chapter, however, is limited to one of the major channels through which political factors influence the capacity of rural households to benefit from economic liberalization—namely, how political status affects the returns to household labor.

How the Rural Labor Market Works: The Example of Zouping County

How much households earn from their labor is determined by the market demand for labor, individual characteristics such as education and experience, and choices that households and individuals make concerning the allocation of labor among activities. When markets are competitive, neoclassical economic theory predicts that maximizing households will allocate their labor to the activities that bring the highest returns. Choices about labor allocation should then be determined by market prices or the wage rate.[19] If all households face similar prices and wages, as should be the case under conditions of competitive markets, we would not expect to see systematic variation in the returns to labor by household, controlling for individual characteristics such as age and education.

On the other hand, however, if markets are imperfect or incomplete as is the case in China, households may face different prices for the same good.[20] For example, cadres may pay less for inputs such as fertilizer, or their transaction costs in marketing activities may be lower. When the labor market is segmented and households do not have equal access to preferred types of employment, the returns to labor will vary among households according to identifiable characteristics.[21] If political connections determine access to wage employment, and households with such access move labor out of agriculture, therefore also raising the marginal returns to farm labor for the household, then we should see the returns to labor varying according to a household's political characteristics. The degree to which labor markets are competitive and how resources are allocated when markets are imperfect are thus crucial determinants of household income.

China's Imperfect Labor Markets

China's rural labor market is characterized by a high degree of segmentation and a large rural labor surplus.[22] During the collective era, China appeared to have found a development path that avoided the problems, typical of developing economies, of surplus rural labor, high rates of migration, and rapid urbanization. These problems became apparent, however, once some of the restrictions on residence, labor mobility, and access to off-farm employment relaxed. The rural labor surplus is now estimated at 30 to 50 percent of the rural labor force, whereas the highly visible "floating population" *(liudong renkou)* of migrant labor is estimated at up to 100 million people.[23] Despite the expansion of off-farm employment and the increase in labor mobility, the household registration *(hukou)* system and the state allocation of jobs remain effective barriers to migration and deny rural residents access to most formal state employment.[24] These conditions and their implications for household employment and income are illustrated in the following case of Zouping County.

The Labor Market in Zouping County

Zouping has experienced rapid economic growth and diversification, particularly since the late 1980s. While agriculture remains the primary income source, households are shifting out of basic crop cultivation (wheat, corn, and cotton) into such commercial agriculture as vegetable and fruit production and raising chickens and livestock. They also engage in family nonagricultural enterprises and wage employment in collective and private enterprises. A construction boom, including the building of a major highway from Ji'nan to the coast, has generated short-term wage work. The number of rural laborers working as street vendors, running market stalls and restaurants, or providing other services has also risen dramatically in recent years.

The overall employment structure at the county and township level replicates the segmented urban state structure. Entry into "formal" employment in state and collective enterprises (*guoying* and *da jiti qiye*) remains highly restricted, with rural residents essentially excluded from many jobs.[25] Table 6.1 illustrates the structure of employment in Zouping County in 1993. Over 90 percent of the labor force is classified as agricultural *(nongye)*, of whom 76 percent are engaged primarily in agricultural activities; 5 percent are employed in rural industry, mostly in the township and village sector; and 5 percent have jobs in the state- or county-level collective sector.[26] The remaining 14 percent of the agricultural workforce is employed in private activities such as construction, transport and retail services, and small household enterprises. Smaller private household enterprises (*geti hu* or *hezuo qiye*) employ 9 percent of the agricultural labor force, with over 13,000 private enterprises registered in June 1993.[27]

Table 6.1 Structure of the labor force in Zouping, 1993

Category	Number employed	Percent of total
Agricutural labor force	331,461	91.4
Agriculture	(250,533)	(69.0)
Industry	(17,258)	(4.8)
Construction	(22,082)	(6.1)
Transport	(6,800)	(1.9)
Retail/services	(5,824)	(1.6)
Other Nonfarm	(28,944)	(8.0)
Nonagricultural labor force	31,171	8.6
State enterprise	(21,184)	(6.2)
County-level collective	(8,744)	(2.4)
Total labor force	362,632	100

Source: Zouping County Statistical Bureau *Zouping tongji nianjian 1993* (Zouping County statistical yearbook [Ji'nan: Zouping xian tongjiju, 1994].

The household survey data reveal higher levels of off-farm employment than those described in county-level data, probably because individuals who undertake more than one activity can be identified. Individuals who are primarily engaged in agriculture but undertake some off-farm activity in the slack season are unlikely to be included in official statistics on off-farm employment. Among the households surveyed in 1990, 97 percent of the individuals in the labor force undertake some agricultural labor, while 67 percent are engaged solely in agriculture; 24 percent have wage jobs, and 10 percent work in household enterprises (Table 6.2). The data at the household level show a higher level of off-farm employment and suggest that households attempt to spread their labor among a range of activities. Among the 257 households sampled in 1990, only one household received no income from agriculture, while less than 40 percent of the households depended solely on agriculture. Almost 50 percent had members in wage employment and 18 percent had members engaged in household enterprises.

The data clearly illustrate the relationship between employment

Table 6.2 Individual and household employment by activity, 1990

Type of employment	Individuals in labor force (n=712)		Households (n=257)	
	Number of individuals employed	As % of total labor force	Households with members in employment	As % of all households
Agriculture[a]	688	96.6	256	99.6
Agriculture only	477	67	102	39.7
Self-employment	75[b]	10.5	46[c]	17.9
Wage employment	169[b]	23.7	125[c]	48.6

Source: All tables are based on 1990 household survey data.

a. Refers to all individuals or households who spend any time doing agricultural labor but who may also undertake other forms of employment, as opposed to "Agriculture only," which refers to individuals or households with no other form of employment.

b. Nine individuals undertake both household sideline and wage employment.

c. One hundred seventy-one households have members who are engaged in nonagricultural activities: 46 in household sidelines, 125 in wage employment, and 16 in both.

type and income, with the poorest households heavily dependent on crop agriculture. The bottom per capita income quartile received 85 percent of its income from agriculture, declining to 60 percent for the third quartile (Table 6.3). Interestingly, this share then increases in the fourth quartile. Similarly, the share from wage employment increases from 8 percent of income for the bottom quartile to 30 percent for the third quartile but decreases in the top quartile. Only the figures for self-employment reveal a consistent pattern, dramatically increasing as the share of income for the top quartile. The total income from off-farm employment increases from 12 percent in the bottom quartile to 38 percent in the third, and then declines to 32 percent in the fourth quartile.

These patterns can be partially explained with reference to Table 6.4, which shows the share of income from different sources received by households in each income quartile. Basic crop income is rela-

Table 6.3 Composition of household income by per capita income quartile, 1990

Per capita income quartile[a]	Average per capita household income [b]	% of per capita income from		
		Agriculture[c]	Wages	Self-employment
1	533.3	85.5	8.4	3.5
	(133.7)	(27.6)	(20.4)	(14.4)
2	791.3	78.8	15.9	4.7
	(65.4)	(24.8)	(22.7)	(13.3)
3	1141.5	60.7	29.3	8.6
	(149.9)	(25.9)	(25.9)	(19.7)
4	2180.8	65.4	16.2	15.9
	(695.4)	(30.4)	(20.1)	(30.7)
Total	1161.7	72.6	17.4	8.2
	(724.4)	(28.9)	(23.5)	(21.2)

a. There are sixty-four households in each quartile. One household with missing information is excluded.

b. Standard deviations are given in parentheses.

c. The last three columns do not sum to 100 percent (total household income) as only earned income sources are reported here. The difference between the sum of these three columns and total income is therefore unearned income, such as gifts, transfers from the government, and remittances.

tively equitably distributed among quartiles. Income from animal husbandry—an activity that generally requires higher capital inputs and carries greater risks than crop production—is concentrated in the top quartile. Income from off-farm self-employment reveals a similar pattern, with the top quartile receiving 67 percent of such income.[28] These patterns suggest a hierarchy of household preferences for different types of employment and indicate the constraints faced by individuals in entering preferred jobs. Wage jobs appear to provide relatively stable, low-risk employment that may be the best route out of agriculture for poorer households but may not be so highly sought after by wealthier families, who have greater capacity to hedge against the risks involved in private business.

The types of employment in which household members engage are correlated with village of residence. Activities vary widely among villages, depending on factors such as agricultural conditions, location, access to markets, and local leadership.[29] For example, residents in villages close to the county seat, such as Dongjing and Tengjia, have access to employment in Zouping as well as in their own village enterprises. Dongjing village has several collectively owned enterprises in which all households are guaranteed at least

Table 6.4 Quartile share of income by source, 1990

Per capita income quartile[a]	% share by quartile of					
	Total income	Agricultural income	Crop income	Livestock income	Wage income	Self-employment income
1	11.1	13.9	18.3	-2.2^{b}	4.9	3.1
2	18.0	20.6	25.1	1.5	15.5	7.6
3	24.1	20.8	23.2	10.2	39.4	21.9
4	46.8	44.7	33.4	90.5	40.2	67.4
Total	100.0	100.0	100.0	100.0	100.0	100.0

a. Household size does not vary systematically with income level, which would distort the share of total income by per capita quartile.

b. This figure is negative, as several households spent more on livestock than they received in income from animal husbandry during the year.

one enterprise job. Villagers have priority over nonvillagers when additional jobs are available. By contrast, in the neighboring township of Qingyang, about 60 percent of the labor force undertakes nonagricultural sidelines owing to poor agricultural conditions.[30] In Qingyang, a relatively land-poor village in Qingyang township, most households engage in private businesses such as restaurant or food-stall management, transportation, and commerce.

In some villages the dominant form of off-farm work is casual, temporary wage labor, often in construction or transportation. Households undertake these activities on a seasonal basis or as necessary to the household economy. The construction boom of the early 1990s has increased demand for such employment. In Liang-mao village, for example, most male laborers were reported to be working outside the village for seven or eight months a year, primarily in construction teams. According to several villagers, the increase in such employment during the past few years has made work readily available for those who want it without the need for personal or political connections.[31]

Specialization in nonstaple agricultural production is another important category of employment that correlates to village of residence. Examples include Dongjing village, where households raise silkworms or grow fruit; Lican, where they engage in market gardening and the breeding of long-haired rabbits; and Baojia, where the specialty is watermelon production. In Jiaoqiao, chicken farming has become the village's primary economic activity. These activities are frequently initiated by one or two households, whose success leads others to follow suit. In some cases, village governments intervene to support the activities by facilitating access to credit, markets, or information. Such interventions have been important elements in the expansion of chicken breeding in Jiaoqiao. Alternatively, local governments may play an important role in initially promoting the activities. In Lican, for example, the township government provides interest-free loans to selected households to engage in market gardening and rabbit breeding.

Controlling for village-level variation in the demand for labor and the human capital of the labor force, political factors are expected to play a role in determining access to certain types of employment.

Casual wage labor—the demand for which has increased rapidly—is one area in which political connections might be relatively insignificant. By contrast, in the formal or collective wage sector, local government officials exercise the most direct control over household access to employment, and political connections should be correspondingly more important. For private enterprises, the nature and scale of the enterprise should determine the importance of family or official connections. Larger enterprises are more likely to be dependent on local government for bureaucratic inputs and services such as licenses and tax assessments. Specialized agricultural activities are subject to fewer regulations than nonagricultural enterprises and are therefore less likely to be dependent on the support of local officials. Nonetheless, for all types of enterprises, connections with officials who frequently control scarce resources or have access to them at preferential prices may still prove advantageous. The effects of such political relationships on the returns to labor are explored in the remainder of this chapter.

Estimating the Returns to Labor

The preceding sections have presented arguments as to why political status or connections with people in positions of authority might affect labor productivity and thus household income. Using household survey data, econometric analysis was undertaken to estimate the marginal returns to labor in different activities.[32] The empirical methodology involved, first, using production functions to estimate the output value from household agricultural and off-farm activities.[33] The second step in the analysis uses the results from the production functions to calculate the marginal returns to labor in the different activities. The determinants of these marginal returns are then estimated to investigate whether households make efficient choices about the allocation of inputs, particularly labor, into production. The results indicate that labor productivity is indeed affected by political connections, particularly party membership.

The relationships between inputs and the output value of two types of household production are examined. The output measures are, first, the value of agricultural production *(agrival)*[34] and, second, revenue from household nonagricultural enterprises or sideline activities *(hhval)*. The key inputs into the agricultural production process are labor, land, and variable costs. Descriptions and summary statistics of the variables used in the analysis are presented in Appendix 6.1.

Labor input is measured as the number of hours worked in each activity by all adult household members (aged sixteen to sixty-five) and by any nonhousehold member who worked for the household. The total number of hours is divided by eight to provide a standard measure of days worked. In order to capture differences in human capital, two measures of education are controlled for. First, the maximum number of years of education achieved by adult household members *(maxed)* provides a general measure of the education level of the household. Second, the education of the household head *(headed)* is included as a measure of the "management effect" in household production.

Cultivated land is allocated to the household by the collective on a per capita basis. A few households either contract or bid for additional land from the collective or recontract their original land to other households. In addition to the total cultivated land area *(land)*,[35] two measures of land quality are included: the number of plots *(plots)* captures potential diseconomies from land fragmentation, and *flat* (the percentage of cultivated flatland) provides a measure of land productivity. The value (in yuan) of variable inputs into crop production *(cropcost)* includes seeds (both bought and retained), pesticides, fertilizers, fuel, and fees paid for the services of animal or machine-driven farm equipment. Animal husbandry costs such as feed, veterinary services, and other related expenses are included in the value of agricultural production.[36]

In addition, variables are entered in the regressions to control for household demographic characteristics that might affect the technical relationship between labor and production. These are the proportion of adult workers who are male *(malepw)* and the area of cultivated land per adult *(landpa)*.[37] Finally, village fixed effects control for variation among villages in factors such as location, market access, soil quality, irrigation, and village leadership.

Political variables are not expected to affect technical productivity directly. They could, however, operate indirectly, for example, by providing better access to education, which may in turn raise the productivity of labor and influence household or individual choices about the allocation of labor among activities. Political and institutional variables thus enter at the second stage of the analysis.

The results of the production function estimations are presented in Appendix 6.2. In agricultural production, land and input costs have coefficients that are significant at the 5 percent level and together explain a large proportion of the variation in income. Variation in land quality *(flat)* within villages does not affect agricultural output, whereas plot fragmentation significantly reduces output. The third main input, labor, has a small and not statistically significant coefficient. (I discuss this result further later in the chapter.) In household enterprise production, input costs and labor explain most of the variation in output value, with both coefficients around 0.4 and significant at the 5 percent level.

The male *(malepw)* proportion of labor is not statistically significant in the regression for agricultural production, a result that is consistent with the existence of surplus labor in the household.[38] In both agricultural and sideline production, the coefficient on the education level of the household head *(headed)* is small and negative but not statistically significant. This finding is at odds with the hypothesis that education improves management and work skills. It may be the case that the skills acquired through education are not relevant to these activities—an explanation that is stronger in the case of agriculture than for household sidelines, and one that is reinforced by the negative and statistically significant coefficients on the maximum years of education *(maxed)*. A possible explanation for this result may also be that households with better-educated heads are more likely to move their most productive members into off-farm employment, leaving agricultural work to less healthy or elderly household members—a phenomenon that has been observed in parts of China where off-farm employment is plentiful.[39] The effect of education on household sideline production remains puzzling and warrants further investigation.

Shadow Wages

The most important results for the purposes of this discussion are the coefficients on labor, from which the marginal product of labor, or shadow wage, can be calculated.[40] In agricultural production, this coefficient is small (0.07) and not statistically significant, implying that changing the amount of labor employed in agriculture, holding other factors constant, has little impact on output. For household enterprises, the coefficient on labor is considerably larger (0.4) and statistically significant.

The shadow wages derived from these coefficients reveal the large gap between the returns to labor in agricultural and nonagricultural employment.[41] For agricultural production, the shadow wage is extremely low, at approximately one yuan per eight-hour day. This figure contrasts with the marginal product of labor in household enterprises of approximately 7.80 yuan per eight-hour day, which is slightly higher than the average wage rate for nonagricultural wage labor of 6.75 yuan per eight-hour day (Table 6.5). For further comparison, the average wage rates for different types of wage employment are presented in Table 6.6.

Tests for the difference in means between the marginal product of labor in agricultural and nonagricultural activities confirm that

Table 6.5 Marginal and average products of labor (yuan per day)

Marginal product of labor[a]	Mean	SD	Min	Max	Average product of labor[b]
Agriculture	0.97	0.7	0.19	4.63	13.0 (9.7)
Household enterprise	7.84	7.7	0.73	33.7	19.7 (19.4)
Wage (n=166)[c]	6.75	3.3	1.5	24.0	—
Wage (n=124)[c]	7.04	3.3	2.8	24.0	—

a. The marginal products of labor are calculated by multiplying the regression coefficient on labor by the average product of labor. All figures are in yuan per eight-hour day. The marginal product of wage labor is assumed to be the wage rate (normalized per eight-hour day).

b. Standard deviations are given in parentheses

c. The first wage rate (n=166) is the average across all individuals who engage in wage labor. The second (n=124) is the average for all households that have members in wage employment.

the difference is statistically significant. This result contradicts the assumption of the neoclassical model that, with well-functioning markets, households equalize returns across activities.[42] In nonagricultural activities, the difference between the returns to household self-employment and wage employment is not statistically significant, indicating that, in the nonagricultural sector, market forces may play a more important role in wage determination.

The preceding analysis supports the claim that markets for labor are imperfect, with surplus labor in agriculture facing barriers to entry into higher-paying employment. In addition, if sufficient labor were moved out of agriculture and into higher-paying activities, we would expect the marginal returns to household labor that remains in agriculture to increase. In fact, having household members working off the land did not significantly affect the returns to agricultural

Table 6.6 Average daily earnings from wage employment (yuan)

	Average daily wage (per eight-hour day)	Number of observations
Agriculture[a]	6.18	13
Household enterprise[a]	6.75	9
Teacher	3.70	6
Transport	4.67	3
Commerce	5.30	9
Industry	5.89	40
Doctor	6.00	2
Food and drink	6.76	9
Other	7.08	2
Construction	7.27	37
Administration	7.60	42

a. Wages for agriculture and household enterprises are the average wages paid to individuals in the survey employed by other households in agricultural activities, or the wages paid to nonhousehold members by households in the survey for agricultural or sideline employment.

labor, suggesting that even households with nonagricultural opportunities employ excess labor on the land.

Political Determinants of the Shadow Wage

The final question to be addressed is whether political factors affect the returns to labor in different activities. I first examine whether the average shadow wage varies systematically among households according to their political characteristics—namely, cadre position, party membership, and class background. Tests for differences in the means of shadow wages among households according to their political characteristics (not controlling for other factors) are presented in Table 6.7. Party membership is most consistently related to higher returns to labor. In agricultural production, both party membership

Table 6.7 Tests for differences in means of marginal product of labor by household political characteristics

| Activity | Group variable | Group variable = 1 | | Group variable = 0 | | T test[b] |
		No. of households	Avg. MPL[a]	No. of households	Avg. MPL[a]	
Agriculture	Cadre	48	1.16	207	0.92	2.08**
	Party member	56	1.27	199	0.88	3.63**
	Good class background[c]	151	0.92	104	1.03	1.25
Household enterprise	Cadre	7	4.69	38	8.42	1.18
	Party member	12	12.1	33	6.29	2.34**
	Good class background[c]	24	7.00	21	8.80	0.78
Wage employment	Cadre	46	7.86	77	6.5	2.13**
	Party member	39	7.6	84	6.9	1.22
	Good class background[c]	103	5.10	64	5.53	0.89

a. Avg. MPL is the average of the marginal product of labor in each activity in yuan per day.

b. T statistics are reported for the tests of whether the differences between the mean marginal products in each group are statistically significant.

** significant at the 5 percent level

c. Good class background refers to hired laborers or poor farmers and cadre position bring statistically higher returns, with the difference on average being 0.40 yuan per day for party members and about 0.30 yuan per day for cadres. These results suggest that even in agriculture, where markets are now relatively free, political connections do provide some advantage.

For household sidelines, party membership again has a significant effect, doubling the average daily returns to labor. Interestingly, cadre position is negatively correlated with the returns to household sidelines, in contrast to other studies that have found cadres to have advantages in private business. One possible explanation is that cadres are, for the most part, wage employees and may have little time to engage in household business. In wage employment, the reverse results hold: households with cadres have higher average wages than those without, whereas households with party members do not. Possible explanations for these results and their implications I discuss further in the text that follows.

These differences in shadow wages by household political status can be further explored, controlling for other household characteristics, in a regression analysis of marginal product of labor in which household demographic characteristics and endowments, and measures of market access and political status are the independent variables. The results of these regressions are reported in Appendix 6.3.

In agricultural production, land endowment and household demographic structure (the dependency ratio and proportion of male workers) do not significantly affect the marginal product of labor. Nor do the measures of asset value. The main variable affecting the marginal returns to labor in agriculture is party membership, which leads to an increase of 0.26 yuan per day, or 27 percent of the average shadow wage of 0.97 yuan per day. Cadre status does not have a significant effect. Consistent with other findings, households with poor class backgrounds have lower marginal returns than those with rich peasant or landlord status, receiving on average 0.14 yuan less per day.

For households with enterprises, Communist party membership again has a statistically significant effect on the returns to labor, with an average increase of five yuan per day, compared with the average daily shadow wage of eight yuan. Having a cadre in the household, however, is negatively related to the returns to labor in household sidelines, leading to a reduction in the shadow wage of about five yuan per day.

The positive effect of party membership in both agriculture and private enterprise may reflect current benefits to party membership, perhaps in terms of access to information, inputs, and markets. In addition, these households were most likely to have had access to collective assets that could have been used to undertake specialized agricultural or nonagricultural activities. A further possibility, however, is that the causality runs in the other direction, with the more able farmers becoming party members.

The contrary results for cadre status may in part be due to the small sample size (only seven households with cadres engage in sideline enterprises). Three possible explanations can be explored further. First, the skills that cadres have acquired are less suited to private enterprise. This explanation would appear to be contradicted by evidence of cadre activity elsewhere. Second, cadres are too busy with relatively unremunerative cadre work.[43] Third, cadres can capitalize best on their positions within the collective enterprise sector, and the returns are not captured in basic income statistics. The latter argument would appear to be supported by the significant difference in wage levels by cadres. Cadres may also use the collective industrial sector for personal gain in ways not identified through this survey.

The results for cadre status may also reflect the introduction of regulations governing the role of local government officials. For example, in Zouping, cadres increasingly depend on formal election mechanisms and on their success in promoting economic growth for the retention of their positions. Tenure for township leaders is limited to six years to prevent entrenched political relationships.[44]

Implications for Elite Power and Economic Stratification

The preceding analysis illustrates how political status, by raising the returns to labor, affects the incomes of rural households. Through this channel, political status helps enable some households to take advantage of new market opportunities, and thus in part determines emerging patterns of economic stratification.

The impact of political status on the returns to labor varies considerably by type of employment. Households that engage solely in crop cultivation tend to be in the lowest-income quartiles, to have very low marginal returns to labor, and to receive negligible benefits from political connections. One reason that the impact of political variables on household farming may be small is that many of the interventions that affect the returns to crop agriculture—for instance, collective ploughing and harvesting or the provision of inputs—are undertaken at the village level. Well-connected or able village and township leaders frequently pursue such policies that may reduce inequality within a village but increase intervillage differentiation. Support for agricultural activities makes it easier for household members to engage in off-farm activities. Village-level promotion of collective enterprises and the allocation of collective jobs to villagers similarly affect household incomes. Further implications of these village-level characteristics remain to be explored in greater detail.

For many rural households, political connections appear to provide a key route out of low-paying agricultural work. They may either facilitate the move out of crop agriculture and into more productive activities or increase the returns to labor in a particular activity. The result is a dramatic average increase in the marginal returns to labor from under one yuan per day in agriculture to seven or eight yuan per day in nonagricultural work. Furthermore, for self-employment households that include party members, the returns to labor are on average over twice as high as for households with no party member.

The variance in returns to self-employment is much higher than in wage employment (Table 6.5), in keeping with the argument that households undertaking private activities can be broadly categorized in two groups. One group engages in low-paying, involutionary activities to supplement their income from agriculture and to absorb surplus labor. Such households—for instance, subsistence farmers—lack political or personal connections. The type of activities undertaken include making reed mats and rope from hemp, selling popsicles, collecting bottles, and digging gravel—activities that require no investment or connections. More highly remunerative household enterprises require higher levels of capital and generally involve greater risks. These include establishing small factories to undertake one stage in the manufacture of electrical goods, making furniture, and running a restaurant. For households undertaking such activities, political connections appear to make an important contribution to their success. Such a picture also supports patterns found elsewhere of earnings from household sidelines contributing more than other income sources to inequality in the distribution of income,[45] and it suggests the importance of differentiating between types of self-employment in order to identify the households that benefit from new income-enhancing opportunities.

At the same time, outside the agricultural sector a more competitive labor market does appear to be emerging. The argument that the strengthening of market forces weakens the dependence of farm households on local government officials requires further consideration. The rapid growth in Zouping's economy has generated a boom in the demand for unskilled labor, for example, in transport and construction. This expansion of labor demand potentially provides a channel through which households with no political connections can gain access to off-farm employment and increase their incomes. Higher incomes may then open new doors to more productive activities, for example, by easing cash or credit constraints and allowing households to invest either in their land or in off-farm enterprises. Thus households with poor political connections are not necessarily excluded from economic opportunities. They may simply face higher costs in obtaining them than do households with good political connections.

Conclusions

The empirical findings presented in this chapter provide strong support for the existence of a large rural labor surplus and restricted labor mobility. The daily shadow wage in agriculture, at less than one yuan, is a fraction of the shadow wage in nonagricultural activities, which averages between seven and eight yuan. Surplus rural labor and barriers to mobility create conditions under which nonmarket mechanisms become critical for allocating economic resources.

The results suggest that political status acts in this way, determining a household's returns to labor and thus its income. As the effect of the labor input on agricultural output is small, the overall effect of political variables on the value of agricultural output is negligible. In household sidelines, however, labor makes a larger contribution to income—doubling the labor input leads to a 40 percent increase in output value. Thus the effect of party membership, by more than doubling the marginal returns to labor, leads to a large overall increase in income from household sidelines.

While these results support the view that political connections continue to play an important role in determining the distribution of income in the transitional rural economy, the nature of this role is complex. The political elite continues to control key economic resources and opportunities, but sources of elite power are changing. Checks on cadre power seem to come, on the one hand, from the challenge of markets during periods of rapid economic growth, such as that Zouping County has experienced in recent years, and, on the other, through institutional changes in the Chinese countryside—changes that aim to increase cadre accountability. Local officials are responsible for managing economic development, and their personal power and income derive largely from their success in promoting economic growth. These factors may inhibit redistributive behavior to the extent that it would harm local growth. At the village level, cadres are also responsible for ensuring minimum levels of welfare for all households.

Whether, or to what extent, the preceding changes can prevent economic and social stratification from becoming more entrenched along the lines of political status remains an open question. More direct interventions may be needed to assist households that might otherwise be excluded from the benefits of reform. The ability of local cadres to assist households with the fewest resources depends on their having sufficient control over financial resources, and on the incentives for them to allocate resources in this way. Perhaps the most important arena for policy intervention, however, is the promotion of greater labor mobility. Further research is needed to understand the extent to which government regulations, such as the household registration system, act as binding constraints on the transfer of labor out of agriculture. Within localities, promoting the private wage sector and facilitating access to inputs, credit, and information should also help poorer households to transfer labor out of unremunerative agricultural employment and so increase their incomes.

Appendix 6.1 Summary of variables used in the regressions

Variable	Description	Mean	SD	Min.	Max.
cropval	Value of crop production (yuan)	4285	2151	625	12695
agrival	Value of agricultural production (yuan)	5434	4537	893	41828
hhval	Value of sideline production (yuan)	4935	5075	400	18720
croplabor	Days labor in crop cultivation	382	175	50	1325
agrilabor	Days labor in all agricultural activities	450	185	50	1344
hhslabor	Days labor in household enterprises	243	174	35	750
cropcost	Cost of inputs into crop cultivation	837	398	172	2878
agricost	Cost of inputs into agricultural production	1454	1689	267	17085
hhscost	Cost of inputs for household enterprises	1736	2909	20	13720
land	Cultivated land (mu)	6.99	2.7	1.9	17
flat	Share of land that is flat	0.97	0.09	0.46	1
plots	Number of plots cultivated	3.56	1.34	1.0	9
landpa	Land (mu) per adult worker	2.5	1.0	0.9	8.5
malepw	Proportion of workers who are male	0.77	0.26	0	1
maxeduc	Max. years education of adult workers	7.16	2.0	2.0	14
depratio	Ratio of nonworkers to workers	0.72	0.18	0.33	1
draftval	Value of draft animals	515	614	0	4000
kvalue	Value of assets in agricultural production	1517	1544	0	10156
hhkvalue	Value of assets for enterprise or sideline production	219	866	0	5000
headed	Years education of household head	6.05	2.39	1	14
cadre	1 = household has cadre	0.19	—	0	1
dccp	1 = household has party member	0.22	—	0	1
rich	1 = landlord/rich farmer background	0.09	—	0	1
middle	1 = middle farmer background	0.31	—	0	1
poor	1 = poor farmer or hired laborer	0.59	—	0	1
dwage	1 = household member in wage job	0.37	—	0	1
dhhent	1 = household sideline or enterprise	0.18	—	0	1
log	Natural log of variables	—	—	—	—

Appendix 6.2 OLS regressions of Cobb-Douglas production functions

Variable	Crop cultivation	Agricultural production	Household enterprise
Log costs	0.44 (0.07)**	0.7 (0.04)**	0.36 (0.05)**
Log labor	0.05 (0.06)	0.07 (0.06)	0.4 (0.12)**
Log land	0.52 (0.10)**	0.41 (0.09)**	—
Log plots	−.01 (0.08)	−0.16 (0.08)**	—
Log share of flatland	−0.1 (0.3)	0.28 (0.29)	—
Log land per adult	−0.08 (.07)	−0.01 (.07)	—
Log share of adults who are male	−0.06 (.05)	−0.06 (.05)	−0.75 (0.25)**
Log education of household head	−0.01 (0.44)	−0.01 (0.04)	−0.04 (0.23)
Log maximum years of education	−0.13 (0.07)*	−0.18 (0.07)**	0.09 (0.33)
Constant	4.6 (1.59)**	1.9 (1.4)	6.5 (1.38)**
Village fixed effects	YES	YES	NO
Number of observations	253	253	44
Adj. R^2	0.78	0.84	0.70

Notes:

Coefficients are given with standard errors in parentheses.

* 10 percent significance level

** 5 percent significance level

Agricultural production includes crop cultivation and other agricultural activities such as animal husbandry.

Appendix 6.3 OLS estimation of marginal products of labor

Variable	Cultivation (n=254)	Agriculture (n=254)	Sideline (n=45)
Land	0.02 (0.013)*	0.024 (0.02)	−0.49 (.44)
Dependency ratio	−0.26 (0.15)*	−0.31 (0.27)	2.08 (7.4)
Share of workers who are male	−0.16 (0.1)	−0.22 (0.18)	−0.91 (4)
Value of draft animals	−0.00 (00)	−0.00 (00)	−0.03 (0.02)*
Value of productive assets	−0.00 (00)	−0.00 (00)	0.000 (.00)
Party member	0.1 (0.06)*	0.26 (0.11)**	5.03 (2.4)**
Cadre	−0.07 (0.06)	−0.01 (0.11)	−5.2 (2.8)*
Good class background	−0.03 (0.05)	−0.14 (0.08)*	−0.14 (2.3)
Household enterprise	—	−0.15 (0.18)	—
Wage employment	—	−0.17 (0.14)	1.0 (2.4)
Village fixed effects	YES	YES	NO
Adj. R²	0.34	0.32	0.31

Note: Coefficients are given with standard errors in parentheses.
* 10 percent significance level
** 5 percent significance level

7 | Preventive Health Care: Privatization and the Public Good

During the Maoist era, China's success in improving its health profile without steady rises in average per capita income was almost unique among nations. In Europe and North America, mortality rates declined, and life expectancies rose over a period of several hundred years, owing to gradual improvements in living conditions.[1] In contrast, in late developing nations, mortality rates did not begin to drop until the 1960s, and then mainly as a result of technology inputs such as immunization and oral rehydration therapy rather than improvements in socioeconomic conditions.[2] By the 1970s, this trend had stalled, however, and even reversed in the 1980s in some areas. China was one of only a few nations whose mortality rates continued to decline.[3]

While average per capita income in China improved somewhat under Mao, investment in health increased substantially. Many authors attribute this achievement to *redistribution* of resources toward such cost-effective measures as environmental sanitation, food distribution, and campaigns against endemic and epidemic diseases and away from such expensive features as high-technology medicine, elite medical training, and investment in sophisticated urban medical centers.[4]

This capacity to redistribute resources was facilitated by two features of the Chinese political system: centralized planning and the creation of a rural commune economy in the late 1950s. The first provided the political capacity to redirect investments from urban to rural medicine. The second established the framework for a well-articulated health system and also provided collective income to fund rural community health programs, including insurance. China was thereby able to develop preventive as well as curative health care at the basic level. The linchpin and symbol of this program was the "barefoot doctor" who worked in village clinics as part of a referral network that connected the village, commune (township), and county hospitals. In addition, the regime's ideological commitment to preventive health was politicized through "patriotic public health campaigns"[5] and institutionalized in a widespread network of rural public health departments and maternal and child health (MCH) clinics.[6]

The prevention of endemic and epidemic infectious diseases—China's "first revolution in health care"—resulted in a rapid mortality decline among infants and women of childbearing age.[7] This produced, in turn, structural demographic changes as both men and women survived in larger numbers into their sixties and seventies. The shift in age structure was associated with changes in the leading causes of death, as more people experienced chronic health problems, including cancer, heart disease, and stroke. This transition from acute to chronic conditions—called the epidemiologic or health transition—was also fueled by changes in behaviors that are risk factors for chronic disease, most notably smoking and dietary changes. By the 1980s, although life expectancy had nearly doubled, there was also increasing concern that China might be unprepared to meet the demand for care of chronic conditions that this "revolution" had produced.[8]

Furthermore, not everyone in China had experienced to the same degree such rapid health improvements. Although differences within urban and rural areas were held down during the Maoist period, the income gap between urban and rural China widened considerably.[9] These income differences were reflected in very different health outcomes. Some of the urban-rural disparities were lessened in the 1980s, as rural incomes doubled and tripled under the decollectivized economic system. At the same time, intrarural inequalities grew, leaving poorer rural counties and some poor households within better-off areas at a disadvantage.[10] And while health care spending rose rapidly all over China during the 1980s and 1990s, it was increasingly directed toward more expensive, hospital-based, urban services.[11]

Reports on health care claim that during the 1980s the economic reforms have eroded primary health care and preventive health services in rural areas.[12] These reports argue that the shift from the collective to the private household system and the introduction of market forces into the delivery of rural health care services have undermined preventive services. Evidence for this assertion is based on five observations.

1. *Spending for prevention relative to other services has declined.* The 1992 World Bank report on health in China demonstrates a sizable shift in expenditures during the 1980s—away from preventive services and toward hospital-based, technology-intensive medical care. This is partly due to an increase in the demand for such care. It is also a result of changed financing policies that encourage medical institutions to invest in income-generating services rather than services that will benefit the health of a population but may not be profitable for an individual hospital.

2. *Similar processes can be observed in rural counties, particularly in the agencies that were responsible for carrying out community-based prevention work under the Maoist system.* According to the 1992 World Bank report, the introduction of market incentives in health care has affected local public health and MCH departments to the detriment of population-based service-delivery planning. The report notes that local agencies tend to emphasize new, profitable services at the expense of needed ones. For example, "Anti-epidemic disease stations . . . spend their time testing water samples from industries who can pay fees for the service . . . and performing laboratory examinations and chest x-rays for industrial workers' annual physical checkups, another money earning activity . . . Maternal and child health centers offer programs which require mothers and children to come to the centers rather than concentrating on (more effective) outreach services."[13] When these moneymaking activities are a major source of extrabudgetary funds, the community is less able to focus

on continuing communicable disease problems and the emerging burden of chronic illness.

3. *New incentives at the village level also undermine prevention.* Many village clinics are now managed by village doctors rather than by the collective. When doctors are no longer on salary, their incomes depend on the sale of medicines. These changes have been shown to be related to decreases in the provision of preventive services. One study[14] found that fewer preventive services are provided in privately run clinics than in collectively run ones. According to the 1990 National Village Doctor Survey of more than 90,000 practitioners, about three-fourths of village doctors' income is derived from providing curative services (including the sale of medicines). The rest is derived from county or township subsidies for preventive services.[15] The rise of for-profit medicine in villages appears to have contributed to the decline in immunization rates in China in the early 1980s, and the increase in adult and childhood infectious disease rates during the same time period.[16]

4. *Since the implementation of the economic reforms, the number of village medical personnel has dropped.* Between 1978 and 1988, the number of rural midwives dropped from 743,498 to 466,974, and the number of village doctors and health workers dropped from a high of 1,559,214 in 1975 to 1,247,045 in 1988.[17] With fewer basic-level health personnel, attention to the less remunerative work of prevention declines.

5. *The cooperative rural insurance program has, for the majority of rural citizens, disappeared.* During the 1970s, cooperative insurance *(hezuo yiliao),* funded in part by the rural welfare fund, was reported to cover 85 percent of the rural population.[18] The demise of collective agriculture brought about the breakdown of this program. According to a 1989 survey of insurance in eight provinces (Jiangsu, Shandong, Liaoning, Henan, Hubei, Hunan, Guangxi, and Guizhou),[19] only 7 percent of village residents enjoyed any type of insurance, and fewer than half of these were farmers covered by cooperative insurance programs. The remainder were cadres or workers covered under public or labor insurance programs. For people of limited means, expensive care is often out of reach. A number of recent studies in China have documented that those without insurance

coverage are less likely to be hospitalized for similar illnesses than those with medical insurance.[20]

While these trends are certainly evident, they are not equally evident in all parts of China. Official statistics report that in 1989 almost 40 percent of village clinics were still "collectively run." In 1991, a survey of village clinics found that almost half reported some or all of their income came from collective funds.[21] Furthermore, even in villages and counties that have become quite privatized, it may be possible that other forces continue to support prevention efforts. To investigate these apparent contradictions, we conducted an in-depth study of health care in Zouping County in 1990. We use this case to describe the changes in the management and financing of preventive health care services and to characterize the mixed medical market in one part of rural China.

An investigation of the viability of preventive health care services in China is particularly important as the prevalence of the chronic diseases typical of developed nations increases relative to that of the acute, infectious conditions that were prevalent in the past. The 1992 World Bank report clearly demonstrates that without effective programs to prevent heart disease, cancer, stroke, and various chronic respiratory conditions, the disease burden in the coming decades will exact a very heavy financial as well as physical toll. Because of this, in addition to investigating a range of preventable acute conditions that represent more "traditional" prevention areas, we also studied a major chronic disease—hypertension—in order to assess the transferability of prevention activities to chronic conditions.

Health and Health Care in Zouping County

Zouping is one of 137 counties in Shandong, a primarily agricultural province with overall economic and health indicators similar to average figures for China as a whole. Between 1976 and 1986, total county expenditures (including health expenditures) and per capita income all rose dramatically (see Table 7.1). Rural agricultural income rose from 50.7 yuan per capita in 1976 to 552 yuan in 1989, compared with national figures of 133.6 for 1978 and 601.5 for

1989.[22] The birth rate in Zouping was lower than national reports for other counties, although it showed the same rise and fall during the 1980s. The average death rate was higher than for other counties in 1980 but lower by 1989.[23]

Table 7.2 shows the steady decline in the incidence of infectious disease in Zouping between 1965 and 1989.[24] Although some infectious diseases (hepatitis, dysentery, and tuberculosis) persist, their incidence declined markedly after the onset of economic reform. It is much harder to get comparable figures for the incidence of chronic conditions, but these diseases have clearly become very important. Table 7.3 presents evidence of this trend, showing the percent of total admissions to the two county-run general hospitals in 1986 (N = 7363), in different diagnostic categories (with the corresponding percentages from 1986 national data). While hospital admissions represent a biased sample of ill persons in the county, these

Table 7.1 Zouping County socioeconomic and health indicators

	1976	1980	1986	1988
Total population[1]	619,517	634,068	649,115	664,281
Birthrate[1]	—	11.9	15.05	12.88
Death rate[1]	—	7.4	6.93	6.20
Per capita income (yuan)[1]	50.7	105	434.5	552[a] 1,797[b]
Total county expenditure (yuan)[2] (per capita)	8,311,000 (13.42)	13,518,000 (21.32)	27,619,000 (42.55)	43,971,000 (66.19)
County health expenditure (yuan)[2] (per capita)	739,000 (1.19)	1,017,000 (1.6)	1,112,606 (1.7)	2,425,000 (3.6)
County and township hospitals (yuan)[2] (% of total)	—	—	789,007 (71%)	1,718,000 (71%)
Prevention services (yuan)[2] (% of total)	—	—	220,296 (19.8%)	414,000 (17.1%)

Sources: [1]*Zouping tongji nianjian 1989* (Zouping Statistical Yearbook [Zouping: Zouping xian tongjiju, 1980]); [2]Interviews with local health department officials, May 1990.
   a. From agriculture.
   b. From industry.

data illustrate the extent to which county resources are devoted to the treatment of chronic disease.

Like most other counties in China, Zouping continues to maintain the general structure of the health care system of the Maoist era. It has four county-level hospitals *(xian yiyuan)*, including two general hospitals, one traditional-medicine hospital, and one small infectious-disease hospital); six "branch" hospitals *(xianfen yiyuan)*, formerly township hospitals but larger and more developed; ten township hospitals *(xiangzhen yiyuan)*, including a psychiatric hospital; approximately 900 village clinics *(weishengsuo);* and 73 private *(getihu)* clinics, located mainly in the county seat. In addition, the county bureau of health runs a public health department or "anti–epidemic disease station" *(fangyi zhan)*, a maternal and child health station *(fuyou baojian zhan)*, and disease prevention/health promotion stations *(fangbao zhan)* at all sixteen township hospitals. These stations

Table 7.2 Infectious disease incidence per 10,000 people in Zouping County, 1965–1989

	1965	1970	1976	1981	1986	1989
Meningitis	4.46	0.94	3.79	0.19	0.11	0.062
Pertussis	13.31	1.15	9.77	1.44	0.08	0
Measles	78.05	37.14	17.68	0.02	0.79	0.092
Influenza	23.34	99.60	102.40	47.22	15.96	0
Dysentery	20.74	1.49	44.00	84.24	12.86	1.46
Hepatitis	3.19	1.14	7.73	6.01	2.53	3.52
Polio	0.39	3.71	0	0	0	0.015
Encephalitis	0.39	0.82	0.71	0.17	0.08	0.046
Malaria	20.00	32.78	4.58	0.45	0	0
EHF	0	0	0	0	7.80	0.015
Total	163.47	177.94	189.95	139.57	40.10	5.54

Source: Infectious Disease Surveillance Reports, Zouping County Anti–Epidemic Disease Station, Epidemiology Department, 1965–1989.

Table 7.3 Hospital admissions by diagnostic categories, for county-level hospitals, 1986

	Admissions	
Diagnosis	Zouping[1]	China[2]
Digestive (acute gastroenteritis, appendicitis, ulcer)	25% (1914)	22.19%
Circulatory (CHD, stroke)	15% (1070)	4.94%
Respiratory (pneumonia)	14% (1048)	18.10%
Infectious disease (EHF, TB, dysentery)	11% (815)	9.91%
Injuries (fractures, accidents, burns)	9% (694)	11.56%
Obstetics (special cases)	5% (403)	8.21%
Tumors (including malignant tumors: stomach, liver, lung, breast, leukemia)	4% (324)	3.35%
Other (urology, parasites, neurology, psychiatry, ophthalmology, dermatology)	17% (1252)	21.74%
Total	100% (7363)	100%

Sources: [1]Zouping County Hospital Records, collected during interviews conducted in 1988; [2]*Zhongguo weisheng nianjian 1988* (China Health Yearbook [Beijing: Weisheng tongji chubanshe, 1988]).

Note: Zouping has separate tuberculosis hospitals and infectious disease hospitals so these underrepresent the cases with these diagnoses.

in turn oversee the various community-based services offered to village residents by the village doctors, including immunization, well-child checks, infectious disease surveillance reporting, and health education work. The hospital and clinic system manages curative health care services; the public health department and MCH station oversee preventive services.

Health Promotion and Disease Prevention in Zouping

The goal of this study was to investigate the management and financing of preventive services at the basic level in Zouping County. As in the Maoist era, these services include community-based as well as clinic-based activities that promote surveillance, treatment, and prevention of acute, infectious diseases. To investigate the possible broadening of prevention activities to include chronic conditions, we also studied the treatment of hypertension. Because it is very common in North China and has a low-cost, easy-to-use screening tool (a blood pressure check), it would be likely that if such a broadening occurred, hypertension screening would be among the first chronic disease prevention activities to be targeted.[25]

We began at the entry level of health care, conducting structured, open-ended interviews with twenty-one primary care providers from sixteen villages and three factory clinics. We used this same structured interview to gather information from physicians at five township hospitals and two county hospitals, representing the middle and highest levels of care in the county. We interviewed administrators at each of these seven hospitals and discussed approaches to prevention and treatment of infectious and chronic diseases with the leaders of the disease prevention/health promotion stations and the MCH stations in each of the five townships and at the county level.[26]

We present our results about "traditional" health promotion and disease prevention activities in the form of answers to the five assertions about the impact of the reforms on prevention.

1. *Was there a decline in funding for prevention?*

There was only a slight decline in prevention funding relative to funding for other services. In 1986, the county spent the majority (71 percent) of its budget supporting its hospitals[27] (see Table 7.4). In contrast, 19.8 percent of the budget supported preventive services (including the disease prevention station and two clinics), and 3 percent was devoted to maternal and child health. As noted earlier, the trend in the post-Mao era has been for hospital budgets to account for a greater proportion of total expenditures.[28] This was not the case in Zouping between 1986 and 1989, however. Table 7.1 shows that while total expenditures for 1989 were substantially higher than for 1986 (2,425,000 yuan compared with 1,112,606 yuan), the total percent spent on hospitals was identical (71 percent), although the proportions spent for the various types of hospitals differed. Prevention spending declined slightly, from 19.8 percent in 1986 to 17.9 percent in 1989, and MCH funding dropped from 3 percent to 1.4 percent. Thus, although prevention services account for less than 20 percent of the budget, and they lost some ground, the changes were not striking.

On the other hand, during the 1980s and 1990s, the county has emphasized curative services, particularly diagnostic and treatment services for chronic conditions. Between 1984 and 1986, the first county hospital spent over 300,000 yuan on new equipment, including a new X-ray, ultrasound, endoscope, ambulance, emergency generator, and electrocardiogram machines. They completed construction of a building for radiology and "health protection." Interviews in 1990 revealed plans for acquisition of additional diagnostic equipment and for construction of a new surgery building. These plans reflect the national trend toward investment in profitable, hospital-based technology.

2. *Did financial incentives undermine county-level prevention work?*

Health promotion and disease prevention activities in Zouping are defined and administered by the layers of health bureaucracy,

Table 7.4 Hospitals in four townships

	Jiuhu	Matou	Sunzhen	Changshan
Number of staff	21	23	45	33
Number of beds	25	24	50	32
Number of outpatients/days	85	60	70–80	100
Number of inpatients/year	1,200	520	597	—
Occupancy rate	46%	40%	20%	41%
Average length of stay	3–5 days	5 days	3–5 days	7 days
Hospital income 1986	<39,000	120,000	170,000[a]	100,000
Hospital income 1989	264,770	180,000	284,400	200,300
Township amount contributed 1989	37,344	25,000	47,000	3,000–5,000
County amount contributed 1989	35,000	37,000	0	46,000
Bed cost/day	2 yuan/day	0.9 yuan/day	2 yuan/day	2 yuan/day

Source: Data collected during interviews in 1988 and 1990.
a. For 1987.

beginning at the provincial level and extending down to the local village clinic. Despite expectations to the contrary, the county remains strongly involved in this work.

Village doctors are supervised in prevention activities (immunizations, maternal and child health checks, infectious disease reports, and general health education work among them) by the disease prevention/health promotion stations *(fangbao zhan)*. The missions of township *fangbao zhan* combine the authority of the county MCH station and the anti–epidemic disease station in one township-level department. Each month the local doctors communicate with their supervisors, either through reports or in regular meetings, when the township doctors review the designated county health education materials and propaganda information. In the spring, topics include dysentery prevention; in the fall, antipneumonia work. The *fangbao zhan* staff do periodic checks of village health work and carry out tasks set by the county departments.

The county MCH station is responsible for health checks, premarital exams, contraception, and prenatal and postnatal care. It is staffed by fourteen people working in a ten-bed outpatient clinic, with an emergency vehicle, surgical department, and diagnostic department (equipped with an ultrasound machine). The MCH station also sends six people out to supervise MCH work at the townships. In Zouping town, all births take place in the county hospital. In the villages, 69 percent of births take place at the township or county hospitals. Those at home are attended by midwives trained by the MCH and hospital personnel. The midwives continue to be supervised by the MCH personnel, and they meet once a year for continuing education. Women are recruited into prenatal care early enough to identify those with at-risk pregnancies; these deliveries, for the most part, occur in hospitals.

The county anti–epidemic disease station, or public health department, with more than fifty employees, oversees all other prevention work, including immunizations, infectious disease reporting (epidemic disease outbreaks), endemic disease control, food and labor hygiene, and health education work.

Immunization work began before 1965. In the mid-1980s, coincident with the dismantling of the collective agriculture system, Zouping experienced a rise in childhood infectious diseases. With

UNICEF funding, the county established a system to ensure safe and timely delivery of refrigerated vaccines. Using bicycles with cold packs attached, village doctors keep the "cold chain" unbroken. Once every two months, the doctors attend meetings at the township *fangbao zhan,* where they pick up vaccine supplies. They then return to their villages by bicycle and administer the immunizations within two days. Immunization coverage improved dramatically under this system. According to posted UNICEF guidelines, they conduct random checks of thirty villages six times a year, checking seven children in each village. In 1989, Zouping reported immunization coverage for polio at 95 percent, tuberculosis at 95.6 percent, DPT (diphtheria, pertussis, and tetanus) at 92.5 percent, and measles at 94.3 percent. These rates are very high and are corroborated by Zouping's infectious disease reports.

Infectious disease surveillance is required by law. While fifty-six diseases are on the reporting form, in Zouping, the most common conditions are influenza, dysentery, and hepatitis. As Table 7.2 shows, the overall decline in infectious disease incidence since the implementation of the economic reforms is striking. In contrast to claims of a deterioration in this system,[29] All of the village doctors interviewed in the spring of 1990 indicated that they turned in infectious-disease surveillance forms to the township *fangbao zhan* two to three times per month. Only one noted that if there were no outbreaks, he did not contact the township office. The reliability of infectious-disease surveillance, particularly over time, is far from perfect.[30] One may also question the validity of self-reported behavior by the local doctors. Nevertheless, the overall trends in lowered incidence, particularly regarding easily identifiable conditions such as polio, are hard to dispute.

During the 1980s, however, these trends had one noticeable exception: between 1984 and 1987, the county experienced an epidemic outbreak of the viral disease epidemic hemorrhagic fever (EHF). EHF is caused by a strain of the Hanta virus and results in acute renal failure. Regardless of advances in therapy, the mortality rate can be as high as 15 to 20 percent.[31] The county's response to this outbreak illustrates the continued viability of the its public health system, as well as its capacity to mobilize across and between different levels of administration.

The first case of EHF appeared in Haosheng township, on the southeast border of Zouping County, and was diagnosed at the army hospital in Zibo City. As the epidemic progressed, most of the cases were referred to the county hospital to confirm the diagnosis. During 1984, there were 184 confirmed cases.

EHF is a seasonal disease, transmitted to humans by contact with a parasite that lives on rats. By the winter of 1985, the whole county was mobilized in a campaign to kill rats, by order of the Shandong anti–epidemic disease prevention station. A county small group (*xiaozu*) was established, headed by the county manager and composed of people from health, public security, transportation and communication, supply and marketing, and food grains. Corresponding small groups were formed in each township, each led by a representative from the county small group. By 1986, every village in the county had a person in charge of killing rats, and every family in the county had a rat-box trap with poisoned grain inside. By 1987, the incidence of EHF began to fall (from thirty-seven in 1987, five in 1988, and one in 1989), and the county "met the rat standard for Shandong."

This case clearly demonstrates the county's ability to implement a Maoist health campaign strategy to prevent the spread of a communicable disease. County-level prevention work is very responsive to problems for which tried-and-true solutions already exist. Our interviews also revealed, however, that the county prevention stations are not free from the kind of financial pressures described in the 1992 World Bank report. In response to budget constraints, several sections of the county public health department developed moneymaking activities. These included screening clinics; health checkup clinics; health exams designed for workers in village-run enterprises; yearly child physicals; blood and other lab work for food workers; and old-age checks.[32] Involvement by the county public health department in such profit-oriented activities draws attention and energy away from prevention work.

3. *Did the incentives of for-profit medical care overshadow prevention in rural villages?*

The answer to this question is yes and no. It is true that a mixture of public and private incentives characterizes village medical markets in Zouping. Yet, while incentives may have changed with the break-down of the collective, village doctors continue to provide health promotion and disease prevention services.

Under the old system, local doctors had few, if any, opportunities to profit from medical work. They were on salary from the village and performed a mix of curative and preventive services for the local community. After the reforms, the collective system of financing and management was retained in some villages, while in many it was replaced by private funding of doctors' salaries, supplies, and equipment. This process unfolded unevenly across China, as illustrated in Table 7.5. Thus, in 1988, while national statistics reported that 37.2 percent of village clinics were collectively run and 45 percent were individually managed, in Anhui, 81.4 percent were private, and in Shanghai, 79.6 percent were collective. In Shandong, 77.1 percent of the clinics were reported to be collectively owned, and 17.4 percent were private.[33]

In Zouping in the early 1990s, completely private clinics comprise

Table 7.5 Village-based health resources

	Zouping[1]				China[3]	
Health personnel	1988	1989			1985	1988
Village doctors	702	769			1,293,094	1,247,045
Health workers	546	475				
Midwives	309	373			513,977	466,974
	Zouping[1]		Shandong[2]		China3	
Clinics	1986	1989	1986	1988	1986	1988
Collectively run	n.a.	88.8%	64.9%	77.1%	37.4%	37.2%
Privately run	n.a.	10.4%	24.4%	17.4%	43.9%	45.0%
Other	n.a.	0.8%	10.7%	5.5%	19.7%	17.8%

Sources: [1]*Zouping tongji nianjian 1989* (Zouping Statistical Yearbook [Zouping: Zouping xian tongjiju, 1989]); [2]*Shandong tongji nianjian 1990* (Shandong Statistical Yearbook [Ji'nan: Zhongguo tongji chubanshe, 1990]); [3]*Zhongguo weisheng tongji nianjian 1989* (China Health Statistical Yearbook [Beijing: Zhongguo weisheng chubanshe, 1989]).

Note: The total number of villages is 857.

only 10 percent of all village clinics. In these cases, the village doctor is able to buy the medical supplies and equipment from the village outright and run the clinic as a private business.[34] According to the reports cited earlier, it would be these doctors who would be most likely to neglect the public health activities that are not financially rewarding, such as infectious disease reports and childhood immunizations.

In contrast, the majority of local clinics in Zouping are managed under a mixed system called *baoben jingying* ("guaranteeing the basic capital"). Officially—according to the Zouping County Yearbook—*baoben jingying* is categorized as "collective." It differs substantially, however, from a system in which the village provides a clinic building, medical supplies, and doctors' salaries. Instead, under *baoben jingying,* villages provide some start-up money for local doctors to run their clinics, either in their homes or in village offices. Income is generated by profits from the sale of drugs (10 to 15 percent above cost) and from providing other services. In many villages, an additional salary subsidy is provided to the doctors by the village, partly to compensate them for carrying out preventive services. In our interviews, we found this subsidy ranged from eight to one hundred yuan per month, depending on the doctors' number of hours worked and the wealth of the area. Most doctors supplement their income with other employment (including farming and nonagricultural employment) and practice medicine during off-hours. Several doctors interviewed noted that they had been trained at the expense of the collective, and their main motive was to provide care rather than to make a profit.

A small number of villages operate in the true "collective" mode, paying their doctor a full-time salary. In Zouping, these tend to be the wealthiest villages. One doctor interviewed reported his salary to be ninety yuan per month.

In sum, the majority of Zouping village doctors operate in a fee-for-service mode for curative services, and many are given subsidies by the collective to reinforce public health work. Because there is so much variation in the way local communities contract with doctors to provide care, it is difficult to generalize about the impact of privatization on providing less-profitable services.

Yet financial reward is only one potential motive for providing such services. Our interviews convinced us that regardless of the financial incentives, village doctors in Zouping County are still very much a part of the countywide public health *system*. As described earlier, the township-level health department and the county department above that continue to regulate actively and encourage their work in health promotion and disease prevention.

4. *Was there a decline in the number of basic-level personnel?*

While Zouping may have experienced the decline in the number of personnel that characterized the nation during the early phase of the economic reforms, almost every village in the county has a clinic with at least one qualified village doctor or health worker. Several of the larger villages have more than one full-time doctor.

Table 7.5 presents village-level data on clinics and on the number of village doctors and rural midwives in 1988 and 1989. Unfortunately, data from earlier years were not collected. Interview data indicated that the number of village personnel had declined slightly, and that many Zouping doctors diversified their employment options, combining part-time clinic work with farming and maintaining small businesses. Furthermore, as Huang Shumin demonstrates in an earlier paper on four village clinics in Zouping,[35] the county's larger and better developed clinics often serve as referral centers for smaller, nearby villages.

More recently, the number of village doctors and midwives has increased. For the doctors, this is due in part to health workers passing the qualifying exam; for the midwives, however, the change is a result of a policy to have eventually at least one midwife in each village. The number of personnel in the anti–epidemic disease prevention stations and the MCH stations, as well as those in township and county hospitals, all increased about 5 percent between 1986 and 1989.[36] Equally important, the county health training school *(weisheng xuexiao)* is once again providing training for continuing education and for a new cohort of health personnel.

5. *Was there a breakdown in rural insurance?*

Like elsewhere in rural China, very little medical insurance coverage is available to the residents of Zouping, outside of that available to nonagricultural employees. County-level cadres have public insurance *(gongfei yiliao)*, which provides comprehensive coverage. The eighteen state-run factories in Zouping all offer some type of insurance for their workers *(laodong baoxian)*—a plan that offers a fixed amount of coverage with provision for additional coverage if costs exceed that amount.

Most farmers (90 percent of the population) have no insurance; they pay for medicines and hospital stays out of pocket. In the case of wealthy villages, the clinics are supported, and collective funds (averaging twenty yuan per person per year) are distributed to families as a form of health subsidy, with additional compensation for long-term illness also provided. This is especially apparent in the wealthiest villages, whose main form of income has shifted from agriculture to village-run enterprises. In these villages, health coverage has begun to resemble the factory insurance programs of town and urban areas. The system of coverage is not new, however; it is an extension of the old cooperative insurance program *(hezuo yiliao)*.

Several new insurance programs have recently been organized, in Zouping as well as in many parts of China. These are programs particularly targeted at pregnant women and at children. Immunization insurance, for example, costs three yuan for children under one year of age, two yuan for ages one to seven, and one yuan for ages seven to twelve. It provides for payment in case of side effects from vaccines. Maternal and child insurance, purchased for one hundred yuan, begins with MCH checks prior to delivery and includes normal delivery services and well-baby checkups to age seven. These policies, administered by the townships, are available in most of Zouping's villages. In three townships we visited (Sunzhen, Changshan, and Xidong), the women pay out of pocket for the insurance; in one township (Jiuhu), the villages paid for the policies. Village doctors and township hospitals receive a percentage of the payments; seventy yuan goes to the hospital, fifteen yuan go to the *fangbao zhan*, and fifteen yuan go to the MCH station.

Many accounts of health services utilization, in China and elsewhere, observe that utilization declines without insurance.[37] In all of our interviews with local doctors, with health officials at all levels, and with patients, we repeatedly asked if the loss of insurance had produced hardships for people who needed care. Uniformly, the answer was no. A recent study of health services utilization in eight provinces in China[38] demonstrated a similar, apparently widespread availability of access to basic-level care, and ability to pay for that care, despite the changes in the management and financing of the system at the basic level. On the other hand, other studies have shown that in very poor areas, the cost of services—particularly the cost of expensive in-patient care—acts as a barrier to access.[39]

Prevention and the Challenge of Chronic Conditions

The challenge for prevention work in China's rural areas lies in the rising crisis of chronic disease. The system was well-developed to structure responses to infectious disease outbreaks and to monitor maternal and child health.

Our case study investigating the definition, diagnosis, and treatment of hypertension in Zouping addresses the issue of how county practitioners respond to increasingly prevalent disease. We interviewed twenty-one primary-care providers regarding their standard practices for hypertension. Over half (fourteen) of the twenty-one doctors interviewed were graduates of three-year training schools. Six were trained for one year or had a combination of some training plus continuing education classes.

The case definition of hypertension was similar for all our interviewees, and was consistent with international standards. All defined it as somewhere between 130 and 160 (systolic) over 90 to 100 (diastolic). With the exception of two respondents who said they based their standard solely on experience, all the doctors said that the standard they used was developed from their own experience, textbooks, and government standards.[40]

Although no population-based data on the incidence of hypertension were available, the majority of doctors in our survey (sixteen) said that, based on their clinical observations, they believe that hypertension is increasing in the county. Four said there was no change, and one believed that the incidence in his village was down. Of those who reported an increased incidence, all thought the increase was due to lifestyle changes, particularly those relating to diet.

Most doctors do not routinely check blood pressure. Perhaps because of this lack of screening of nonsymptomatic patients, virtually all the doctors we interviewed considered hypertension to be a symptomatic illness. In other words, it was defined by patient symptoms rather than by the blood pressure measurement. Twenty out of the twenty-one doctors spontaneously noted the symptoms (pain, numbness, and insomnia) that prompt them to treat hypertension. For four of the doctors, symptoms were the only criteria for treatment. Most understood that incidence increased with age, but only one doctor said that age was more important than symptoms. Lifestyle factors—including decreased activity and dietary changes, especially increased intake of animal fat—were considered the most important causes of hypertension. Smoking, while not prompted as an answer, was mentioned by only five of the twenty-one. All respondents knew that stroke and heart attack were complications of hypertension. Village doctors estimated the prevalence of symptomatic hypertension from between 0.5 percent to 20 percent of their village populations.

For patients diagnosed with hypertension, doctors provide an explanation of the disease, its causes and consequences, and counseling about exercise and modification of fat intake. Referral is rare. Medications to control hypertension combine western and traditional Chinese therapies. Treatment was reportedly not linked to ability to pay.

Our interviews revealed that at this time in Zouping County, no systematic guidelines were available for primary-care doctors for the diagnosis and treatment of nonsymptomatic hypertension. Prevention of the most common chronic condition in North China was not a target of either clinical or health education propaganda. In clinical care, doctors were responding to only the tip of the iceberg. Ironically, the popular perception in Zouping was that hypertension is a rising problem. A sample of lay health magazines available in the county all contained at least one article on stroke or hypertension. On the other hand, little, if any, community health education about the condition was provided, and no provider-oriented campaign was under way to identify and treat cases. The problem awaits concerted action from above.

Conclusions

Zouping probably did experience a decline in the number of basic-level health personnel since the implementation of the reforms. Yet most of the villages have doctors, the level of training has improved, and the number of midwives has increased. Regarding health expenditures in the county, the data show that overall expenditures on health care have risen, while the proportion of spending on preventive services relative to curative, hospital-based services has declined slightly.

Financing of clinic services at the village level involves a mix of market and collective incentives. Small subsidies are provided for prevention work. When areas get wealthy, they often increase rather than decrease their collective benefits. Even where clinics are individually owned and salaries are derived from the sale of medicines, this does not automatically mean that less profitable prevention work is ignored. The hierarchy of medical supervision continues to extend to the villages, and to the private clinics in the county town as well. Village doctors function as integral members of the county health infrastructure, extending down from the county anti–epidemic disease prevention stations to the township *fangbao zhan* to the village clinic. While some of the market forces identified by critics cited earlier are clearly operating, we believe that these authors underestimate the strength of county health institutions.

The campaign to eradicate epidemic hemorrhagic fever illustrates these strengths. The limited diagnostic and treatment approaches to hypertension, the most common chronic condition in North China, illustrates the problems that lie ahead. The top-down mobilization style of health education and prevention work has advantages and disadvantages. The system has the capability, but individuals at the bottom are not in the habit of launching innovative programs in response to perceived needs.

We conclude that despite the introduction of a more market-oriented primary health care system, prevention of infectious disease and maternal and child health problems continues to be strongly emphasized. The state mandate to carry out this work continues to be enforced both ideologically and institutionally. We also conclude that although the system has the capacity to direct its preventive health system toward an array of chronic diseases, it is unclear whether limitations caused by a top-down system, and by limited knowledge on the part of lower- and mid-level health care workers, will permit such development.

LYNN W. PAINE

8 | Making Schools Modern:
Paradoxes of Educational Reform

Schooling in Zouping, like rural education throughout
China, has at one level undergone remarkable changes in
the past decade—changes that have made education appear more widely distributed, more efficiently organized,
more standardized, and increasingly bureaucratized. During recent years, Zouping's schooling has become more
tightly integrated into national and international systems
of education. These changes have occurred at the same
time that authority for educational funding has been devolved to lower levels. These reforms have tended to legitimize policies of differentiation. The result has been
increased stratification of educational opportunities in
Zouping. The policy changes have aimed at making
schools modern, more accessible, and more responsive to
local community development. Yet the combination of
reforms has paradoxically supported traditions of inequality and the idea of education to serve as an individual's
flight from rural life. Despite the rhetoric about recent
reforms in education serving the needs of rural development, the decisions of county officials, schools administrators, teachers, students, and parents appear to approach
teaching and learning as activities dedicated to winnow-
ing out academic talent and providing opportunities for
such talent to leave the rural community.

Background

Echoing chords from the late nineteenth century and subsequent waves of reforms, education reformers in the 1980s claimed that "the 21st century is around the corner. The destiny, fall or rise of China depends to a large extent on the development of education today."[1] This kind of argument has helped to push through an array of structural and policy changes in China's educational system. The Educational Reform Decision of 1985 and the passage of the Compulsory Education Law in 1986, the first of its kind in the country, represent two of the most important sets of changes. While the reforms are multifaceted and potentially far-reaching, at their heart is the commitment to providing nine years of basic education for all children, separating more clearly academic from vocational tracks in secondary schooling, and an effort to give authority for education to lower levels of governance and, within limits, to school administrators and teachers themselves.[2] The reforms are explained as necessary to increase education's efficiency and its potential to support economic and social transformation. The goal is to serve local and national development needs. Education, in the range of reform policies put in place over the last decade, has been approached as a tool of microeconomic change.

Given the scope and significance of these changes, it should not then be surprising that rural education has been dramatically affected. Rural schooling accounts for the vast majority of basic education activity in China, with 91 percent of all primary schools, 78.4 percent of primary pupils, 76.4 percent of primary teachers, 66.3 percent of junior secondary students, and 62.7 percent of junior secondary teachers located in rural areas in 1990.[3] Yet examining the case of Zouping County, one finds interesting questions and rather paradoxical findings about the degree and type of changes in rural education. How do reforms in education in Zouping contribute to (notions of) development, modernization, and the construction of the modern citizen? The picture of schooling in Zouping as a process of making things "modern" is decidedly mixed.

This chapter considers the organization, allocation, and process of education in Zouping County as a way of asking questions about the role of schooling in the process of rural development. I consider first how education is organized in Zouping and the nature of reforms introduced by the county. In the second section, I turn to the consequences of reforms aimed at modernizing the system of schooling. In the conclusion I consider the contradictions inherent in the challenge of making rural schools "modern." I argue that the reforms in Zouping's educational system appear to have produced greater participation in schooling, more local control of education, and more efficient delivery of schooling. Yet these reforms also perpetuate and perhaps exacerbate inequalities in access to good teachers and good students. The reforms' efforts to reconceptualize Zouping's schools in terms of modernization for rural development have proved more difficult, and their lack of success signals popular rejection of the idea and an embrace of schooling as a vehicle for social mobility and an exodus from rural life.

The chapter is based on Zouping fieldwork conducted over a nine-week period, during two field trips in 1990 and 1991. While a thorough understanding of the implications of educational policy decisions will require further fieldwork over an extended period of time, the data already collected present striking questions about the consequences of educational reform for the meaning of schooling and students' access to educational opportunities and types of knowledge.

Research involved fieldwork at the provincial, county, township, and village levels, and included interviews and document collection from government offices as well as intensive observation and interviewing in schools. Provincial-level interviews involved representatives from different sections of the Provincial Education Commission. County interviews and document collection focused primarily on three county bureaus (education, finance, and labor) and two government offices (that of the magistrate in charge of education and the vocational education office). At the township level, documents were collected, and lengthy interviews were conducted with heads and members of education commissions (the *xiangjiaowei*, or the lowest-level administrative office for education) for seven of the county's seventeen townships, and follow-up interviews allowing for more detailed and longitudinal analysis were conducted in two of these townships. In addition to interviews, historical records of township and county-level education (particularly school, student, and teacher populations and funding patterns) were solicited. Finally, much school-level data were collected. This came in part through interviews I conducted in 1990 with people working in thirty-four schools representing the range of school types and levels within the county.[4]

For more focused analysis of daily practices and policy implementation, follow-up interviews and observations in 1991 were made at seven of these schools. In each of these schools, I observed classes and interviewed school administrators, teachers, and students. In one focal school, a township-level junior high, I spent more time and was able, in addition to the formal observations and interviews, to conduct much informal interviewing with teachers and students in their offices and classrooms during their lunch and evening breaks and during extracurricular activities. I also interviewed parents of some of this school's students in their homes in one village. Finally, curricular documents (including the complete set of textbooks used by the classes [ban] that I followed over time), teacher reference and evaluation materials, and township- and county-level school-related data were also collected.

Tapes of classroom discussions were transcribed to allow for analysis of interaction patterns, the forms of knowledge introduced in classes, and the allocation of time. Student writing was translated and coded for emergent categories related to views of knowledge.[5] Simple descriptive statistics were calculated for data on provision of township education between 1985 and 1990.

Becoming Modern: The County View of Educational Reform in Progress

At the level of educational provision, policy, organization, and governance, there appears to be important change afoot in Zouping over the past decade. Inspired by a particular set of images related to modernization, Zouping reformers in the 1980s worked to change education. Their policies have increased participation in basic education,[6] worked to make the county education system more rational, and focused on improving the quality of education offered.

Participation

The enrollment rate of school-age children in elementary school went from 98.3 percent as a county average in 1985 to 99.9 percent in 1990, and during the same period the rate of elementary student promotion to junior secondary schooling went from 69.4 percent to 82.1 percent.[7] As Table 8.1 suggests, this increase in the late 1980s

Table 8.1 Promotion rate to junior high school, 1978–1991

Year	Rate
1978	94.19[a]
1979	82.16
1980	60.149
1981	78.39
1982	69.976
1983	64.826
1984	62.257
1985	69.73
1986	—
1987	77[b]
1988	83.7
1989	83.1
1990	84.0[c]
1991	86.0

a. Statistics for 1978–1985 based on data from Zouping Educational Annals Editorial Leadership Group, eds,. *Zouping jiaoyuzhi* (Educational Annals of Zouping County [Shandong Publishing House, Huimin Prefecture Branch, 1990]), 146–147, 178–79.

b. Statistics based on county Education Bureau documents for 1986–1990.

c. Based on interviews with county Education Bureau officials.

represents a distinct rise from the early 1980s, when the promotion rate ranged between 60 percent and 78 percent. In interviews in 1991, county officials at the Bureau of Education (BOE)[8] claimed that the enrollment rate for junior high that year had reached 86 percent so that "now basically everyone who wants their kid to go to junior high can." Elementary schooling had been popularized by the end of the 1980s, with county officials in 1990 stating that, in addition to the enrollment rate, the rate at which students stay on in elementary schools in the county had reached 99.8 percent and graduation rates from elementary school were 99.7 percent. (Compare this with elementary enrollment rates in the 1950s that ranged from 64 percent to 75 percent and elementary school graduation rates that, even for students entering in the late 1970s, ranged from 66 percent to 85 percent.)[9]

This expansion of educational participation appears striking when one considers how educational access for students today differs from that of their parents. Of the students I followed most closely (those in a township central junior high), the majority had parents who twenty years prior had not even completed the full cycle of elementary school. Of the students I interviewed formally and informally, it was the rare student in the central or ordinary junior highs who had a parent who had attended junior high school. (Not surprisingly, this was not as rare for students at the elite junior high schools in the county seat.)[10]

The access issue became salient in interviews with parents of junior high students. In the seventeen homes in which I conducted interviews in Fengjia village, I found that the majority of mothers were illiterate, or at most had four or fewer years of schooling. In the junior high school that their children attended, however, girls were well represented. (In fact, they outnumbered boys slightly in the graduating class.) While even the rate at which boys reach junior high school certainly is higher than that of their parents' generation, the presence of so many girls in junior high school stands out, given the low levels of educational attainment for women in this community one generation earlier.

The increased access to basic education, of which county officials are so proud, represents changes over the past decade. These county policies aimed at popularizing education reflect national and provincial policies and targets. Their success, and the success of the next and more difficult to achieve target of compulsory education, is described as depending in part on making education more rationally and efficiently organized and with higher-quality standards.

Rationalizing the System: Decision Making and Efficiency

The goal of rationalization of schooling in the county is best expressed through two sets of changes that have taken place over the past decade: a policy of decentralized administration and decision making and a restructuring of provision through school consolidation and differentiation of school types. The first represents a shift in the governance and financing of schools. The second reflects a change in organizational structures. Both are seen as producing greater quality and efficiency.

Decentralization. The decentralization reform, referred to as *fenji banxue,* or having separate administrative levels running their own education, encourages each government or administrative level to take responsibility for its own schools, typically schools of a single level. The rationale for *fenji banxue* is that devolution more efficiently mobilizes the resources of a community.

In Zouping's case, the policy has produced a situation in which there are three main tiers of schools and educational administration. The county takes charge of schools designated as county-run: all five academic senior secondary schools, all vocational and technical senior secondary schools (a total of four in 1991), two elite junior high schools (the junior high school attached to the sole key senior secondary school and the junior high attached to the county's No. 1 experimental school), two elementary schools (the No. 1 and No. 2 experimental schools), and a teacher in-service training school. In other words, the county Bureau of Education oversees all senior secondary education in the county (with the exception of the secondary normal school, run by the prefecture), as well as elite junior and elementary schools based in the county seat and teacher in-service training. Township-run schools represent all other junior high schools, which are categorized as "central" *(zhongxin)* schools (with one of these per township) or as ordinary junior highs; each township also runs one "central" elementary school. The rest of elementary education, which represents the majority of Zouping's educational provision, is the responsibility of villages.[11]

The notion of "responsibility" for running schools refers primarily to financial responsibility. Curriculum is in fact set by provincial dictate and inspected by the county Bureau of Education. But the significance of this devolved responsibility should not be underestimated. Townships now are responsible for financing their own schools, for dealing with personnel issues and problems related to teaching qualifications, and for handling party and youth league issues. Villages bear the brunt for funding their elementary schools (although all state-supported or *gongban* teachers get their salaries from state funds, not village coffers).

This administrative reform began in the first half of 1988, with personnel and financial decision making being formally assigned to the townships. For the townships, as well as the county Bureau of Education, this represented what county officials in interviews described as a new situation, as by their account all education had formally been controlled by the county in the years between 1949 and 1987. While there had been previous periods, notably 1958 and 1968–1978, when administrative control of schooling was decentralized, for much of the time between 1949 and the mid-1980s schools were administered primarily by the county (or, in the case of secondary schools, by the county and prefecture).[12] While the creation of separate levels running education in the late 1980s has broadened the number of organizations involved in running schools and given greater formal responsibility to local-level officials (spawning the creation of township education commissions, themselves a new organizational entity), the policy has also had the effect of legitimizing patterns of inequality in the name of rational efficiency and local control. I discuss this consequence of reform in more detail later in the chapter.

Restructuring of the System. A second expression of the goals of rational provision of education is the restructuring that has taken place over the 1980s and early 1990s. This restructuring process, aimed at rationalizing the allocation of resources, involves school consolidation and differentiation. In the first of these, education officials argued that schools can only have legitimacy and quality when they have a minimum number of students. Drawing on this economies-of-scale argument, county officials have moved away from the expansionist approaches of the 1970s, when Zouping's schools were most numerous, and worked quickly to reduce the number and to consolidate schools. As Table 8.2 indicates, the number of elementary schools has fluctuated somewhat throughout the period from 1949 to 1985, although the number of schools began to taper off from 805 in 1975 to 766 in 1985. Between 1985 and 1990, the reduction was much more drastic, with more than 100 schools closed down and only 665 schools remaining by 1990.[13] The traditional village school now no longer exists in every community, as children from an increasing number of villages must walk to neighboring communities for their primary education.

More dramatic have been the efforts to consolidate secondary schools, as Table 8.3 suggests. From the height of 72 senior high and 234 junior high schools in 1978, by 1985 the county had 5 senior and 102 junior highs. Although the senior high schools remained stable at the beginning of the 1990s, the junior high consolidation continued at a fast pace, with only 63 junior high schools admitting an entering class of students in 1990, only 41 enrolling new students in 1991, and a plan for only 32 total in 1992.[14]

County officials, although acknowledging that these school closures often distress parents whose community is losing a neighborhood school, defend their policy on the grounds of efficiency and educational quality. Using surveys of community needs based on a metric related to population size, bureau officials see the policy change as scientifically based and pedagogically justified. Elementary schools are seen as needing five classes *(ban)* to be a legitimate school; communities that cannot support such a large school (because of their smaller population) face school closure or, as a temporary measure, having their school serve as a "teaching station" *(jiaoxuedian)*. In the junior secondary sector, where closures have been far more dramatic, the county has been motivated by a similar

Table 8.2 Number of elementary schools and students in Zouping, 1950–1990

Year	Number of schools	Enrollment
1950	705[a]	34,046
1955	910	56,915
1960	916	82,505
1965	732	64,310
1970	756	85,937
1975	805	95,723
1976	778	94,344
1977	715	90,591
1978	784	99,844
1979	764	99,874
1980	768	99,792
1981	791	98,686
1982	783	94,694
1983	784	91,123
1984	775	85,830
1985	766	78,653
1986	772[b]	80,067
1987	757	76,963
1988	744	69,845
1989	707	65,613
1990	674	62,233

a. Numbers for schools and student enrollments for the years 1950–1985 come from *Zouping jiaoyuzhi,* 144–147.

b. Numbers for schools and student enrollments for the years 1986–1990 come from county Education Bureau documents for the academic years 1985–1986 through 1989–1990.

Table 8.3 Number of secondary schools and students in Zouping, 1978–1990

Year	Senior high schools	Students enrolled	Junior high schools	Students enrolled
1978[a]	72	11,236	234	33,249
1979	21	5,977	163	32,893
1980	17	5,651	121	33,123
1981	11	4,448	109	32,828
1982	7	3,268	109	28,612
1983	5	2,623	105	28,330
1984	5	3,200	105	28,772
1985	5	3,200	102	28,772
1985–86[b]	—	—	103	30,290
1986–87	5 academic	3,339	100	32,635
	3 agricultural	807		
1987–88	5 academic	3,941	95	28,810
	4 voc./tech.	1,380		
1988–89	5 academic	3,510	80	27,485
	4 voc./tech.	1,297		
1989–90	5 academic	2,242+[c]	68	27,485
	4 voc./tech.	1,180+[d]		

a. Information for the 1978–1985 years comes from *Zouping jiaoyuzhi,* 178–179.

b. Information for the academic years 1985–1986 through 1989–1990 come from documents in the county Education Bureau.

c. County records for this year only provide enrollment data for three of the five academic high schools, although it is clear that the other two schools did in fact have students enrolled at this time. Therefore, 2,242 represents some portion (estimated, based on other data, as approximately 60 to 70 percent) of the total number of students enrolled in the academic high schools in that year.

d. County records for this year do not provide enrollment data for one of the vocational schools, which in the previous year accounted for 27 percent of the students enrolled in vocational and technical secondary programs. But because these kinds of schools were both new and had such fluctuating enrollments, it is unwise to try to estimate enrollments. Rather, it is certain that the enrollments in 1989–1990 were greater than 1,180.

interest in trying to reduce the number of schools and to increase the scale of individual schools. A community of 12,000 to 20,000 is seen as needing one junior high school, which ideally would have five *ban* per grade. The educational argument is that small schools cannot sustain or develop quality instructional standards, nor can they have access to enough financial support, to have the facilities most conducive to students' educational achievement. Once the number of junior highs is reduced, officials suggest, every junior high will be able to have dormitories—something thought to improve a student's chance to study and currently a feature only of the few, central schools.

Differentiation of School Types. Concomitant with countywide consolidation has been a process of school differentiation, similarly justified as part of a larger policy of educational rationalization and efficiency aimed at improving quality. As part of the 1980s reforms and closely associated with the policy of *fenji banxue,* the state has moved to designate multiple layers of key schools, known locally as *zhongxin,* or central schools. While there is only one official "key" *(zhongdian)* school in the county, which was designated by the province, these county-assigned central schools provide additional, if subordinate, levels of privileged status. With the reorganization of education in the 1980s, each township was to have both a central (as opposed to an ordinary) junior high and central elementary school, typically in the township's own community, and each school district (*xuequ* or *bashequ*) within each township was to have a central elementary school. Awarded the better teachers, often accorded privileges in recruiting the academically strongest students, and receiving more financial support than their ordinary counterparts, this increased number and type of elite school strata represents a new development of the 1980s, although the consequences are familiar to anyone who has studied key schools nationally.[15]

With the creation of central schools, the county has simply extended the degree of differentiation. The educational argument, as in the national case of key schools, is that central schools serve as models for ordinary schools, beacons of educational experimentation and improvement, and as such can augment the role that the county's two experimental schools play and more widely distribute the benefits of good educational practice. Clearly threaded through this argument is the notion of rational diffusion of expert knowledge.

Differentiation has occurred in another significant way as well— through the reorganization of secondary education. Here Zouping, like the rest of China, has moved to transform a previously uniformly academically focused secondary education sector into one that includes academic high schools and vocational and technical schools. Zouping's school consolidation and reductions meant a sharp decrease in the number of academic high schools over the past decade, as seen in Table 8.3. For example, in 1978 the county had 72 senior high schools enrolling 11,236 students. Just one year later, the number of schools and students dropped to 21 and 5,977, respectively. By 1985, only 3,200 students were enrolled in the county's 5 senior highs,[16] and according to education officials, that number remained around 3,600 at the end of the 1980s and into the early 1990s.

But these figures do not represent the related change in—and the major reform of—senior secondary education, that is, the establishment of vocational and technical senior high schools. The county has introduced a range of vocational and technical options, some sponsored by the Bureau of Education and others (such as the school of public health) jointly administered with other bureaus. These schools do represent alternative institutions and additional senior secondary student populations. As Table 8.3 indicates, their enrollments grew quickly in the late 1980s. Their relative share of the secondary school population also grew, as Table 8.4 demonstrates. County officials reported that the vocational/technical schools accounted for 43 percent of senior secondary education in 1990 and that 1,400 of the 2,600 (or 53.8 percent) of the junior high graduates admitted to any form of senior secondary schooling in 1991 were matriculating at vocational or technical schools. (Note how the number of students admitted in 1991 was larger than that for all students enrolled in such programs just a few years earlier.)

The justification for these schools is directly connected to a vision of education's economic role. In moving to reshape secondary education, county officials claim that these new schools can supply much-needed personnel for the technical transformation of the county's agricultural and industrial sectors. Human capital theory arguments and assumptions guide their work; a restructured education system is intended to increase productivity, particularly as the rural economy itself is changing.

Quality as a Goal

These policies of administrative reorganization for educational governance and finance, of school consolidation, and of the creation of differentiated levels and types of schools illustrate a major feature of the county's effort to make education more "modern." Another important feature of the county's view of modernizing education is related to a wide range of efforts to make explicit and to raise standards of educational quality. The concern for quality control has been expressed in a wide-ranging set of measures aimed at creating standard procedures, norms, and targets.

One example of this objective that county officials talk about most readily concerns the creation of "standardized" *(guifanhua)* schools.

Table 8.4 Changes in the structure of Zouping secondary education, 1986–1990

Year starting	Academic senior high school enrollment	Vocational and technical senior high school enrollment	Percentage enrolled in voc./tech. schools
1986	3,339[a]	807	19.46
1987	3,941	1,380	25.93
1988	3,510	1,297	26.98
1989	—	—	—
1990	—	—	43[b]

a. Enrollment figures for the academic years 1986–1987 through 1988–1989 come from county Bureau of Education yearly documents, and percentages for the share of students attending vocational and technical programs are based on these.

b. Based on interviews with the county Bureau of Education.

The concern for standardized schools has a precursor in the early 1980s, with a policy aimed at schools meeting a set of six rather basic targets related to school facilities, such as every student having a desk. The *guifanhua* campaign began in 1988, in the aftermath of this initial policy. Including but going beyond a sole focus on the physical plant, the goal for the standardized school takes into account academic standards of school administrators and teachers, management, teaching quality, and operational issues. Still a goal to work toward, the campaign for standardized schools has occupied a major portion of county bureau activity. The standards were set by the prefecture, and special funds were allocated by it to support the county's effort to comply. The first year that each township had at least one junior high meeting the target was 1991.

The drive toward "standardized" schools is perhaps the most comprehensive approach to create common norms for quality. Yet in many other aspects of the county's educational life, additional evidence suggests that this is a major preoccupation of the county. The move during the 1980s to rank all teachers against some new and explicit standards of professional preparation and practice is one such example. Similarly, the county's decision to ban the hiring of *minban,* or community-supported teachers (typically coming with lower academic credentials than their state-supported counterparts) suggests its desire to bring teacher quality under its control.[17]

A detailed observation form used by the county Bureau of Education to evaluate classroom teaching represents an example of the county's ability to penetrate even classroom practice in an effort to develop some standard norms for education; Bureau of Education officials describe spending sizable portions of the year observing classrooms, using this form both as evaluation material and as a method of disseminating common notions about good teaching. Finally, in 1991, the county moved toward unified entrance exams and policies for its senior secondary schools. Admitting that the schools resented having to give up some of their authority (as previously they had been able to set their own entry requirements), the county officials interviewed appreciated this approach for its greater efficiency and for the fact that it allows a more rational identification and allocation of student talent.

Whether it be related to issues of school provision, staffing, class-room teaching, or student achievement, these and other efforts directed at improving (and controlling) quality all require greater amounts of information and supervision than was necessary before the reforms. At even the most basic level, one notes a marked change in the quantity of detail and number of categories about school life for which the county collected data from each township over time. In Bureau of Education records I had access to for 1985–1990, even over just that five-year period, the amount of information generated to support education planning and to provide an explanation of educational activity clearly expanded.

In addition, the Bureau of Education created a supervision or superintendency *(dudao)* section in 1989 to support a process of more aggressive and systematic inspection of school reform. The members of that section are charged with overseeing the work of educators at the next level down (the township). They are part of a newly created national-level inspectorate aimed at investigating the experience of reform, and their participation in training classes on supervision, which are centrally organized and run by the State Education Commission, reflects how Zouping's efforts at quality control are themselves connected to the national system of education and to a central reassertion of authority in the face of devolution of financial responsibility for schools.[18]

School-Level Reform for an Integrated System

The appearance of educational modernization is striking on any school visit in the county. Everywhere you look schools are under construction, most often with a familiar architectural design.[19] Making schools beautiful, with newfound attention to gardens, is an important symbolic aspect of these physical changes. The vision of the multistoried concrete school building with rooms designed to support modern audiovisual equipment stands in sharp contrast to the one-story brick rows of schools that have characterized most of Zouping's education since the 1970s. If the architects' plans represent one symbol of Zouping's aggressive move toward educational transformation, the symbols within the school walls are equally telling.

In the late 1980s and early 1990s, schools in the county took on three major reforms: a principal responsibility system, where more decision-making authority devolved to the principal (the "education expert," as opposed to the party representative or higher-level administrators); a teacher appointment system that instituted new, local-level processes for appointing teachers to particular posts; and a unit target responsibility system, in which schools have a clearly specified set of goals against which they and their teachers are held accountable. These reforms, instituted in the late 1980s, figured prominently in interviews with school, township, and county educators and officials, and documents recording the reforms' purposes and progress toward implementation lined the walls of many school offices as symbols of a systematic effort to improve education. In every school I visited I could find charts that outlined targets, merit plaques noting the achievements of individual teachers in reaching these goals, or detailed lists outlining the school goals or individual objectives by which people would be measured.

These wall plaques, as well as the bundle of reforms they represent, are suggestive of the more significant reforms in Zouping's educational organization, provision, and governance. With these policy changes, education within the county has grown increasingly systematic, rational, differentiated, and bureaucratic. The changes, though relying significantly on greater fiscal responsibility at lower levels of government, represent a closer integration into both national and international systems of education. A concern for "scientific management," at the heart of the "three reforms" stressed by the county, was expressed in numerous interviews with county bureau officials and school principals. The elaboration of targets, while officially a responsibility now devolved to the school level and the principal, is subject to rationalization and penetration from superior levels. "Scientific management" in fact encourages closer connections within the professional community of educators. Thus, as the county has rationalized its educational organization, the role of the "teaching research section" (jiaoyanzu) has expanded.

Reinvigorated, the jiaoyanzu creates an organizational structure by which educators work across individual schools to develop instructional approaches. The *jiaoyanzu,* a basic organizational unit of teachers within a school, is replicated within the school district, the county, the prefecture, and the province. In Zouping, this has meant that reforms that reshape the goals of teaching can be introduced at the provincial level and disseminated quickly to every school in the name of "scientific management." A striking example of this occurred as I listened to teachers in dusty ordinary schools in Zouping's villages talk about the U.S. educational psychologist Benjamin Bloom's teaching reforms that center on "mastery learning." Imported from the University of Chicago, his ideas had entered via the provincial capital, summarized in a book distributed provincewide to teaching research sections and studied within the county under the supervision of the Bureau of Education.

Stratification as a Consequence

If becoming modern in Zouping means knowing about Bloom's ideas, it also means accepting differentiation as a necessary aspect of educational improvement. The pattern of changes that appeared during the past decade in the county's educational work has as major themes rationality, efficiency, and devolution. Together, these combine to encourage differentiation and to legitimize systematic inequality and stratification. It is important to note at the outset of this discussion that inequality in education is not new to Zouping, nor to rural education in China more generally. Rather, what I argue here is that the recent logic of reform in the county provides conceptual justification for differentiation and inequality and, in some cases, exacerbates existing patterns of stratification and increases disparities.

The concern for efficiency and rational allocation that is at the heart of the county's reform of education has led to calls for an increased range and type of sources of financial support for schooling in Zouping. Buttressed by the national policy of society running (or supporting) education *(shehui ban jiaoyu),* county education during the 1980s and 1990s turned to an ever-wider range of possible revenues.[20] Off-budget funds grew in their significance, as schools would draw not only on money that came from state finances but also from student fees, school-run enterprises *(qingongjianxue)*, social contributions *(shehui jizi)*, and an educational surcharge *(jiaoyu fei fujia)* on personal and industrial income.[21] In 1991, state finances accounted for 15,488,000 yuan of educational investment, but the education surcharge brought in an additional 7,800,000 yuan and school-run enterprises 2,400,000 yuan. Not even considering student fees[22] and social contributions (which alone over 1989–1991 came to 22 million yuan), off-budget funds represented 40 percent of total educational investment.[23]

Fees and school-run enterprises have been a part of Zouping's school support for some time, although they are now being regulated more systematically and, especially in the case of enterprises, encouraged in their development. But the presence of social contributions (typically one-time-only collections taken to support a particular school goal) and the education surcharge are new and highlight the critical role a school's local environment now plays in its welfare. These changes in patterns of school finance, when combined with the policy of devolution of authority for education, produce a situation in which schools are increasingly vulnerable to their surroundings. The changing responsibility structures of schools drive school leaders to scan their environment for exchange relations that might benefit their school's interests. Yet given differences in those environments and existing differences among schools, greater differentiation results.

Transforming the Role of the Environment

Zouping schools have sought to establish tighter horizontal relations with others in their organizational environment. This process transforms the local community in ways that allow the environment, teachers, and students to be seen as potential resources. Although schools, for example, are given admissions quotas for the numbers of students they can take in, schools are allowed to admit students beyond the quota for additional fees or to exchange student places for favorable relations with a nearby unit. But for schools to be able to capitalize on this, they need to have "seats" that are seen by parents as desirable (something more likely for schools with a record of high rates of promotion to higher levels of education) or to be situated near units with something to trade. For schools in Zouping, this naturally put schools in the county town, and particularly the elite schools with established records of consistently high promotion rates, at a distinct advantage.

As one example of how schools with comparative advantage can be enterprising in generating additional income, consider the case of the key school's enrollment of a special category of student. Until 1990, when county policy officially restricted this, each year the key school would admit a group of senior high repeaters who were staying on an additional year in the hopes of finally testing into some form of higher education. With a success rate consistently over 50 percent, in contrast with other high schools ranging from 15 to 25 percent, the key school was able to market itself significantly better than its "competitors."[24] The school's repeater option was attractive to parents and students, as well as to the school, which could support these fee-generating students with little additional cost to the school in terms of classroom space or teacher salaries. Administrators of the school described it as a way to bring in "lots of money" through the additional tuition and school fees. All schools officially had the right to engage in such entrepreneurial efforts, but none was in the position of this school.

Similarly, school leaders and township officials all agreed that a school's success in developing its own enterprises is dependent on the economic strength of the surrounding area, the market for goods and services in the community, the school's location, the availability of transportation, and access to a good manager. Not all of this is a matter of serendipity. Certainly one's proximity to an economically developed area makes a difference, but so, too, does the ability to exploit personal ties to surrounding units in ways that assure a market. The county key school's agreement with a local textile factory is one clear example; the relationship allowed the school enterprise (producing burlap wrapping) to have a stable market through the factory's orders. Half of the school enterprise's product could be sold directly to the factory, something school leaders described as "especially good in these competitive years."

That the match between school and factory was brokered by county official illustrates the differential concern given elite and mass institutions, for which no such lucrative relationship was arranged. The county chose to find enterprise partners for each of its own schools, and had the means to do this with the most profitable enterprises in the county, as these were all located in the county seat. Townships have less chance of locating such partners for their schools, and schools not run directly by the county, although encouraged to make links with business, are not in a position to do so. Thus the policies that have created different types of schools and encouraged different administrative levels to take responsibility for their well-being legitimize differential access to funding, teachers, and students.

Clearly, now that the local environment is defined as a resource and schools are more dependent on their resources than before, the difference between environments—not simply the urban/rural dichotomy—is crucial. Viewing this process from a resource dependence model[25] allows us to recognize that a school's location in its organizational field accounts for a great deal of its ability to succeed or fail in the competition for scarce resources. Traditional but simple dichotomies between key and ordinary schools no longer capture the complexity of school differentiation that now occurs. In competition for resources, not all ordinary schools are equal. With the advent of the educational surcharge or tax on income, location itself determines much. With the surcharge based on a percentage of local and industrial income or consumption, it can generate more income for schools in wealthy areas, and it offers little in the way of support for schools serving poorer and less industrialized townships.

Given variation in local development within the county, the degree to which Zouping schools could rely on educational surcharge funds thus varied widely. For six townships for which I have detailed data, their 1990 surcharge generated between 209,500 yuan and 540,000 yuan. With this range in income generated by the surcharge and a comparable range in other sources of off-budget funds, the relative significance of the surcharge also varied, comprising between 15.7 percent and 45.5 percent of educational funds for each of the townships.

As a logical extension of power of environment and location, it is clear that the policies of reform tend to privilege schools (and their communities) that are already privileged or successful. Breaking out of a cycle of resource shortage or academic failure becomes increasingly difficult in a climate of intensified resource competition, entrepreneurial incentives, and devolved authority. It therefore is not surprising that townships with consistently higher promotion rates, with more qualified teachers, and that in other ways appear "successful" are able to maintain their position, while townships that historically have ranked low on these measures are not supported by the current reforms to break out of the bottom ranks.

Access to Resources: County-Township and Within-Township Disparities

The policy of *fenji banxue,* combined with new approaches to types of educational funding, further separates schools in terms of "winners" and "losers." For the three tiers of schools (county-run, township-run, and village), a school's access to three key types of resources (funds, qualified teachers, and able students) increases with the level of organizational unit responsible for a school. Interviews and county, township, and school records suggest that each level attempts to concentrate its funds and connections (or *guanxi*) on its own schools. Township schools, for example, tended to have a larger portion of their overall income coming from student fees or school-run enterprises (that is, funds they could generate themselves) than the county schools, which could rely on rather large amounts of county money. For the county key school, for instance, 77.7 percent of its expenses were covered by state funds, whereas a rather typical township central junior high school had only 13.7 percent covered by its township (state) money and had to rely heavily on its fees (which represented 22.2 percent of its total budget) to cover expenses.

The agreement between the key school and the textile factory is another illustration of this pattern. In this case the county matched up its own schools (including the full range of senior secondary, junior high, and elementary schools) with the major local enterprises to encourage industrial support of education. The top schools were paired with the most profitable units, which then provided the schools with services, markets for their school-run enterprises, outright contributions, and above-quota students who could be admitted in exchange for fees or other kinds of support. As a result of this matching, other schools in the county said that they had no way to establish links with productive units; all economically viable units had been "given away."

The increased separation of county-run schools—in terms of access to funding, privileges, teachers, and students—from the rest of the educational institutions in Zouping and of key and ordinary senior secondary schools in the county parallels the ways in which the logic of reform policies has encouraged greater disparities between township-run central schools and ordinary junior highs. This holds true in terms of teachers, funding, and access to academically capable students.

Teachers

For example, townships now have authority over personnel decisions. As a result, recently graduated qualified teachers have been disportionately assigned to township central schools, a decision made by the township Education Commissions, whose formation represents institutionalization of an interest group that can affect stratification within the township. Typical was the decision of one township Education Commission that, when allocating seven new graduates of a secondary teacher training school, chose to assign four to the central junior high (literally next door to their office), two to their central elementary school (down the road, but in the same community), and one to an ordinary junior high in a village. They explained that their decisions are based on need, although every township junior high school needs newly qualified teachers.

This differential access to qualified teachers becomes an important issue in Zouping, as in much of China, as many teachers are considered academically unqualified (or lack a sufficient level of schooling needed for teaching the level at which they work). County officials reported in 1990 that 23 percent of the county's elementary teachers were unqualified (that is, they lacked the equivalent of a senior secondary degree) and 77 percent of the junior high teachers were unqualified, in that they lacked the equivalent of two years of college training.

It has long been the case that Zouping's teachers, like teachers in other parts of China, have not been equally distributed across schools in terms of their academic preparation; thus, for example, key schools traditionally have had a higher proportion of academically well-prepared teachers than do ordinary schools. But the new policy (of devolved personnel decision making), in addition to this already unequal distribution of human resources, has produced a very uneven portrait of teaching in the county. While the county's average percentage of junior high teachers who are considered qualified has risen steadily since 1985 (increasing between 1985 and 1989 from 8.8 percent to 12.2 percent to 19.6 percent to 20.3 percent to 21.0 percent), the majority of township-level teachers are considered unqualified. The disparities between teacher qualifications in central and ordinary schools are clear; in one township, for example, the central school had 23.5 percent of its junior high teachers ranked as Grade 1 teachers (the second out of four possible rankings, and the highest ranking for any junior high teacher in the township), while only between 0 and 18 percent of the teachers in the four ordinary junior highs were considered qualified to this rank.[26]

The disparities within a township should not mask, however, the disparities between township-run junior highs and county-run junior highs. Here, in terms of teacher qualifications, the countywide 1989–1990 average for township junior secondary schools was 21 percent (with a range of 14.8 percent to 35.4 percent), while the two county-run junior high schools had 100 percent and 89.9 percent of their teachers with the appropriate academic degrees and training.

Funding

The tendency is to support the concentration of resources locally. This pattern is seen clearly in terms of funding for schools. In one township, for example, township monies given for operating expenses for the central and ordinary schools differed dramatically.

For elementary schools in the township, the ordinary elementary school received 52.6 yuan per month operating funds from the township in 1985, and this decreased to 50 yuan per month in 1990, while the central elementary school was receiving monthly support of 150 yuan in 1985, which increased to 200 yuan in 1990. For the area's junior highs, the support of ordinary schools (measured in terms of contributions per school) increased as the number of schools was reduced; throughout the period 1985–1990, however, central schools always received significantly more support than ordinary schools, as Table 8.5 suggests.

Student Access

Reform policies support differentiation in access to funding and to qualified teachers, both in terms of a county-township distinction and in terms of distinctions within a township. Not surprisingly, similar patterns exist in terms of students' access to high-quality schools (or, if seen in resource terms, schools' access to strong students). I have already mentioned the relatively high rate of key school graduates' admission to higher education when compared

Table 8.5 Funding for ordinary and central township junior high schools, Sunzhen township, 1985–1990

	Monthly operating funds	
Year	Allocated central school (yuan)	Funding per ordinary school (yuan)
1985	600	168.3
1986	700	200.0
1987	700	250.0
1988	850	253.5
1989	860	251.0
1990	891	529.5

Source: Interviews at Sunzhen Township Educational Commission and local schools; documents provided by commission.

with graduates of ordinary senior high schools. It is important to note that access to the key school, while officially a matter of open competition, was far more likely for students from the county town and, in particular, from two junior high schools. While students graduated from sixty-three junior high schools in the county in 1990, 18 percent of the key senior high's entering class for the fall of 1990 came from just two schools (the key and experimental schools), and 31.8 percent came from these two schools and the county town. Eighty-five percent of that entering class came from a central school. Thus chances for access to the key school for an ordinary township school student are statistically poor. In fact, in 1988–1989, the county average by township for promotion from junior high to some form of senior secondary school was 18.9 percent, but for students from a central township school it was 31.8 percent.[27]

Students living in the county town are certainly educationally advantaged in terms of being able to attend the only schools in the county with a surplus of teachers and a comparatively high proportion of qualified teaching staff, and there is a greater likelihood that they will proceed to the elite senior high school. One paradox of the implementation of compulsory education is that students in the county town can now be admitted to the elite junior highs (that is, those associated with the key school and the experimental school) not by examination but simply by virtue of the proximity of their homes to the school. While administrators of elite schools talked about what this change means for junior high programs, it has not changed the benefits (of teachers and facilities) that these schools offer. By making education now available to everyone on a compulsory basis, privileges for some are granted solely on the basis of residential location—something that had not been so clearly sanctioned before the reform.

Just as unequal patterns of opportunity occur between county and township-based students, similar patterns of differentiation occur within townships. Here, congruent with the policy of decentralized decision making, admissions policies for access to the township central school are subject to local decision making. Although township approaches to this practice do vary, the majority of townships have developed policies that are selective and elitist (that is, they use competitive examinations to select students for many of the places in the best schools) while still typically giving preference to local students. One approach represents a compromise between self-serving elitism and meritocracy: of eight *ban* of students admitted to the township's central school, six came exclusively from the township seat and an adjoining district, while two entered from the entire township (which has six districts) on the basis of a competitive exam. Entrance to any of the eight classes hinged on a student's exam score, but for those young people from the township seat or its neighboring district, the probability of having access to the resources of the central school is much higher than that of their counterparts in the other districts.[28]

These admissions policies combine in significant ways with other resource decisions justified on the basis of efficiency and modernization. Students at the township central school are taught by a staff of teachers, 40 percent of whom are deemed qualified, while students in ordinary junior highs in the township work under school staffs of which only 16 percent of the teachers are qualified. Thus, in human as well as material resources, this central school, though certainly poor and lacking the official privilege and status of the county key junior high, stands apart from its peers. The record of its graduates' entry rate to senior high school indicates that its students also stand apart from their peers. Its graduates went on to senior secondary schooling at a rate of 37.5 percent in 1989, while the overall township rate that year was 15.4 percent.

In a system where access to the next level of education and, eventually, to social and economic mobility hinges on a standardized test, these admissions, teacher allocation, and funding decisions have significant consequences. Whether it is in the school, the township, or the county, a pattern of differentiation has developed, supported by local decisions and a logic of reforms aimed at rationalization and efficiency. Fueled by unequal access to resources, the unequal opportunities for learning within a single county become part of a broader picture of stratification. While education reforms were created out of a concern for making the county's schools more "modern," these policies have produced a traditional picture of education as a social sorter—one that offers valued opportunities to some and less valued opportunities to others.

The Challenge of Making Rural Schools "Modern"

In the past decade Zouping's educators and policy makers have put tremendous energy into making their system of schooling more modern. Self-consciously connecting their reforms to those in the rest of the province, the nation, and other countries, they have sought to make schooling more widely accessible, of a higher quality, and more likely to increase individual and community economic productivity. In order to achieve these goals, they have assumed notions of rationality in planning, administration, and allocation of resources. Central to this rationality is an assumption about the importance of involving and supporting the local community. "Society should run education and education should be run for society," goes the popular slogan. For Zouping, as in many places in China, making schools "modern" means being aware of the local contexts. This results in curricular reforms that acknowledge the schools' rural base and designs—for example, labor-skills classes meant to serve better the productive needs of rural dwellers. Taking the rural context seriously also means designing rural vocational programs to attract junior high graduates rather than continuing to support and expand a large number of academic secondary schools whose graduates are unable to enter university but who are ill-prepared to contribute to the rural economy. The challenge for Zouping's educators, however, has been to construct a viable concept of modern rural schooling—one that is an alternative to an academically oriented, university-driven educational system in the service of individual social mobility.

One area in which county officials felt that they could begin to articulate this alternative vision of schooling is in the introduction of a new labor skills course embedded within a strengthened junior high curriculum. As a required course designed to serve better the needs of the community's economic construction, it is to offer "scientific" knowledge about practices that are central to rural life.

Offered to all students in their last year of junior high school—which is the jumping-off point for the majority of students—it aims at making valuable knowledge available to all. The idea of the course brings with it an image of modern schooling efficiently distributed—schooling that connects rural students to cosmopolitan systems of practice and strengthens the ability of students to serve their local communities. It is an image familiar to readers of human capital theory, of rational planning, and of county officials who argue for the powerful role of schools in the process of economic development and modernization. But the implementation of this course has produced unintended effects. The students devalue it, the schools give it to teachers who are unprepared to teach it, and its contents are trivialized.[29]

In one junior high I observed, the labor skills teacher had no prior preparation in the area and received no assistance to learn to teach the course, which had been designed by the prefecture. In one class I observed, the actual teaching time was quite short; the instructor stopped class rather abruptly and let students do their own work (as it turns out, on a range of unrelated things). It was clear that he had little to say about the content of the lesson—when to water and fertilize particular crops. His suggestion was that students should find out about this topic by asking their parents. An education official observing the class was shocked, because, as he put it, by telling students that the source of knowledge for the course is one's parents, the teacher is suggesting that there is no reason to learn this subject through formal schooling. Formal schooling remains important only for what it exposes the student to in terms of high-status academic knowledge. The time, organization, and pedagogical decisions about this course all suggested that to the teachers, parents, and students, junior secondary schooling is not, as county education reform policy would dictate, basic education or preparation for work or a way to make a contribution to the local community but an opportunity to invest time in learning the high-status knowledge that is tested on entrance exams for higher-level schooling.

In short, this course, by being a caricature of a "regular" course, reinforced a sense of division between knowledge that students might generate on their own (or from their families' experience)—that is, the knowledge that comes from their daily lives—and knowledge that is valuable. In other words, the labor-skills lesson, as a parody of knowledge, confirmed what other classes may subtly have suggested to students—that as rural students, their positions are marginal and that if they are smart, they should try to distance themselves from that experience.

This rejection of schooling that is both "modern and rural" is nowhere clearer than in the very real problems that county education officials face in getting students and their families to be enthusiastic or supportive about technical/vocational schools. The traditional *zhiye zhongzhuan* holds increasing attraction for Zouping's students, as it is seen as offering job possibilities in rural commerce, industry, and so on. Yet the newer creations of the county, the *zhiye zhongxue,* have not been able to fill their classrooms with students. While national policy has aimed at increasing the number and role of such schools, in Zouping, hardly anyone even lists these schools as an option they will entertain in thinking about continuing their education. Educators face the problem of enticing students to attend these schools at the same time that they are beginning to acknowledge that they need to rethink this policy.

The failure of *zhiye zhongxue* and the anecdote from the labor-skills class remind us of the difficulty county educators face in defining the purposes of education for rural areas. In fact, in interviews with ordinary senior high school teachers and administrators—people whose graduating students overwhelmingly complete academic senior high school as their terminal degree and return to their villages—I regularly asked how the national slogan of education serving rural development and the county policy of encouraging schools to serve local economic needs was understood at their school. Most commonly, these teachers and principals were speechless. As we would continue to talk, their conversations made it clear that, in this process of a rhetorical shift in the purpose of education and continued real competition around academic goals, they were literally at a loss in defining what their schools were for.

Time and again in interviews, parents, teachers, and administrators explained the commitment to education with the traditional adage *wangzi chenglong,* the hope that one's child can "become a dragon" or a great success. That this saying assumes that the dragon was first a carp and is dramatically transformed suggests that the hope for those who buy into the process of schooling in Zouping is for a transformation equally great—not one that would enable them to improve their local community but one that would instead qualify them to jump out of it.

The paradox of Zouping's education reforms is that in constructing modern schools, policies of localizing and decentralizing education have had contradictory results. The modernizing reforms of Zouping have indeed made schooling more accessible, systematic, and rationally organized, but they have also produced more and new forms of inequality, all the while failing to find a new way of reconceptualizing a way for rural schools to serve the rural community and a means by which privilege can be muted and opportunity enhanced.

Appendix 8.1 Graduation rate from elementary schools in Zouping,
1976–1985

Year entering elementary school	Percent of class graduating
1976	74.7[a]
1977	81.3
1978	66.4
1979	85.7
1980	84.4
1981	92.2[b]
1982	82.2
1983	82.5
1984	84.1
1985	99.7[c]

Note: Rates are calculated as percentage of students entering first grade in a year to graduate five years later.

a. Data for classes entering between 1976 and 1980 are based on data in *Zouping jiaoyuzhi*, 146–147.

b. Statistics for entering classes between 1981 and 1984 are based on data in *Zouping jiaoyuzhi*, 146–147, and data from county Bureau of Education documents for 1985–1990.

c. Based on interviews with officials in county Bureau of Education.

Notes

Contributors

Notes

Preface

1. In addition to the authors of the present volume, Guy Alitto (history), William Chang (environmental science), Judith Farquhar (medical anthropology), Andrew Kipnis (social anthropology), Michel Oksenberg (political science), and Lester Ross (law), among others, have worked in Zouping. Publications by these individuals based on their work in Zouping include Judith Farquhar, *Knowing Practice: The Clinical Encounter with Chinese Medicine* (Boulder, Colo.: Westview, 1994); Judith Farquhar, "Eating Chinese Medicine," *Cultural Anthropology* 9 (1994): 471–497; Judith Farquhar, "Market Magic: Getting Rich and Getting Personal in Medicine After Mao," *American Ethnologist* 23 (1996): 239–257; Andrew B. Kipnis, "Within and against Peasantness: Backwardness and Filiality in Rural China," *Comparative Studies in Society and History* 37 (1995): 110–135; Andrew B. Kipnis, "The Language of Gifts: Managing Guanxi in a North China Village," *Modern China* 22 (1996): 285–314; and Andrew B. Kipnis, *Producing Guanxi: Sentiment, Self, and Subculture in a North China Village*, (Durham, N.C.: Duke University Press, 1996).
2. The latter approach is taken by Marc Blecher and Vivienne Shue, *Tethered Deer: Government and Economy in a Chinese Village* (Stanford, Calif.: Stanford University Press, 1996).
3. This account is based on information provided by Guy Alitto, who visited the village in 1987 and who was familiar with the county as the site of Liang Shuming's rural reconstruction movement in the 1930s. Alitto has conducted research on the county's modern history, and has written two historical background papers for members of the project, one of which I draw upon in my introduction. See Guy S. Alitto, "Rural Reconstruction during the Nanking Decade: Confucian Collectivism in Shantung," *China*

Quarterly 66 (1976): 213–243, and Guy S. Alitto, *The Last Confucian: Liang Shu-ming and the Chinese Dilemma of Modernity* (Berkeley, Calif.: University of California Press, 1979).

1. Zouping in Perspective

1. Zouping County, Shandong Province Historical Gazeteer Editorial Committee, *Zouping xianzhi* (Zouping County gazeteer; Beijing: Zhonghua shuju, 1992), chart 40.

2. See Joseph Esherick's illuminating sketch of the geographic regions of Shandong province in chapter 1 of his *The Origins of the Boxer Uprising* (Berkeley: University of California Press, 1987), and Kenneth Pomeranz's even more detailed analysis of western Shandong in his *The Making of a Hinterland: State, Society and Economy in Inland North China, 1853–1937* (Berkeley, Calif.: University of California Press, 1993). Pomeranz analyzes the introduction of cotton into the region on pp. 72–82. Qidong County was actually just across the Yellow River from Esherick's "Northwest Region," although Qidong appears to share many of its characteristics. Up until the mid-1980s, the area was still relatively impoverished; during our first year of research in Zouping, county officials referred to townships along the Yellow River as their "Siberia."

3. Despite lying south of the Yellow River and outside of the Boxer heartland, the three counties of the period that comprise present-day Zouping (Qidong, Zouping, and Changshan) nonetheless experienced significant Boxer activity in 1900. Contemporary official accounts record fifteen incidents in Qidong, eleven incidents in Zouping, and nine in Changshan; suggestively, the number of incidents declines as one moves south, away from the impoverished regions where the Boxers originated. During the same period, just north of the Yellow River in Linyi County, on the edge of the Boxer heartland, thirty-two incidents were reported. See Modern History Research Center, Chinese Academy of Social Sciences, *Shandong yihetuan an juan* (Archives of the Shandong boxers [Ji'nan: Qili shushe, 1980]), 147–156, 168–179, 181–191, 282–315.

4. See also Esherick's characterization of the prosperous "North Slope" region, *Origins*, 7–11. Unless other citations are provided, these four paragraphs are based on Alitto, "Zouping in Historical Perspective."

5. See Susan Mann, *Local Merchants and the Chinese Bureaucracy, 1750–1950* (Stanford, Calif.: Stanford University Press, 1987), 76–77, 81.

6. Mann, *Local Merchants*, 74–77, esp. the map on p. 75.

7. Zhoucun was a Qing Dynasty phenomenon, and something of a puzzle. A landlocked town reachable only over hilly terrain and poor roads, with no

noteworthy economic endowments and not even the seat of a county government, it nonetheless grew into a flourishing center of trade and manufacturing by the early eighteenth century. At the beginning of the nineteenth century, it was described as the second largest market center in the province, after Jining (Esherick, *Origins*, 10–11), and at the beginning of the twentieth century, Japanese surveyers described a walled city of 25,000 (mostly entrepreneurs) that was the "busiest interior market in Shandong province" (Mann, *Local Merchants*, 82). Efforts to explain Zhoucun's puzzling rise range from the argument that local gentry created an efficient market administration free from tax predation, to the rise of sericulture and coal mining in the nearby hills (Mann, *Local Merchants*, chap. 5).

8. Shandong Province Statistical Bureau, *Shandong tongji nianjian 1995* (Shandong statistical yearbook [Beijing: Zhongguo tongji chubanshe, 1995]), 541.

9. A photograph of these walls, apparently dating from the 1940s, shows them to be some three stories tall and almost as thick (*Zouping xianzhi*, 377).

10. According to published mortality and fertility figures, most of this number must have migrated. Mortality rates during this period were triple those of the mid-1950s, but the numbers of reported deaths account for only a small proportion of the population loss (*Zouping xianzhi*, 190). If these mortality figures are accurate, most of the missing population would have migrated permanently elsewhere, or would have died on the road while begging for food. Regardless of whether the drop in population is due to mortality or out-migration, it is testament to the catastrophic scale of the famine. The best single analysis of the Great Leap famine is Thomas P. Bernstein, "Stalinism, Famine, and Chinese Peasants: Grain Procurements during the Great Leap Forward," *Theory and Society* 13 (1984): 1–38. Bernstein argues that the effects of bad harvests were exacerbated by overprocurement of grain based on earlier inflated output reports. It seems likely that population declines explain reduced subsequent harvests.

11. Statistical series provided by county agencies.

12. A similar portrait of 1970s agriculture is given in Anita Chan, Richard Madsen, and Jonathan Unger, *Chen Village* (Berkeley: University of California Press, 1984).

13. Statistical series provided by county agencies.

14. While the details are not clear in the county gazeteer (*Zouping xianzhi*, 27–29, 213), it is evident that the county government was badly disrupted during 1968, and that organized violence was considerable. The economic damage, however, was limited in extent and duration compared with the

Greap Leap. Both the grain harvest and industrial production declined by some 20 percent in 1968, recovered to 1967 levels by 1969, and resumed their upward trend of the mid-1960s by 1970.

15. Zouping County Statistical Bureau, *Zouping tongji nianjian 1980* (Zouping statistical yearbook [Ji'nan: Zouping xian tongjiju, 1981]), 1, 4, and Table 1.1.

16. Statistical series provided by the county government.

17. Zouping's agriculture and rural economy were less diversified than national averages in 1980, and its agriculture was more oriented to the production of staple grains. Where 80 percent of Zouping's agricultural output was from the cultivation of crops (mostly corn and wheat), the national figure was 76 percent. Zouping's animal husbandry represented only 10 percent of agricultural output, while nationwide it was 18 percent. Where 6 percent of Zouping's rural labor force worked outside of agriculture, the figure was 9 percent nationwide. Calculated from figures in Table 1.1 for 1980, *Zouping tongji nianjian 1980*, 1, 4, and State Statistical Bureau, *Zhongguo tongji nianjian 1995* (China statistical yearbook [Beijing: Zhongguo tongji chubanshe, 1995]), 27, 84–85.

18. Statistical series provided by county agencies and *Zhongguo tongji nianjian 1995*, 32.

19. Statistical series provided by county agencies and *Zhongguo tongji nianjian 1995*, 280.

20. These averages are calculated by taking total value of output for township and village industry (including sideline industry) and dividing by the total rural population, and the data come from Tables 1.1, 1.2, and *Zouping tongji nianjian 1980*, 4–5; *Zhongguo tongji nianjian 1995*, 332, 365.

21. See Terry Sicular, "Agricultural Planning and Pricing in the Post-Mao Period," *China Quarterly* no. 116 (1988): 671–705.

22. *Zouping xianzhi*, 33.

23. Cotton output rose less rapidly through 1988, and in fact has declined since then (Table 1.1)—a victim of low state monopoly pricing, as Sicular suggests in Chapter 5.

24. The baseline figure of 105 yuan for 1980 is from statistical series provided by the county government; the 1993 figure of 836 yuan is from *Zouping tongji nianjian 1993*, 13, and was deflated by the national cost of living index.

25. Interview with the director of the cotton textile mill, June 8, 1988.

26. *Zouping tongji nianjian 1980*, 168–169, 176–177.

27. Interview with the director of the brewery, June 10, 1988. By 1992, the cotton textile mill ranked third in realized profits and taxes, despite its huge size. See my more detailed discussion of the brewery in Chapter 3, and the figures presented in Table 3.3.

28. *Zouping tongji nianjian 1992*, 262.
29. *Zouping tongji nianjian 1993*, 253.
30. Ibid., 254.
31. Ibid., 257.
32. Whereas China's rural industrial output (that is, excluding urban state and collective sectors) grew a very impressive 5.6-fold in constant yuan from 1985 to 1993, Zouping's rural industrial output grew 12-fold in real terms, more than double the national increase. Calculated from data in Table 1.2 and *Zhongguo tongji nianjian 1990*, 412; *Zhongguo tongji nianjian 1995*, 375.
33. Similar conclusions about a rural county in adjacent Hebei province are offered in Marc Blecher and Vivienne Shue, *Tethered Deer: Government and Economy in a Chinese Village* (cited on p. 239) (Stanford, Calif.: Stanford University Press, 1996), esp. 205–215.
34. See also Jean C. Oi, "The Role of the Local State in China's Transitional Economy," *China Quarterly* no. 144 (1995): 1132–1149.
35. See Jean C. Oi, "Fiscal Reform and the Economic Foundations of Local State Corporatism in China," *World Politics* 45 (1992): 99–126.
36. *Zouping tongji nianjian 1993*, 33.
37. See, for example, Jean C. Oi, "Commercializing China's Rural Cadres," *Problems of Communism* 35 (1986): 1–15; Jean C. Oi, "The Fate of the Collective after the Commune," in *Chinese Society on the Eve of Tiananmen*, ed. Deborah Davis and Ezra Vogel (Cambridge, Mass.: Harvard University Press, 1990), 15–36; Oi, "Fiscal Reform"; Victor Nee, "Organizational Dynamics of Market Transition: Hybrid Forms, Property Rights, and Mixed Economy in China," *Administrative Science Quarterly* 37 (1992): 1–27; William A. Byrd and Qingsong Lin, "China's Rural Industry: An Introduction," in *China's Rural Industry: Structure, Development, and Reform*, ed. W. Byrd and Q. Lin (New York: Oxford University Press), 1–18; and Christine P. W. Wong, "Between Plan and Market: The Role of the Local Sector in Post-Mao China," *Journal of Comparative Economics* 11 (1987): 385–398.
38. See the writings in this vein quoted and cited in Andrew G. Walder, "China's Transitional Economy: Interpreting its Significance," *China Quarterly* no. 144 (1995): 963–979, and in Thomas G. Rawski, "Implications of China's Reform Experience," *China Quarterly* no. 144 (1995): 1150–1173.
39. The argument that an entrenched Communist bureaucracy is the natural enemy of market reform was once widespread, and it motivated much of the argument in favor of shock therapy in Eastern Europe. See the literature characterized and cited in Steven M. Goldstein, "China in Transition: The Political Foundations of Incremental Reform," *China Quarterly* no. 144 (1995): 1105–1131, at 1109–1110.
40. See Jeffrey D. Sachs and Wing Thye Woo, "Structural Factors in the

Economic Reforms of China, Eastern Europe, and the former Soviet Union," *Economic Policy* 18 (1994): 102–145.

41. Ibid., and Nee, "Organizational Dynamics of Market Transition."

42. The argument is laid out more systematically in Andrew G. Walder, "Local Governments as Industrial Firms: An Organizational Analysis of China's Transitional Economy," *American Journal of Sociology* 101 (1995): 263–301.

43. See Oi, "Fiscal Reform."

44. An important empirical study that also reviews these trends is Keith Griffin and Zhao Renwei, eds., *The Distribution of Income in China* (New York: St. Martin's Press, 1993).

45. See, for example, Ivan Szelenyi and Robert Manchin, "Social Policy under State Socialism: Market, Redistribution, and Social Inequalities in East European Socialist Societies," in *Stagnation and Renewal in Social Policy*, ed. G. Esping-Anderson, M. Rein, and L. Rainwater (Armonk, N.Y.: Sharpe, 1987), 102–139; Jean C. Oi, *State and Peasant in Contemporary China: The Political Economy of Village Government* (Berkeley, Calif.: University of California Press, 1989); Jadwiga Staniskis, "'Political Capitalism' in Poland," *East European Politics and Societies* 5 (1991): 127–141; Akos Rona-tas, "The First Shall Be Last? Entrepreneurship and Communist Cadres in the Transition from Socialism," *American Journal of Sociology* 100 (1994): 40–69; and Yanjie Bian and John R. Logan, "Market Transition and the Persistence of Power: The Changing Stratification System in Urban China," *American Sociological Review* 61 (1996): 739–758.

46. See Victor Nee, "A Theory of Market Transition: From Redistribution to Markets in China," *American Sociological Review* 54 (1989): 663–681, and Victor Nee, "Social Inequalities in Reforming State Socialism: Between Redistribution and Markets in China," *American Sociological Review* 56 (1991): 267–282.

47. See the two publications cited in the preceding note.

48. See Nee, "Social Inequalities in Reforming State Socialism," and Victor Nee, "The Emergence of a Market Society: Changing Mechanisms of Stratification in China," *American Journal of Sociology* 101 (1996): 908–949.

49. Yu Xie and Emily Hannum, "Regional Variation in Earnings Inequality in Reform-Era Urban China," *American Journal of Sociology* 101 (1996): 950–992.

50. Compare the southern coastal regions examined in Thomas P. Lyons and Victor Nee, eds., *The Economic Transformation of South China: Reform and Development in the Post-Mao Era* (Ithaca, N.Y.: East Asia Program, Cornell University, 1994).

51. See, for example, the symposium published in *American Journal of Sociology* in January 1996.

2. The Evolution of Local State Corporatism

1. See my "Fiscal Reform and the Economic Foundations of Local State Corporatism," *World Politics* 45 (1992): 99–122, and "The Role of the Local State in China's Transitional Economy," *China Quarterly* 144 (1995): 1132–49.

2. This is often called the Sunan model, named after practices found in Jiangsu. Detailed case studies can be found in John Wong, Rong Ma, and Mu Yang, eds., *China's Rural Entrepreneurs: Ten Case Studies* (Singapore: Times Academic Press, 1995). Also see George Brown, "The Sunan Model and Rural Development," paper presented at the Association for Asian Studies annual meeting, Washington, D.C., April 2–5, 1992. A good description of how the model works at the village level is found in James Kung, "The Structure and Evolution of Property Rights in China's Village Enterprises: The Case of Wuxi County," paper presented at the Conference on Property Rights in Transitional Economies: Research Insights from China, Hong Kong, June 1996.

3. See Jean C. Oi, "The Shifting Balance of Power in Central-Local Relations: Local Government Response to Fiscal Austerity in Rural China," paper presented at the Association for Asian Studies annual meeting, April 11–14, 1991, New Orleans.

4. Between 1980 and 1988, township and village-run enterprises increased their gross output by 169 million yuan in real terms, while output of cooperative and individual enterprises grew by only 80.5 million yuan. The public sector's contribution to growth was therefore double that of the nonpublic sector. Calculated from data in Table 1.2.

5. Between 1988 and 1993, township and village-run enterprises increased their gross output by 421 million yuan in real terms, while output of cooperative and individual enterprises grew by 489 million. The private sector's contribution to growth was therefore 16 percent higher than that of the public sector. Calculated from data in Table 1.2.

6. This account relies heavily on interviews with officials and managers at the provincial, prefectural, county, township, and village levels. I made five research trips to Ji'nan, Binzhou, or Zouping between 1988 and 1996. Most of the more than 160 interviews were conducted at county, township, and village bureaus. I concentrated on the bureaus and agencies directly involved with the day-to-day development of rural industry under the jurisdictions of townships and villages: the Rural Industry Management Bureau, the Finance Bureau, the Tax Bureau, the Agricultural Bank, the Auditing Bureau, the Individual Entrepreneurs Association, and the Industrial and Commercial Bureau. In townships, I interviewed many of the

lower-level branches of the county bureaus just named, and various financial institutions, including the savings and loan cooperatives and the credit associations. While I visited numerous villages and townships over the years, I concentrated on Dongguan village in Zouping township, and Fengjia village in Sunzhen township.

7. For an elaboration of this, see Jean C. Oi, "The Role of the Local State in China's Transitional Economy," *China Quarterly* 114 (1995): 1150–1173.

8. Those areas of rural China that relied heavily on private enterprises from the beginning of the 1980s tended to be places where little industrial development was initiated under the communes, and that had strong ties to overseas communities of emigrants in Southeast Asia and Hong Kong. The strategy was therefore initially common primarily along the coast of Zhejiang, Fujian, and Guangdong. On Wenzhou, see Liu Yialing, "Reform from Below: The Private Economy and Local Politics in the Rural Industrialization of Wenzhou," *China Quarterly* 130 (1992): 293–316. On Fujian, see Chih-jou Jay Chen, "Local Institutions and Property Rights Transformation in Southern Fujian," paper presented at conference on Property Rights in Transitional Economies, Hong Kong University of Science and Technology, June 1996; and David Wank, "The Social Organization of Property Rights in China's Non-State Urban Economy," paper presented at conference on Property Rights in Transitional Economies, Hong Kong University of Science and Technology, June 1996.

9. In 1979, the number of townships enterprises ranged from a high of twelve in Zouping to a low four in Weiqiao and Libatian. The number of village enterprises ranged from a high of fifty-five in Weiqiao to none in Changshan, Yuancheng, Jiuhu, Libatian, Taizi, and Matou townships.

10. China Interview 6288.

11. China Interview 10688. The timing of contracting seems to have varied widely. For example, Zouping township, which had many township enterprises, started to contract them out in 1985. Sunzhen, which had few, waited until 1988. Fengjia village, in Sunzhen township, contracted out its first factory in 1985. However, even in villages like Dongguan, which started contracting in 1983, the party secretary personally managed the new cotton mill until it was fully operational.

12. In highly industrialized Dongguan, only one of its seventeen enterprises, the flour mill, was leased, beginning in 1987, after it lost considerable sums of money and fell into deficit. Originally, like the others, it had been contracted out for individual management. China Interview 4688. In Xiwang, another highly successful village in Handian township, only one of the village's ten enterprises—a transport operation—was leased. China Interview 62494.

13. Christine Wong makes a similar point in her "Interpreting Rural Industrial Growth in the Post-Mao Period," *Modern China* 14 (1988): 3–30.

14. Not all of Zouping's seventeen townships actually shared revenues with the county. Some could not collect sufficient revenues to meet basic expenditures. Of the seventeen townships, the ten poorest received subsidies from the county. The seven that actually have paid taxes to the county since the revenue-sharing system started in 1986 are those that have the largest number of rural enterprises. The tax status of the seventeen townships has remained constant. China Interviews 6288 and 19696.

15. For a more detailed description of some of the early types of contracting arrangements, see my "The Fate of the Collective after the Commune," in *Chinese Society on the Eve of Tiananmen,* ed. Deborah Davis and Ezra Vogel (Cambridge, Mass.: Harvard University Press, 1990), 15–36.

16. One such place was Zouping township, which tried *dabaogan* from 1985 to 1987. China Interview 14688.

17. China Interviews 14688 and 52590.

18. China Interview 4688.

19. Yuancheng township uses a slightly different system. It apportions 50 percent of the basic profits to the township and 50 percent to the factory. Of the percentage that goes to the factory, 20 percent is given to the contractor and 30 percent goes to the workers. The amount that the township economic commission received was reduced from 20 percent to 10 percent in 1989. China Interview 52490.

20. Such limits have been a source of some tension, and factory managers express frustration with them. The focus of the frustration, however, was the collective spirit that demanded limits on wage inequalities, not the industrial committee or the village party secretary. China Interview 8691.

21. China Interview 17788.

22. China Interview 52490.

23. Dongguan has classified its enterprises into three categories based on output, profits, and fixed capital. The amounts that they are asked to loan vary with their rating. China Interview 8691.

24. China Interview 52090.

25. This began in 1988. In 1991 the average interest on these savings plans in Dongguan was around 12 percent.

26. Village workers bought anywhere from 5,000 to 10,000 yuan in bonds.

27. China Interview 52090.

28. China Interview 23696.

29. China Interview 52590.

30. China Interview 81391.

31. This is for fixed-capital loans. They do not have to sign for circulation funds that enterprises routinely borrow. According to local officials, new rules prohibit the township economic commission from acting as guarantors for loans. An enterprise is supposed to find another economic entity—that is, another firm with sufficient assets—to agree to be guarantor.

32. China Interview 17788.

33. In some counties the township economic commission may operate under different names, such as the industrial office. A vice–party secretary or vice–township head is often also the head of the township economic commission. He is often the only state cadre in the commission. The rest of the staff are considered local cadres. China Interview 4688.

34. This commission is funded mostly by local revenue from its enterprises. Each enterprise pays 1 percent of *before-tax* profits to the township economic commission as a management fee *(guanli fei)*. Part of this is supposed to be turned over to the county Rural Enterprise Management Bureau. Each contractor must pay an additional 10 percent of his enterprise's *before-tax* profits to the township government. The amount paid to the township government varies. For example, in Zouping township, 20 percent of the after-tax profits go to the township economic commission, but 30 percent of this amount is turned over to the township government, which does not take the usual 10 percent of before-tax profits that most other township governments in the county take. Village enterprises do not pay profits or fees to the township, but in some of the highly industrialized villages each factory pays a management fee of 1 percent of the total enterprise income to the village Industrial Committee. China Interviews 4688 and 8991.

35. Around 1988, each township economic commission received 300 yuan that could be divided among the staff.

36. China Interview 52290.

37. China Interview 52290.

38. China Interview 6688.

39. China Interview 52190.

40. To facilitate the work at the county level, a similar process occurred at the township level for all but the small and unprofitable enterprises served by the subbranch of the Agricultural Bank; the township economic commission and the Agricultural Bank's branch office *(yingyesuo)* participated. China Interview 6388; China Interview 22688.

41. China Interview 21696.

42. Exceptions are villages such as Fengjia, which is developed and highly regarded. Fengjia was wealthy enough for Sunzhen township to ask it for loans.

43. China Interview 22688. Statistics from Zouping township belie this generalization, but it must also be remembered that the township has the largest number of village enterprises in the county. These enterprises have long commanded respect and have solid credit ratings. According to township officials, in 1989, 6.7 million yuan was for township enterprises, 14.7 million yuan was for village enterprises, 250,000 yuan was for *lianheti*, and 770,000 yuan was for *geti*. China Interview 52590.

44. Private entrepreneurs who should have technically done their business at the Agricultural Bank also used other specialized state banks, such as the Construction Bank. Unlike collective enterprises, private businesses do not need guarantors, but they must provide collateral. These loans consisted of both fixed-capital loans and circulation fund loans.

45. China Interview 81391.

46. This Construction Bank was established in 1979, but only after 1985 did it accept savings and make loans. Prior to that it was simply a bank of the Finance Bureau that made grants to designated projects. China Interview 81391.

47. China Interview 81391.

48. China Interview 81391.

49. Local officials take extraordinary measures carefully. Only the best are able to secure such loans, especially during periods of retrenchment and credit shortage.

50. Zouping does not seem to have had much, if any, of the IOU problem for the procurement of grain.

51. China Interview 8991.

52. This was not the first time that the factory received a loan; this second loan was made in part to protect an earlier investment in the factory by the Construction Bank. China Interview 81391.

53. China Interview 81391.

54. China Interview 52290

55. China Interview 8891.

56. China Interview 6288.

57. The interest rate varied depending on use: for agricultural projects it was 2.5 percent; for husbandry, 3.5 percent; and for industrial projects, 4.2 percent.

58. The upper levels have since stopped this practice.

59. According to tax officials, a regulation was in force since 1980 that allowed the county tax office to keep a small percentage of these taxes. The amount was decided by the Shandong Provincial Tax Bureau. China Interview 52290.

60. China Interview 6288.

61. China Interview 52290.

62. The importance of these channels is also noted by Hua Sheng, Xuejun Zhang, and Xiaopeng Luo, *China: From Revolution to Reform* (London: Macmillan, 1993).

63. Unless otherwise noted, the information in this section is from China Interview 52490.

64. See Jean C. Oi, "Cadre Networks, Information Diffusion, and Market Production in Coastal China" (*Private Sector Development Occasional Paper No. 20* [World Bank: Washington, D.C., December 1995]), for a fuller discussion of how rural enterprises obtain technical assistance and market information.

65. At least one former county magistrate/party secretary is in a prominent position within the province, having first served at the prefecture after leaving Zouping.

66. This is not surprising given that county investment is concentrated in the brewery. While this county has a number of other factories, the bulk of investment over the last few years has gone into the brewery.

67. China Interview 62294.

68. China Interview 62494.

69. See Barry Naughton, "Implications of the State Monopoly over Industry and Its Relaxation," *Modern China* 18 (1992): 14–41.

70. Changing market conditions, backward technology, and lack of technological expertise were cited by a leading county bank official as well as by officials in the Rural Enterprise Management Bureau. China Interviews 21696 and 24696.

71. China Interview 21696.

72. In the case where debts cannot be repaid and an enterprise closes, bankruptcy is declared. A bank will receive a portion of the proceeds once an enterprise declares bankruptcy, but it is the last in line to receive payment. Consequently, banks recover only a portion of the original loan. China Interview 21696.

73. China Interview 23696.

74. In 1996, Dongguan was one of seven villages that qualified for such a classification in the county. China Interview 24696.

75. For example, county leaders recently have begun a big push to develop commercial agriculture. Under the aegis of the Bureau of Agriculture, the county has mobilized resources at all levels of government to facilitate vegetable production and distribution. This new direction was spurred by the opening of a joint-venture plant making dried vegetables used in instant noodle soups. The 1994 tax reforms designated taxes on agriculture as local taxes that need not be shared by the center. This further diversified strategy not only will add more revenues, but it is particularly

beneficial for those townships, such as Matou, that have failed to develop rural industry and remain largely agricultural. China Interview 23696.

76. As of the summer of 1996, 153 enterprises had been leased out, sixty-one of them township-owned. Twenty-six enterprises had adopted the shareholding system, and of these, nine were township-owned, while five or six were village-owned; the remainder were formerly jointly owned *(lianheti)*. Fourteen had become conglomerates. China Interview 24696.

77. As of the summer of 1996, seventeen enterprises had been auctioned, and fourteen had gone bankrupt. The assessment is handled by an Asset Assessment Small Group under the Industrial Commercial Bureau of the county. China Interview 24696.

78. According to county officials, the township already had leased out a number of its enterprises by 1994. The township decided to sell these enterprises after the township party secretary went on a study trip to the United States. Only five of the township's enterprises remain collectively owned.

79. China Interview 23696.

80. None has been officially registered. It was unclear to county authorities how many may have been sold informally.

81. The county education commission first assigned vocational school graduates in 1994; a second assignment was done in 1995. This last round yielded 150 students. China Interview 24696.

82. See also David Wank, "Private Business, Bureaucracy, and Political Alliance in a Chinese City," *Australian Journal of Chinese Affairs* 33 (1995): 55–74.

83. China Interview 21696.

84. China Interview 21696.

85. This private tile maker had previously developed close ties with those in the Rural Industrial Management Bureau when he managed a township-owned tile factory. China Interview 62294.

86. China Interview 23696.

87. In 1994, four private businessman changed their household status under this provision. China Interview 24696.

88. Unfortunately, I do not know how many of these are industrial enterprises. China Interview 24696.

89. See Liu Yialing, "Reform from Below."

90. China Interview 6688.

91. In addition, the collective label also allows companies to acquire land more easily, which in the current context may be one of the most important benefits once a private company becomes large enough to secure its own loans. China Interview 7794.

92. China Interview 24696.

3. The County Government as an Industrial Corporation

1. See Andrew G. Walder, "Local Bargaining Relationships and Urban Industrial Finance," in *Bureaucracy, Politics, and Decision Making in Post-Mao China*, ed. Kenneth G. Lieberthal and David M. Lampton (Berkeley, Calif.: University of California Press, 1992), 308–333.

2. See William A. Byrd, "Entrepreneurship, Capital, and Ownership," in *China's Rural Industry: Structure, Development, and Reform*, ed. William A. Byrd and Qingsong Lin (New York: Oxford University Press, 1990), 189–218; Victor Nee, "Organizational Dynamics of Market Transition: Hybrid Forms, Property Rights, and Mixed Economy in China," *Administrative Science Quarterly* 37 (1992): 1–27; Victor Nee and Sijin Su, "Local Corporatism and Informal Privatization in China's Market Transition," *Working Papers on Transitions from State Socialism No. 93-2* (Ithaca, N.Y.: Cornell University, Einaudi Center for International Studies, 1993); Jean C. Oi, "Commercializing China's Rural Cadres," *Problems of Communism* 35 (1986): 1–15; Jean C. Oi, "The Chinese Village, Inc.," in *China in a New Era: Continuity and Change*, ed. Bruce Reynolds (New York: Paragon, 1988), 55–75; Jean C. Oi, "The Fate of the Collective after the Commune," in *Chinese Society on the Eve of Tiananmen*, ed. Deborah Davis and Ezra Vogel (Cambridge, Mass.: Harvard University Press, 1990), 15–36; Jean C. Oi, "Fiscal Reform and the Economic Foundations of Local State Corporatism in China," *World Politics* 45 (1992); 99–126; Yingyi Qian and Chenggang Xu, "Why China's Economic Reforms Differ: The M-Form Hierarchy and Entry/Expansion of the Non-State Sector," *Economics of Transition* 1 (1993): 135–70; Scott Rozelle, "The Economic Behavior of Village Leaders in China's Reform Economy" (Ph.D. diss., Cornell University, 1991); and Christine P. W. Wong, "Between Plan and Market: The Role of the Local Sector in Post-Mao China," *Journal of Comparative Economics* 11 (1987): 385–398.

3. See, for example, Oi, "The Chinese Village, Inc.," "The Fate of the Collective after the Commune," and "Fiscal Reform."

4. See, for example, Nee, "Organizational Dynamics of Market Transition"; Nee and Su, "Local Corporatism and Informal Privatization"; and Victor Nee, "Peasant Entrepreneurship and the Politics of Regulation in China," in *Remaking the Economic Institutions of Socialism*, ed. Victor Nee and David Stark (Stanford, Calif.: Stanford University Press, 1989), 169–207.

5. Zouping County Statistical Materials, unpublished compilation of statistical materials provided by county statistical bureau, 1988, 38.

6. Much of the growth in the private and cooperative sectors came from the reclassification of village-run enterprises into cooperatives in the early 1990s.

7. Tianjin Municipal Statistical Bureau, *Tianjin tongji nianjian 1987* (Statistical yearbook of Tianjin [Tianjin: Tianjin tongji chubanshe, 1987]), 87.

8. See Andrew G. Walder, "Local Governments as Industrial Firms: An Organizational Analysis of China's Transitional Economy," *American Journal of Sociology* 101 (1995): 263–301.

9. See Walder, "Local Bargaining Relationships"; Barry Naughton, "Hierarchy and the Bargaining Economy: Government and Enterprise in the Reform Process," in *Bureaucracy, Politics and Decision-Making in Post-Mao China*, ed. Kenneth G. Lieberthal and David M. Lampton (Berkeley: University of California Press, 1992), 245–79; and Gary H. Jefferson and Thomas G. Rawski, "Enterprise Reform in Chinese Industry," *Journal of Economic Perspectives* 8 (1994): 47–70.

10. Calculated from *Zouping tongji nianjian 1992*, 267.

11. Zouping county statistical materials, 78–84.

12. Oi, "Fiscal Reform."

13. *Zouping tongji nianjian 1992*, 262.

14. *Tianjin tongji nianjian 1987*, 87.

15. See the description in Walder, "Local Bargaining Relationships."

16. Realized profits and taxes are the total of profits earned and taxes paid to the local government. They are reported in official statistics as a measure of firm performance, because real tax burdens vary considerably among enterprises, depending on their debt burden (loan packages often stipulate that debt be repaid in lieu of taxes over a three-year repayment period).

17. And as I have earlier described at some length in "Local Bargaining Relationships." The striking absence of such bargaining in Zouping was one of the first things that I noticed during my interviews there.

4. Fengjia: A Village in Transition

1. See Harry Harding, *China's Second Revolution: Reform after Mao* (Washington, D.C.: Brookings Institution, 1987), and Huang Shu-min, "The Strategy of Prosperity in a Chinese Village," *Journal of Developing Societies* 3 (1987): 119–136.

2. See Peter Ferdinand, "Shandong: An Atypical Coastal Province?" in *China's Regional Development,* ed. David S. G. Goodman (London: Routledge, 1989).

3. See Teodor Shanin, *Peasants and Peasant Societies* (London: Penguin Publications, 1966).

4. Maurice Freedman suggests that this type of single surname village with significant lineage organization and elaborate genealogy is a sociocultural phenomenon predominantly seen in China's southeast frontier, specifi-

cally in Guangdong and Fujian provinces. See his *Lineage Organization in Southeastern China* (London: Athlone Press, 1958) and *Chinese Lineage and Society: Fukien and Kwangtung* (London: Athlone Press, 1966). Recent fieldwork in the North China plain, including our studies in Zouping and Myron Cohen's study in Hebei, indicate that this type of lineage community is quite common. Freedman's main thesis should thus be reevaluated in light of current studies. See Myron Cohen, "Lineage Organization in North China," *Journal of Asian Studies* 49 (1990): 509–534.

5. See Emily Ahern, *The Cult of the Dead in a Chinese Village* (Stanford, Calif.: Stanford University Press, 1973).

6. See Guy Alitto, *The Last Confucian: Liang Shu-ming and the Chinese Dilemma of Modernity* (Berkeley: University of California Press, 1979).

7. The total amount of farmland own by Fengjia is unclear. Officials in the village government claimed that there was a total of roughly 2,600 mu as of 1986. This number was the basis for allocating 2.3 mu for each of the 1,116 villagers in the household registrations. This land size, however, did not include the "flexible land" (*jidongdi,* farmland not formally leased out to villagers, which can be used to meet temporary needs, such as when a village family brings in a new bride and hence is entitled to an additional 2.3 mu). If we estimate that the village government keeps 10 percent of all farmland as flexible land, then the total acreage of farmland in Fengjia is close to 3,000 mu. Based on aerial photography, however, Stewart Odend'hal estimates that Fengjia should have about 3,300 mu of farmland. This seems to confirm Jean Oi's argument that local officials in rural China systematically underreport the amount of farmland to the government in order to lessen tax burdens, a "rationality of evasion." See Jean Oi's *State and Peasant in Contemporary China: The Political Economy of Village Government* (Berkeley: University of California Press, 1989).

8. See Andrew Kipnis, "Producing Guanxi: Relationships, Subjects, and Subcultures in a Rural Chinese Village" (Ph.D. diss., University of North Carolina, 1991), and Stewart Odend'hal, "Fengjia Village, Shandong: A Corporate Village," in *Chinese Landscapes: The Village as Place,* ed. Ronald G. Knapp (Honolulu: University of Hawaii Press, 1992).

9. See Kipnis, "Producing Guanxi."

10. See Anita Chan, Richard Madsen, and Jonathan Unger, *Chen Village under Mao and Deng* (Berkeley: University of California Press, 1992), Huang Shu-min, *The Spiral Road: Change in a Chinese Village through the Eyes of a Communist Party Leader* (Boulder, Colo.: Westview Press, 1989), and Sulamith Potter and Jack Potter, *Chinese Peasants: The Anthropology of Revolution* (Cambridge: Cambridge University Press, 1990).

11. See Huang Shu-min, "Re-Examining the Extended Family in Chinese

Peasant Society: Findings from a Fujian Village," *Australian Journal of Chinese Affairs* no. 27 (1992): 25–38.

12. See Myron Cohen, *House United, House Divided: The Chinese Family in Taiwan* (New York: Columbia University Press, 1976).

13. See Andrew Walder, *Communist Neo-Traditionalism: Work and Authority in Chinese Industry* (Berkeley: University of California Press, 1986).

14. See Oi, *State and Peasant*, p. 9.

15. See Edward Friedman, Paul G. Pickowicz, and Mark Selden, *Chinese Village/Socialist State* (New Haven, Conn.: Yale University Press 1991).

5. Establishing Markets

I would like to thank Sarah Cook for her assistance in preparing this chapter and Andrew Walder, Jonathan Morduch, and Robin Cowan for their helpful comments. This research was supported by the National Science Foundation under grant no. SES-8908438, and by the Committee on Scholarly Communication with China with funds from the U.S. Information Agency.

1. Gross domestic product (GDP) measures the total value of all finished goods and services produced domestically (in this case, within the county) during the year.

2. Because GDP statistics for Zouping are only available after 1988, growth in county output for earlier years is calculated using the traditional socialist output measure "net material product." Net material product measures the final value of goods and some (but not all) services produced.

3. These figures for household income data in Zouping are from the official rural household survey conducted by the State Statistical Bureau. National data are from State Statistical Bureau, *Zhongguo tongji nianjian* (A Statistical Yearbook of China [Beijing: Zhongguo tongji chubanshe, 1992]), 308, and State Statistical Bureau, *Zhongguo tongji zhaiyao* (Statistical Survey of China, [Beijing: Zhongguo tongji chubanshe, 1993]), 50.

4. This section summarizes the main features of the state commercial policies that have been relevant to Zouping. It incorporates information obtained in interviews with officials in the Shandong provincial and Zouping County governments. See Jean Oi, *State and Peasant in Contemporary China: The Political Economy of Village Government* (Berkeley: University of California Press, 1989); Terry Sicular, "China's Agricultural Policy during the Reform Period," in Joint Economic Committee of the U.S. Congress, *China's Economic Dilemma in the 1990s: The Problems of Reforms, Modernization and Interdependence* (Washington, D.C.: U.S. Government Printing Office, 1991), 340–364; and Terry Sicular, "Redefining State, Plan, and Market: China's Reforms in Agricultural Commerce," *China*

Quarterly 144 (1995): 1020–1046, for more extensive discussion and documentation of China's commercial reforms.

5. Since the 1950s, China's commercial administration has undergone numerous reorganizations. During certain periods, the National Federation of Supply and Marketing Co-ops and the Grain Bureau were under the Ministry of Commerce; at other times they were independent. For example, in 1970 the National Federation of Supply and Marketing Co-ops and the Ministry of Grain became bureaus under the Ministry of Commerce. In 1975, the Supply and Marketing Co-op system was split off to become an independent agency, and in 1979 the Bureau of Grain was also split off and assumed its previous status as the Ministry of Grain. In 1982, these organizations were again merged into the Ministry of Commerce. In recent years the trading agencies of these and other government bureaus have been renamed "companies" and have been given more autonomy. For example, in 1992 the Zouping County Grain Bureau was renamed the Grain Company *(liangshi jituan gongsi)*. See Ministry of Commerce Institute of Economic Research, *Xin Zhongguo shangye shigao* (A Commercial History of New China [Beijing: Zhongguo caizheng jingji chubanshe, 1984]), and Contemporary China Series Editorial Committee, *Dangdai Zhongguo shangye* (Contemporary China's Commerce [Beijing: Zhongguo shehui kexue chubanshe, 1988]), vol. 1, for additional discussion on this institutional history.

6. At this time the central government also abolished the use of mandatory production targets. The government announced that it would continue to set area targets for major crops such as cotton, oil seeds, and grain, but that such targets were for guidance purposes and that farmers were no longer obligated to follow them.

7. Recent cotton policies are discussed in Frederick W. Crook, "Reform of China's grain and oilseed markets," in U.S. Department of Agriculture, Economic Research Service, *China: Situation and Outlook Series,* RS-93-4, July 1993; and W. Hunter Colby, "Discouraged by IOU's and Pests, Cotton Farmers Cut 1993 Area," in U.S. Department of Agriculture Economic Research Service, *China: Situation and Outlook Series,* RS-93-04, July 1993, 24–26. These policies were also mentioned by local officials interviewed in Zouping in 1992–1994.

8. County net material product in current prices grew 14.3 percent per year between 1980 and 1992. Retail sales statistics in China apparently exclude intrarural transactions. Thus official data on retail sales understate the level of commercial activity and overstate the relative importance of designated state commerce.

9. Between 1980 and 1992, national retail sales grew 14.6 percent per year (State Statistical Bureau, *Zhongguo tongji zhaiyao,* 93). Between 1980 and

1991, provincial retail sales grew at an average annual rate of 14.7 percent a year (Shandong Province Statistical Bureau, *Shandong tongji nianjian 1992* [Statistical Yearbook of Shandong 1992 (Ji'nan: Zhongguo tongji chubanshe, 1992)], 17).

10. These figures are similar to the national averages. In 1988, social retail sales averaged 53 percent, and in 1992, they averaged 46 percent of national GDP (State Statistical Bureau, *Zhongguo tongji zhaiyao*, 6, 93).

11. For a historical description of periodic markets in Zouping, see C. K. Yang, *A North China Local Market Economy: A Summary of a Study of Periodic Markets in Chowping Hsien, Shantung* (New York: Institute of Pacific Relations, 1944).

12. See Jean Oi's discussion in chap. 2.

13. Note that the term "market" as used here is not limited to trade at periodic markets. Trade at rural market fairs or periodic markets is one component of market trade, but market trade also includes trade that takes place in other locations and through other channels.

14. These numbers do not count direct sales among farmers. Because such sales would be considered nondesignated and nonstate, the statistics in Table 5.8 will tend to overstate the importance of designated and state trade. At the same time, planned sales by state commerce are counted at the below-market planned prices, which would cause understatement of the importance of the designated state transactions. Yet even if, on balance, the numbers in Table 5.8 overstate designated state commerce by as much as 50 or 100 percent, it would still account for at least one-third of total retail sales.

15. Equivalent statistics are not available at the national level. Note again that these statistics exclude intrarural exchange, and that planned purchases by the state are valued at lower prices than market purchases.

16. These quantities exclude seed purchases. Households purchased, on average, twenty-five jin of wheat seed from the county Seed Company. Note that designated state agencies such as the Supply and Marketing Co-ops and Seed Company remain important suppliers of agricultural inputs such as fertilizer, pesticides, seed, and fuel.

17. In the case of grain, farmers had the alternatives of selling to nondesignated buyers or of retaining grain for feed or their own consumption. These options were not relevant for cotton. Handicraft textile production is now practically nonexistent, and households in Zouping retain little, if any, cotton for their own consumption.

18. In addition to the delivery quota or contract, the state has also collected an in-kind agricultural tax that is usually paid in wheat. The county-level data on grain contracts do not include the in-kind agricultural tax.

19. Households were also required to deliver, on average, seventy-nine kilo-

grams of wheat to the state in fulfillment of the agricultural tax. This tax was also uniformly fulfilled.

20. County-level data on the composition of wheat sales are unavailable.

21. Similar problems of underfulfillment have been reported elsewhere in China. See, for example, the report on Jiangsu by Joseph Kahn, "Peasants Rebel against Beijing's Control of Cotton," *Asian Wall Street Journal Weekly,* November 14, 1994, 23, 25.

22. Note that the amount of income lost by the producers exceeds the amount of the implicit tax. The tax received by the government equals the quantity delivered at the state price times the difference between the state and market prices. Producers lose this amount of income, plus any income lost because planning causes them to produce more output than they would in the absence of the plan. The additional income loss owing to the fact that producers change their output levels is a deadweight loss to society.

23. For the sake of comparison, one can make a similar calculation for wheat. The import price of wheat in 1990 was, at the official exchange rate, equal to about 0.90 yuan, which is close to the market price for wheat in Zouping that year (see Table 5.12). Note that such calculations are approximate because (1) the official exchange rate has in general overvalued the yuan, and (2) the quality of imported and domestic products can differ. International prices are calculated from import volume and value data given in U.S. Department of Agriculture Economic Research Service, *China: Agriculture and Trade Report,* Situation Outlook Series, RS-92-3, July 1991, appendix tables 7, 8, and 13.

24. Instances of such entry in cotton markets have been reported in the press. See, for example, Kahn, "Peasants Rebel against Beijing's Control of Cotton," 23, 25.

25. The role of competition among state agencies is discussed in Richard H. Holton and Terry Sicular, "Economic Reform of the Distribution Sector in China," *American Economic Review* 81 (1991): 212–217.

6. Work, Wealth, and Power in Agriculture

I would like to thank Jean Oi, Jonathan Morduch, Terry Sicular, Peter Timmer, and participants in the workshop Economic Development and Institutional Change in China at Harvard University for comments on earlier versions of this chapter. Financial support from the Institute for the Study of World Politics, Washington D.C., is gratefully acknowledged.

1. For comprehensive discussions of the development of markets and the commercialization of the rural economy, see D. H. Perkins, "Completing

China's Move to the Market," *Journal of Economic Perspectives* 8 (1994):23–46, and Terry Sicular, chap. 5.

2. Jonathan Unger provides a useful overview of some of these issues and of the characteristics of a nascent elite class in wealthier regions of China in "'Rich Man, Poor Man': the Making of New Classes in the Countryside," in *China's Quiet Revolution: New Interactions between State and Society,* ed. David S. G. Goodman and Beverley Hooper (New York: St. Martin's Press, 1994), 43–63.

3. The data are from a stratified random sample survey of 257 farm households in sixteen villages throughout Zouping County undertaken in 1991. Detailed information was collected on household economic activities, and income, as well as measures of political status. See Sicular's chap 5. for further information about the survey and data.

4. For analyses of the determinants of household income and the relationship between different types of employment and income, see Denise Hare, "Rural Nonagricultural Activities and Their Impact on the Distribution of Income: Evidence from Farm Households in Southern China," *Chinese Economic Review* (1994): 59–82 and A. R. Khan, "The Determinants of Household Income in Rural China," in *Distribution of Income in China,* ed. Keith Griffin and Zhao Renwei (New York: St. Martin's Press, 1993), 95–115.

5. "Class background" *(chengfen)* refers to the political status assigned to families prior to land reform in 1949. The five categories were hired laborer *(gunong),* poor farmer *(pinnong),* middle farmer *(zhongnong),* rich farmer *(funong),* and landlord *(dizhu).* This assigned status determined a family's social and economic position. For example, those from rich farmer or landlord classes had limited access to education or government position prior to reform.

6. A. Rona-Tas provides an excellent overview of this debate, with particular reference to Hungary, in "The First Shall Be Last? Entrepreneurship and Communist Cadres in the Transition from Socialism," *American Journal of Sociology* 100 (1994): 40–69. The major debates in this literature on China are reflected in the work of Victor Nee and Jean Oi. See for example, Victor Nee, "Peasant Entrepreneurship and the Politics of Regulation in China," in *Remaking the Economic Institutions of Socialism: China and Eastern Europe,* ed. Victor Nee and David Stark (Stanford, Calif: Stanford University Press, 1989), 169–207; Victor Nee, "A Theory of Market Transition: From Redistribution to Markets in State Socialism," *American Sociological Review* 54 (1989): 663–681; Victor Nee, "Social Inequalities in Reforming State Socialism: Between Redistribution and Markets in China," *American Sociological Review* 56 (1991): 267–82; Jean Oi, *State and Peasant in Contemporary China: The Political Economy of Village Government* (Berkeley:

University of California Press, 1989); and Jean Oi, "Fiscal Reform and the Economic Foundations of Local State Corporatism in China," *World Politics* 45 (1992): 99–126.

7. In addition to the work of Victor Nee cited earlier, see his "Organizational Dynamics of Market Transition: Hybrid Forms, Property Rights and Mixed Economy in China," *Administrative Science Quarterly* 37 (1992): 1–27.

8. Nee, "Social Inequalities."

9. Oi, "State and Peasant," and Jean C. Oi, *Rural China Takes Off: The Political Basis for Economic Reform* (Berkeley: University of California Press, 1998).

10. Nee, "Peasant Entrepreneurship," 171.

11. A useful discussion of these issues, and of the use of terms such as "partial reform," can be found in Rona-Tas, "The First Shall Be Last." Rona-Tas also comments on the limitations of the income data used by Nee to support the argument Nee presents in "Social Inequalities."

12. For a discussion of property rights in China, see A. G. Walder, "Evolving Property Rights and Their Political Consequences," in *China's Quiet Revolution: New Interactions between State and Society*, ed. David S. G. Goodman and Beverley Hooper (New York: St. Martin's Press, 1994), 3–18. Reviewing the Hungarian experience, Rona-Tas provides a more sophisticated analysis of transition, differentiating between the erosion of traditional institutions and periods of constructive transition, and between the effects of transition in different economic sectors. See Rona-Tas, "The First Shall Be Last," 47.

13. Oi, "Fiscal Reform," and *Rural China Takes Off*.

14. Khan, "Household Income," and Hare, "Rural Nonagricultural Activities," 74.

15. In his study of Dahe Commune in Hebei, reported in *Continuity and Change in China's Rural Development: Collective and Reform Eras in Perspective* (New York: Oxford University Press, 1993), Louis Putterman finds that these specialized households were among the highest income groups in the rural areas. Similarly, in a study undertaken in Jiangsu province, Flemming Christiansen finds that the development of the private sector was largely due to the emergence of specialized households that had been able to purchase production equipment from the collectives (76–77). See Flemming Christiansen, "Market Transition in China: The Case of the Jiangsu Labor Market, 1978–1990," *Modern China* 18 (1992): 72–93.

16. Yang Minchuan, "Reshaping Peasant Culture and Community: Rural Industrialization in a Chinese Village," *Modern China* 20 (1994): 157–179.

17. Hare, "Rural Nonagricultural Activities," 74.

18. As families with relatives overseas were usually assigned a "bad" (rich farmer or landlord) class background, they are more likely to receive such remittances.

19. I. Singh, L. Squire, and J. Strauss, eds., *Agricultural Household Models: Extensions, Applications and Policy* (Baltimore, Md.: Johns Hopkins University Press for the World Bank, 1986).

20. Ibid., and Terry Sicular, "Why Quibble about Quotas? The Effects of Planning in Rural China," *Discussion Paper 1714* (Cambridge, Mass.: Harvard Institute of Economic Research, 1995).

21. The main conditions for segmented markets are that queuing and rationing exist, giving rise to a situation in which groups have differential access to resources or face different prices for the same good. See Dwayne Benjamin, "Household Composition, Labor Markets and Labor Demand: Testing for Separation in Agricultural Household Models," *Econometrica* 60 (1992): 287–322.

22. The literature on labor markets in developing countries has been dominated by the Lewisian model of dual labor markets, in which labor in the "traditional" agricultural sector faces barriers to entry into the "modern" sector, which leads to rural underemployment. High rates of rural to urban migration occur as surplus agricultural labor seeks higher-paying off-farm employment. See W. A. Lewis, "Economic Development with Unlimited Supplies of Labor," *Manchester School of Economic and Social Studies* 22 (1954): 139–191.

23. For excellent discussions of the size of the rural labor surplus and the methods used in its estimation, see J. Taylor, "Rural Employment Trends and the Legacy of Surplus Labor, 1978–1986," *China Quarterly* no. 116 (1988): 736–766, and Lora Sabin, "China's New Urban Labor Resources: Rural Workers in Cities," in "The Development of Urban Labor Markets in Contemporary China" (Ph.D. Diss., Harvard University, 1995).

24. China has a rigid system of household registration (the *hukou* system) that divides the population broadly into urban and rural residents. There also exists an overlapping but not identical division of the population into agricultural and nonagricultural labor. In 1992, 74 percent of the labor force was classified as agricultural workers. Of these, only 22 percent were engaged in nonagricultural activities. See State Statistical Bureau, Zhongguo tongji gaiyao (A Statistical Survey of China [Beijing: Zhongguo tongji chubanshe, 1993]), 16–17. Published statistics do not always make a clear distinction between the categories. For thorough discussions of the categories and problems of definition, see Cheng Tiejun and M. Selden, "The Origins and Social Consequences of China's *Hukou* System," *China Quarterly* no. 139 (1994): 644–68; R. J. Kirkby, *Urbanization in China: Town and Country in a Developing Economy 1949–2000* A.D. (London: Croom Helm, 1985); and Harry X. Wu, "Rural to Urban Migration in the People's Republic of China," *China Quarterly* no. 139 (1994): 669–698.

25. The following discussion is primarily concerned with those rural residents

who are in the labor force, most of whom are agricultural workers. In the household survey, very few individuals have changed their residence permit to urban, which would give them access to jobs in the state and collective wage sector.

26. In general, rural workers who are employed in the state sector undertake jobs that are unattractive to the urban population, such as mining: in Zouping, over half such employees work in the copper mine (interview, Zouping County Labor Bureau, 1994).

27. This number fluctuates seasonally as some households undertake nonagricultural sidelines only during the slack agricultural season. The number of registered businesses rose to more than 18,000 in December 1993. Larger enterprises employing over eight people *(siying qiye)* were legalized in 1988 and by 1993 employed about 1 percent of the agricultural workforce (interview, Zouping Bureau of Commercial and Industrial Administration, 1994).

28. This pattern of income distribution is consistent with the findings in Hare, "Rural Nonagricultural Activities," based on survey data from Guangdong province.

29. The following description of village and township variations is drawn primarily from interviews with government officials, enterprise managers, and residents of several villages and townships in Zouping County, July–August 1994.

30. Interview, Qingyang Township, July 1994.

31. Interview, Liangmao Village, July 1994.

32. The marginal returns to labor is a measure of the contribution that an additional unit of labor makes to output. In the case of imperfect labor markets, this may be affected not only by prices (as should be the case in a competitive economy), but also by an individual's access to different types of employment.

33. A production function measures the technical relationship between inputs—such as land, labor, and fertilizer—and outputs in the production process. Economists make the basic assumption that producers operate on their production possibility frontier—that is, they are maximizing output for a given quantity of inputs. The functional form of the production functions estimated here is Cobb-Douglas. This specification was tested using the Ramsey regression specification error test for left-out variables. The test results did not reject the Cobb-Douglas specification as the appropriate model. The coefficients in this model have a straightforward interpretation as the elasticity, or percentage change in output generated by a percentage change in the given input.

34. The dependent variable, *agrival,* includes the output value of both crop and noncrop agriculture. While the production inputs and processes are

clearly not the same for all crops or activities, it is impossible completely to separate inputs into different types of agricultural production. Production functions with the value of crop production *(cropval)* as the dependent variable were also estimated, and the results are presented in Appendix 6.2. The discussion focuses primarily on the results of the regression analysis of total agricultural production *(agrival)*.

35. Land area is measured in mu, where 15 mu = 1 hectare.

36. Ideally a measure of the value of capital inputs would also be included. A measure was constructed consisting of the value of draft animals and agricultural implements, such as pumps, small tractors, and threshers. Two problems are involved in this measure: first, that of separating inputs into different activities, and second, of measuring the value of the "services" or actual input into the production process. The variables *(draftval* and *kvalue)* were entered in the regressions using 10 percent, 20 percent, and 100 percent of their value. The results did not vary greatly and were not statistically significant.

37. The proportion of adult workers who are male *(malepw)* controls for potential productivity differences by gender. The area of cultivated land per adult *(landpa)* is included to account for the possibility that, if markets are working imperfectly, households that are unable to move excess labor out of agriculture may employ more than the efficient amount of labor on the land. For example, Sen finds that larger households employed more labor on farms of a given size. See Amartya Sen, "Peasants and Dualism with or without Surplus Labor," *Journal of Political Economy* 74 (1966): 425–450. As land in China is distributed on a per capita basis, the variation in land per adult should be captured largely by the land and labor variables. This appears to be the case, as the coefficient on *landpa* is not statistically significant.

38. If women are left on the farm as men seek alternative off-farm activities, however, we might expect nonagricultural income to be positively correlated with a higher proportion of male labor. The negative and significant coefficient on male labor in the regression on household enterprise production contradicts this explanation in the case of household enterprises, although it may still hold in the case of wage employment, particularly as women may be less likely to travel far to work.

39. See Christiansen, "The Jiangsu Labor Market," and Taylor, "Surplus Labor."

40. The shadow wage is the opportunity cost of time for an individual—in other words, how much that person must be paid to give up an extra unit of leisure time to engage in additional employment. For individuals in wage employment, this is usually assumed to be the observed wage. For those engaged in household production, the shadow wage is determined

within the household. When households are allocating their labor in the optimal way, the shadow wage is equal to the marginal returns to labor. See Hanan Jacoby, "Shadow Wages and Peasant Family Labor Supply: An Econometric Application to the Peruvian Sierra," *Review of Economic Studies* 60 (1993): 903–921.

41. Given the Cobb-Douglas specification of the production function, the marginal product of a factor is the coefficient β(that is, its elasticity) multiplied by the average product of that factor. Despite the low significance levels of the coefficient estimates, they are the best ones that can be derived.

42. A further test of the assumption that households equalize returns across activities was carried out. Following Jacoby ("Shadow Wages," 915), for households with members engaged in wage work, a regression was run with the marginal product of labor from household agricultural or non-agricultural activities as the dependent variable and wages as the independent variable. If households equalize returns to labor across activities, as predicted by theory, then the coefficient on wages should be one. In the regression of the marginal product of labor in household sideline production on wages, the hypothesis that the coefficient on wage is equal to one is rejected at the 99 percent significance level.

43. In interviews, cadres frequently complain of this predicament. Zouping interviews, 1994.

44. Zouping Township interviews, July 1994.

45. Hare, "Rural Nonagricultural Activities."

7. Preventive Health Care

1. Thomas McKeown, *The Modern Rise of Population* (London: Edward Arnold, 1976).

2. See Abdel R. Omran, "Epidemiologic Transition: Theory," in *International Encyclopedia of Population* (New York: Collier MacMillian Publishers, 1982), 174–175. See also Henry W. Mosley and Lincoln Chen, "An Analytic Framework for the Study of Child Survival in Developing Countries," *Population and Development Review* 10 (1984):25–30.

3. In China, between 1950 and 1965, mortality rates declined from slightly over 20 to under 10 per 1,000. See William Lavely, James Lee, and Wang Feng, "Chinese Demography: The State of the Field," *Journal of Asian Studies* 49 (1992): 807–834. During the 1980s, mortality continued to decline, especially in more remote provinces. See Judith Banister, "China: Recent Mortality Levels and Trends," paper presented at the Annual Meeting of the Population Association of America, Denver, 1992.

4. William C. Hsiao, "The Incomplete Revolution: China's Health Care Sys-

tem under Market Socialism," paper presented at the Annual Meeting of the Association for Asian Studies, Boston, 1987. See also Omran, "Epidemiologic Transition" and Dean Jamison et al., *China: The Health Sector* (Washington, D.C.: World Bank, 1984).

5. David M. Lampton, *Health, Conflict, and the Chinese Political System* (Ann Arbor: University of Michigan Center for Chinese Studies, 1974). See also Joshua Horn, *Away with All Pests: An English Surgeon in the People's Republic of China* (New York: Monthly Review Press, 1969).

6. Jamison, *China: The Health Sector.* A system of county disease prevention stations *(fangyi zhan)* was established to monitor and respond to infectious and parasitic disease outbreaks. There were 147 such stations in 1952, 1,626 in 1957, and 3,532 in 1988. A parallel system of maternal and child health stations *(fuyou baojian zhan)* in each county was also established. In addition to the establishment of approximately 2,700 MCH stations between 1957 and 1988, the number of trained obstetricians rose from 4,194 to almost 50,000, and the number of MCH hospitals rose from 96 to 310. *Zhongguo weisheng nianjian 1989* (China Health Yearbook [Beijing: China Medical Publishing House, 1989]), 517–573).

7. Jamison, *China: The Health Sector.*

8. World Bank, *China: Long-Term Issues in Options for the Health Sector* (Washington, D.C.: World Bank, 1992).

9. Carl Riskin, *China's Political Economy: The Quest for Development Since 1949* (New York: Oxford University Press, 1987).

10. Aziz R. Khan, Keith Griffin, Carl Riskin, and Zhao Renwei, "Household Income and Its Distribution in China," *China Quarterly* no.132 (1992): 1029–1061.

11. World Bank, *China: Long-Term Issues.*

12. Amartya Sen, "Women's Survival as a Development Problem," *Bulletin of the American Academy of Arts and Sciences* 43 (1989): 14–19. See also Mary Young, "Maternal Health in China," (unpublished paper); Zhu Naisu et al., "Factors Associated with the Decline of the Cooperative Medical System and Barefoot Doctors in Rural China," *Bulletin of the World Health Organization* 67 (1989): 431–441; Willy De Geyndt, Zhao Xiyan, and Liu Shunli, "From Barefoot Doctor to Village Doctor in Rural China," *World Bank Technical Paper No. 187,* Asia Technical Department Series (Washington, D.C.: World Bank, 1992); and World Bank, *China: Long-Term Issues.*

13. World Bank, *China: Long-Term Issues,* 71.

14. DeGeyndt, Zhao, and Liu, "From Barefoot Doctor."

15. Ibid, 6.

16. Hsiao, "Incomplete Revolution"; *Zhongguo weisheng tongji nianjian 1988; Women and Child Health in China* (Beijing: UNICEF, 1990).

17. *Zhongguo weisheng tongji nianjian 1989*, 572–573.
18. Zhu et al., "Factors Associated with the Decline of the Cooperative Medical Care System."
19. Gail Henderson et al., "Distribution of Medical Insurance in China," *Social Science and Medicine* 41 (1995): 1119–1130.
20. Gu Xingyuan et al., "Financing Health Care in Rural China: Preliminary Report of a Nationwide Study," *Social Science and Medicine* 36 (1993): 385–391.
21. Gail Henderson et al., "Trends in Health Services Utilization in Eight Provinces in China, 1989–1993" (unpublished paper, 1996).
22. Zouping County Statistical Bureau, *Zouping Tongji Nianjian 1991* (Zouping Statistical Yearbook [Zouping: Zouping xian tongjiju, 1991]), 295. *Zouping Tongji Nianjian 1992*, 431.
23. Figures for the birthrate (per 1,000) for 1976 in Zouping were unavailable, but between 1980 and 1986, it rose from 11.9 to 15.05, and then fell again in 1989 to 12.88. During the same period of time, the birthrate in all of China's counties rose from 18.82 in 1980 to 21.94 in 1986 and to 22.28 in 1989. In Zouping, the death rate (per 1,000) declined from 7.4 in 1980 to 6.93 in 1986, and then to 6.2 in 1989. For all China's counties, the death rate rose from 6.47 in 1980 to 6.74 in 1986, but fell to 6.69 in 1989. (*Zhongguo weisheng tongji nianjian 1990*, 90).
24. This information was compiled from primary data collected by Henderson, including the county infectious and parasitic disease reports from 1965 to 1989, hospital admission reports from 1980 to 1989, and interview data on trends in health resources at each of the levels of care, from 1985 to 1990.
25. Hypertension is the most important known risk factor for stroke, currently one of the leading causes of death in China. Stroke is more common in the North. In a 1981 survey of twenty-eight disease surveillance points in rural locations all over China, the leading causes of death were found to be heart disease (23.6 percent), cancer (19.1 percent), and stroke (18.4 percent). Cancer was higher in the South (20.2 percent versus 19.2 percent), while heart disease and stroke were higher in the North (29.1 percent and 19.6 percent in the North, compared with 16.2 percent and 16.8 percent in the South). Jamison et al., *China: The Health Sector*, 123. The more recent World Bank report (*China: Long Term Issues*, 16) notes that stroke and cardiovascular disease account for 28 percent of all mortality in China, and that in rural areas, 40 percent of those deaths are attributed to stroke. Furthermore, comparing males and females in urban and rural areas, rural males are at the highest risk for stroke, at all age groups, but particularly between the ages of sixty-five and seventy-four.
26. In this study, we selected eight townships for investigation, out of a total

of seventeen townships in the county, including the township in which the county seat, Zouping town, is located. These townships were selected to provide a range of income distributions and variation in level of rural industrialization. Within each township, one to three villages were selected for further investigation, again based on a range of income and administrative considerations. Although many of the almost 900 villages in the county were not "open" to foreigners, the villages we visited represented a wide range of levels of income and industrial development. The highest per capita income was 1,700 yuan; the lowest was 350. The interviews focusing on general preventive services included a series of open-ended questions on the following topics: the diagnosis of common infectious diseases; the process of reporting of infectious disease outbreaks; the logistics and implementation of the immunization program; and the delivery of maternal and child health services. In addition, each provider and administrator was asked about the financing of preventive services. The hypertension questionnaire was designed to collect the following data from each health care provider: medical training; definition of hypertension; treatment of hypertension; understanding of the causes and consequences of hypertension; circumstances for checking someone's blood pressure; and treatment standard.

27. Hospital in-patient care is provided by the several county-level hospitals, including two municipal hospitals (250 and 150 beds), a traditional Chinese medicine hospital (eighty beds), and an infectious disease hospital (forty beds). Each of the seventeen townships in Zouping has its own hospital (although one has been changed into a psychiatric hospital), and they range in size from ten to fifty beds. In addition, the county instituted a system whereby five of the larger township hospitals were designated as "branch" hospitals *(fenyuan)* to serve as intermediate referral hospitals for the other township hospitals. These are Sunzhen, Yanqiao, Changshan, Minjiaji, and Linchi township hospitals, with beds numbering thirty-nine to fifty. The remaining township hospitals have ten to thirty-five beds, with an average of twenty-one. Branch hospitals are administered jointly by the county and the township, but at least one (Sunzhen) implemented a new contract management system, and operated its own independent budget. Table 7.4 presents summary data on the four township hospitals (two branch and two regular). Notable are the low occupancy rates, large increases in income between 1986 and 1989, and variation in type of village clinic management system.

28. World Bank, *China: Long Term Issues.*

29. Hsiao, "The Incomplete Revolution," and Zhu et al., "Factors Associated with the Decline of the Cooperative Medical System."

30. A system that depends on local doctors finding, diagnosing, and reporting

cases is clearly susceptible to biases from measurement errors and reporting errors. Influenza and dysentery cases may easily be misdiagnosed or remain unreported. Furthermore, over time, changes have taken place in diagnostic capabilities at the local level (in hepatitis or EHF, for example), thus introducing additional biases in case-finding.

31. Myron S. Cohen, "Epidemic Hemorrhagic Fever Revisited," *Reviews of Infectious Diseases* 4 (1982): 992–998.

32. For example, old-age checks were conducted for 150 yuan in the rich village of Dongguan.

33. *Zhongguo Weisheng Tongji Nianjian 1989.*

34. . . . and pay taxes, which may be why most are still willing to be called "collective."

35. Huang Shumin, "Village-Level Health Care and Rural Reform: Four Villages in Zouping County, Shandong," (paper presented at meeting of Zouping Research Group, Wingspread Conference Center, Racine, Wis., 1988).

36. Between 1987 and 1990, *fangyi zhan* personnel rose from twenty to twenty-four; first county hospital staff increased from 290 to 308.

37. Gu et al., "Financing Health Care."

38. Gail Henderson et al., "Equity and the Utilization of Health Services: Report of an Eight-Province Survey in China," *Social Science and Medicine* 39 (1994): 687–699. See also Henderson et al., "Trends in Health Services Utilization," which demonstrated a similar result for 1989–1993.

39. Gu et al., "Financing Health Care."

40. All the comments reflected a reasonable understanding of hypertension. The head of internal medicine at the county hospital stated that the standard to be used was 160/95. He said that formerly it had included 140/90, but to get in line with international standards, a 1988 conference in China had established borderline hypertension as above 145/90. On the other hand, more than half of the village doctors used a standard somewhat different that this "national" standard.

8. Making Schools Modern

Field research for this chapter was supported by a grant from the Committee for Scholarly Communication with China. Support for some of the analysis came from a National Academy of Education Spencer grant and Michigan State University. I would like to thank these organizations and people in Zouping County for their help, as well as Brian DeLany, Li Wei, Andrew Walder, Wang Jian, and Zhang Naihua for comments on drafts of this chapter and help with analysis of data.

1. Feng Zhijun, *Guangming ribao*, December 3, 1988, 1 (trans. in Foreign

Broadcast Information Service, *Daily Report, China,* December 22, 1988, 26).

2. For review of these reforms and a fuller discussion of their content, see, for example, *Reform of China's Educational Structure: Decision of the Communist Party of China Central Committee (May 1985)* (Beijing: Foreign Languages Press, 1985); *Jiaoyu gaige zhongyao wenxian xuanbian* (Selections from Important Education Reform Documents [Beijing: Renmin jiaoyu chubanshe, 1986]); Zhou Nanzhao, "Historical Contexts of Educational Reform in Present-Day China," *Interchange* 19 (1988): 8–18; Keith Lewin and Xu Hui, "Rethinking Revolution: Reflections on China's 1985 Educational Reforms," *Comparative Education Review* 25 (1989): 7–17.

3. Kai Ming Cheng and Lynn Paine, "Research on Education in Rural China: A Survey of the Literature" (paper delivered at the International Conference on Chinese Education for the 21st Century, Honolulu, November 1991), 1–2.

4. I interviewed at eight senior high–level (including key and nonkey, academic, vocational, and technical) schools, twelve junior high schools (key, central [*zhongxin*], and ordinary), and fourteen elementary schools (also representing the central and ordinary range). During these interviews, typically lasting half a day, I interviewed principals and often teachers.

5. In addition to observations and formal and informal interviews, I asked the graduating classes in the elementary and junior high schools I visited to write brief responses (a few sentences to a paragraph) to questions I posed about knowledge.

6. Basic education is defined in China in light of the Compulsory Education Law as elementary and junior secondary education. The goals of the Compulsory Education Law are for nine years of schooling for each child. In Zouping, because elementary education remains a five-year cycle, at present "basic education" actually includes only eight years of schooling— five elementary and three junior secondary.

7. Statistical data on educational participation and achievement pose many problems, as scholars of Chinese education recognize. Discrepancies were evident in the data I was able to gather from published records, internal documents to which I had access, responses to survey forms I asked education offices to complete, and interviews. I try here to report data that either are confirmed by more than one kind of source or for which the discrepant data represent a small variation that does not change the overall interpretation. Thus, for instance, the promotion rate I was able to calculate from county documents for 1985 (69.7 percent) was not identical to that reported in interviews with county officials (69.4 percent), but the difference is small. I do find it wise to remind ourselves not

to rely too heavily on quantitative measures of change, nor to rely exclusively on a single piece of data or a single data point.

8. In the county education bureau, I had lengthy individual interviews with heads of eight of the sixteen bureau sections and had the opportunity in 1990 and 1991 to have repeated interviews with them. I am grateful to them for supplying me with access both to particular data I inquired about (filling out forms I prepared) as well as for making it possible for me to study their internal records regarding county education policy and provision.

9. The types of data reported in published and internal materials changed over time in Zouping, and unfortunately I have no data on enrollment rates for the late 1970s and early 1980s that could provide a more recent comparison with the reform period studied. As for the graduation rates from elementary school, calculated as the percentage of students entering first grade to graduate five years later, data for the classes entering between 1976 and 1980 (and hence expected to graduate from elementary school in 1981–1985) are drawn from Zouping Educational Annals Editorial Leadership Group, eds., *Zouping jiaoyuzhi* (Educational Annals of Zouping County [Shandong Publishing House, Huimin Prefecture Branch, 1990]), 146–147. For a breakdown of the elementary graduation rate for classes entering between 1976 and 1985 (and graduating between 1981 and 1990), see Appendix 8.1. These data suggest less yearly fluctuation in the late 1980s than in earlier years, and rates were consistently over 80 percent.

10. I interviewed students formally and informally at seven schools, which included both county-level key and experimental schools, township elite or "central" schools, and ordinary schools. I had formal interviews with fifty students in small groups of graduating students (that is, students from the graduating classes) in four junior high schools (two elite schools in the county seat, one township central school, and one ordinary school run by several villages), and three senior high schools (one key academic school, one ordinary academic, and one vocational school).

11. Elementary education represents the major task of education provision in the county. Elementary schools in the early 1990s accounted for 90 percent of all schools in Zouping, and their students represented approximately 64 percent of all students enrolled in precollegiate education.

12. *Zouping jiaoyuzhi*, 48.

13. County bureau records on schools for the 1989–1990 year show 674 elementary schools in the county. County officials in the late summer of 1990 reported that there were only 665 schools. The difference might be a simple error of reporting, but it might also reflect another year's closures, with 665 schools readied to begin the 1990–1991 year. Whether the

larger or smaller number is used does not change the direction of the trend—toward an ever smaller number of schools.

14. The reduction of schools has generally reflected school consolidation, particularly in elementary and junior secondary schooling. Thus, numbers of total students have not dramatically decreased, especially during the 1980s. (It is true that at the time of Zouping's 234 junior highs, there were 34,327 students, also a high watermark.) In 1985, there were 28,772 junior high students in 102 schools, and in 1990 more than 31,000 attended 63 schools.

15. For more background, see Heidi Ross, *China Learns English: Language Teaching and Social Change in the People's Republic* (New Haven, Conn.: Yale University Press, 1994); Suzanne Pepper, *China's Universities: Post-Mao Enrollment Policies and Their Impact on the Structure of Secondary Education* (Ann Arbor: Center for Chinese Studies, University of Michigan, 1984); and Stanley Rosen, "Restoring Key Secondary Schools in Post-Mao China: The Politics of Competition and Educational Quality," in *Policy Implementation in Post-Mao China*, ed David M. Lampton (Berkeley: University of California Press, 1987), 321–353.

16. *Zouping jiaoyuzhi*, 178.

17. It is worth noting, however, that despite the official ban, schools still face shortages of teachers who are qualified; they have gotten around the ban and hired *minban* staff by employing them as temporary workers. The result is that the county can still look like it is taking action to provide schools that fit an image of efficient, modern, rational institutions at the same time that the schools can cope with the realities of rural life.

18. For more on this tension between devolution of authority and the reassertion of central control, see Lynn Paine and Brian DeLany, "Authority, Stratification and Schools in China" (paper delivered at the Annual Meeting of the Comparative and International Education Society, Pittsburgh, March 1991).

19. Given that schools are being closed down, as suggested in the preceding discussion about school consolidation, it may seem puzzling that there is construction going on. But in fact this combination of schools being closed and new ones opened—both processes carried out in the name of creating more modern and better-equipped schools—was part of the distinguishing quality of education in Zouping in the early 1990s.

20. Zouping here reflects the national trend of increasing the importance of off-budget contributions to or investment in schools. Nationally these extrabudgetary funds increased annually during the period 1986–1991, eventually constituting 37.2 percent of all education funding by 1991 (Adrian Vespoor and Mun C. Tsang, *Case Studies of Financing Quality Basic Education* [Washington, D.C.: World Bank, 1993], 62).

21. In interviews, officials explained that the education surcharge (*jiaoyu fei fujia*) is a kind of tax, yet they preferred not to call it a "tax" because of connotations associated with that term and what they said were legal requirements that would have to be met in order for this to be treated officially as a tax.

22. Student fees represent a combination of tuition (which can now only be charged for schooling beyond basic education—that is, as tuition for senior secondary schooling) and fees for a range of expenses (heating, materials, and so on). Interviews with teachers, school administrators, students, parents, and education officials for township and county offices offer a conflicting picture, but one that suggests that fees have risen over time and, in many cases, are higher than the county officially approves. For example, county policy in 1990 set a limit on fees that schools could charge to eight yuan and sixteen yuan per year for elementary and junior secondary schools, respectively, which was higher than the five yuan previously allowed for elementary school fees. Yet different schools reported very different school-level practices, ranging from no fees charged (saying the village bears the costs for the students) to following the county policy to charging more than three times the county policy (twenty-five yuan and fifty yuan for elementary and junior high, respectively, in one township). Parents and students in interviews regularly reported even higher figures, with parents of junior high students typically reporting that they paid between 100 and 250 yuan per year for school costs. The press for schools to locate support has encouraged them to charge a range of fees, which has become a national problem and frequently the topic of criticism and debate. Many places such as Zouping have tried to set relatively low limits on charges, and many have tried to ban the excessive reliance on fees, as well as to ban charging fees for a particularly wide range of activities and materials (such as those singled out in an article about Shijiazhuang, where fees for equipment for eye massages, required Olympic T-shirts, Young Pioneers membership, merit books for Young Pioneers, bicycle storage, middle-school graduation certificates, administrative and school records, and so on were prohibited [*Zhongguo jiaoyubao* (China Education News), July 24, 1993, 17]. In this regard, Zouping's discrepancy between official policy and much of its enacted practice is illustrative of the challenges that schools (and parents) face.

23. While townships ranged in the extent of their reliance on state funds, the range (between 63.5 percent and 34.8 percent for six townships for which I have detailed data) nevertheless suggests that township school systems relied heavily, often primarily, on off-budget funding.

24. See, for example, how in the 1991 graduating class there were 110 repeaters (70 originally from the school and 40 coming as graduates of other

senior highs) and 312 regular students. For that year, the school's overall success rate for passing a test for some form of further education was 57.1 percent (64.4 percent for the regular students and 36.3 percent for the repeater group). School leaders were critical of county objections to marketing this service (that is, accepting repeaters for exam preparation) and said that they saw this as filling a "social need" for which there is a viable market. In the past, they said, this was a lucrative means of additional support for the school.

25. For an overview of a resource dependence framework, see Jeffrey Pfeffer and Gerald Salancik, *The External Control of Organizations: A Resource Dependence Perspective* (New York: Harper & Row, 1978).

26. The idea of a critical mass of strong teachers being able to make a difference is perhaps more significant in Chinese schools, where the organization of teaching is structured to produce much more frequent and extensive collaboration, and teachers have many opportunities to benefit from the strengths and expertise of colleagues, differ from those in the United States, which are characterized by norms of autonomy and a privatization of the practice of teaching (Lynn Paine and Liping Ma, "Teachers Working Together: A Dialogue on Organizational and Cultural Perspectives of Chinese Teachers," *International Journal of Educational Research* 19 [1993]: 675–697). The township's unequal distribution of teachers who are considered very strong thus reflects not only the disparity in numbers and proportion of talented teachers but also inequalities in the opportunities that other teachers have to improve their practice.

27. Promotion is based on students' performance on an examination. In eight of the townships, the rate for promotion for students from the central school was approximately twice as high as that for students who attended the ordinary junior highs.

28. The probability is greater simply because more seats (in the central school) were designated for students from the nearest catchment areas than for students from the other districts in the township.

29. Here and elsewhere where I am making claims about the enacted curriculum of Zouping's schools, I rely heavily on classroom observations and formal and informal interviews with students and teachers. I spent more than ninety hours in classroom observation and for most of that time recorded classroom discourse either through audiotaping or videotaping. While I observed altogether in seven schools, the majority of that time was spent all day daily in one junior high (a township "central" school), primarily with one class (or *ban*) of graduating eighth graders.

Contributors

Sarah Cook is a fellow of the Institute of Development Studies at the University of Sussex, England. She recently completed her Ph.D. at Harvard University on *Employment and Income Distribution in Rural China,* and is currently co-editing a volume on Chinese labor markets. Her research interests include gender, poverty, and social policy in China.

Gail E. Henderson is associate professor of social medicine and adjunct professor of sociology, University of North Carolina at Chapel Hill. Her research interests include medical sociology, health and inequality, health and health care in China, and comparative medical ethics. She is the author of *The Chinese Hospital: A Socialist Work Unit,* has written a number of articles about health care in China, and is the editor of two forthcoming volumes: *The Social Medicine Reader* and *Reexamining Research Ethics: From Regulations to Relationships.*

Huang Shu-min, professor of anthropology at Iowa State University, has conducted rural field research in recent years in Fujian, Shandong, and Taiwan. His publications include *The Spiral Road: Change in a Chinese Village through the Eyes of a Communist Party Leader* (1989) and *Ethnicity in Taiwan: Social, Historical, and Cultural Perspectives* (co-edited with Chen Chung-min and Chuang Ying-chang, 1994).

Stewart Odend'hal, formerly of the College of Veterinary Medicine of the University of Georgia, is director of the European Center of Georgia and assistant to the director of the Office of International Development of the University of Georgia. His recent publications include "Intermediary Agricultural Energetics: A Case Study of Solar Energy Linkage with Chinese Working Cattle."

Jean C. Oi is associate professor of political science, Stanford University. Formerly on the faculty of Harvard University, she was recently a visiting professor in the Division of Social Science, Hong Kong University of Science and Technology. She is the author of *State and Peasant in Contemporary China: The Political Economy of Village Government* (1989) and *Rural China Takes Off: The Political Basis of Economic Reform* (1998).

Lynn W. Paine is on the faculty of the College of Education, Michigan State University, where she specializes in the sociology of education and international-comparative education. Her research examines the links between educational policy and practice. Her recent publications include two book chapters, "Progress and Problems in China's Educational Reforms" and "Teacher Education in Search of a Metaphor: Defining the Relationship between Teachers, Teaching, and the State in China."

Terry Sicular is associate professor of economics at the University of Western Ontario. Her research on the Chinese economy has included studies of commercial development, planning and markets, income distribution, agriculture, and state-owned enterprises. Her recent papers include "Redefining State, Plan and Market: China's Reforms in Agricultural Commerce," *China Quarterly* (December 1995), and "On the Four Major Relationships concerning Income Distribution in Rural China" (with J. Morduch, 1996).

T. Scott Stroup is assistant professor of psychiatry, adjunct professor of social medicine, and research fellow at the Cecil G. Sheps Center for Health Services Research, University of North Carolina at Chapel Hill. He conducts research on the ways in which health systems affect people with severe and persistent mental illness. His recent publications include "Can Managed Competition Reform Mental Health Care?" and "The Impact of a Managed Mental Health Program on Medicaid Recipients with Severe Mental Illness," both with R. A. Dorwart.

Andrew G. Walder is professor of sociology and senior fellow, Institute of International Studies, Stanford University. Previously on the faculty of Harvard University, he recently was professor and head, Division of Social Science, Hong Kong University of Science and Technology. He is the author of *Communist Neo-Traditionalism: Work and Authority in Chinese Industry* (1986) and editor of *China's Transitional Economy* (1996).

Harvard Contemporary China Series

Chinese Society on the Eve of Tiananmen:
The Impact of Reform
Edited and with an Introduction by Deborah Davis
and Ezra F. Vogel

New Perspectives on the Cultural Revolution
Edited and with an Introduction by William A. Joseph,
Christine P. W. Wong, and David Zweig

From May Fourth to June Fourth:
Fiction and Film in Twentieth-Century China
Edited by Ellen Widmer and David Der-Wei Wang

Engendering China:
Women, Culture, and the State
Edited by Christina K. Gilmartin, Gail Hershatter,
Lisa Rofel, and Tyrene White